The Mystery
of BANKING

The Ludwig von Mises Institute thanks
Mr. Douglas E. French and Ms. Deanna Forbush
for their magnificent sponsorship
of the publication of this book.

The Mystery
of BANKING

MURRAY N. ROTHBARD

SECOND EDITION

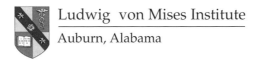
Ludwig von Mises Institute
Auburn, Alabama

For information write the Ludwig von Mises Institute, 518 West Magnolia Avenue, Auburn, Alabama 36832. Mises.org.

ISBN: 978-1-933550-28-2

To Thomas Jefferson,
Charles Holt Campbell,
Ludwig von Mises

Champions of Hard Money

CONTENTS

PREFACE

Although first published 25 years ago, Murray Rothbard's *The Mystery of Banking* continues to be the only book that clearly and concisely explains the modern fractional reserve banking system, its origins, and its devastating effects on the lives of every man, woman, and child. It is especially appropriate in a year that will see; a surge in bank failures, central banks around the globe bailing out failed commercial and investment banks, double-digit inflation rates in many parts of the world and hyperinflation completely destroying Zimbabwe's economy, that a new edition of Rothbard's classic work be republished and made available through the efforts of Lew Rockwell and the staff at the Ludwig von Mises Institute at an obtainable price for students and laymen interested in the vagaries of banking and how inflation and business cycles are created.

In the absence of central-bank intervention, the current financial meltdown could be a healthy check on the inflation of the banking system as Rothbard points out in his scathing review of Lawrence H. White's *Free Banking in Britain: Theory, Experience, and Debate, 1800–1845* that first appeared in *The Review of Austrian Economics* and is included as a part of this new edition to correct Rothbard's initial support of White's work in the first edition. There have been virtually no bank failures in the United

States since the early 1990s and as Rothbard surmised during that period where there was "an absence of failure" that "inflation of money and credit [was] all the more rampant." Indeed, from January 1990 to April 2008, the United States M-2 money supply more than doubled from $3.2 trillion to $7.7 trillion. Bankers were living it up, "at the expense of society and the economy faring *worse*" (Rothbard's emphasis).

Although ostensibly it is dodgy real estate loans that are bringing the banks down this year, in the seminal book that you hold, Rothbard shows that it is really the fraudulent nature of fractionalized banking that is the real culprit for the bankers' demise.

But central bankers will never learn. "We should not have a system that's this fragile, that causes this much risk to the economy," New York Federal Reserve President Tim Geithner said after engineering J.P. Morgan's bailout of the failed Bear Stearns investment bank in the first quarter of 2008 with the help of the central bank. Of course the thought of dismantling his employer, the government leaving the counterfeiting business, and a return to using the market's money—gold—didn't occur to him. More government regulation in which "the basic rules of the game establish stronger incentives for building more robust shock absorbers," is what he prescribed.

Surely Murray is somewhere laughing.

My introduction to *The Mystery of Banking* came in 1992 as I was finishing my thesis at UNLV under Murray's direction. I found the book in the university library and couldn't put it down. The book was long out of print by that time and being prior to the start of Amazon.com and other online used book searches, I was unable to find a copy of the book for purchase. Thus, I fed dimes into the library copier one Saturday afternoon and made myself a copy. When the online searches became available I waited patiently and bought two copies when they surfaced, paying many times the original $19.95 retail price (as I write this AbeBooks.com has three copies for sale ranging from $199 to $225, and Bauman Rare Books recently sold a signed first edition for $650).

When I discovered Rothbard's great work I had been a banker for six years, but like most people working in banking, I had no clear understanding of the industry. It is not knowledge that is taught on the job. Murray may have referred to me as "the efficient banker," but he was the one who knew the evil implications of the modern fractionalized banking system: "the pernicious and inflationary domination of the State."

Douglas E. French
Las Vegas, Nevada
June 2008

FOREWORD

L ong out of print, *The Mystery of Banking* is perhaps the least appreciated work among Murray Rothbard's prodigious body of output. This is a shame because it is a model of how to apply sound economic theory, dispassionately and objectively, to the origins and development of real-world institutions and to assess their consequences. It is "institutional economics" at its best. In this book, the institution under scrutiny is central banking as historically embodied in the Federal Reserve System—the "Fed" for short—the central bank of the United States.

The Fed has long been taken for granted in American life and, since the mid-1980s until very recently, had even come to be venerated. Economists, financial experts, corporate CEOs, Wall Street bankers, media pundits, and even the small business owners and investors on Main Street began to speak or write about the Fed in awed and reverential terms. Fed Chairmen Paul Volcker and especially his successor Alan Greenspan achieved mythic stature during this period and were the subjects of a blizzard of fawning media stories and biographies. With the bursting of the high-tech bubble in the late 1990s, the image of the Fed as the deft and all-seeing helmsman of the economy began to tarnish. But it was the completely unforeseen eruption of the wave of sub-prime mortgage defaults in the middle of this decade, followed by the Fed's panicky bailout of major financial institutions and the onset of incipient stagflation, that has profoundly shaken the widespread confidence in the wisdom and competence of the Fed. Never was the time more propitious for the radical and penetrating critique of the Fed and fractional-reserve banking that Rothbard offers in this volume.

Before taking a closer look at the book's contents and contributions, a brief account of its ill-fated publication history is in order. It was originally published in 1983 by a short-lived and eclectic publishing house, Richardson & Snyder, which also published around the same time *God's Broker*, the controversial book on the life of Pope John Paul II by Antoni Gronowicz. The latter book was soon withdrawn, which led to the dissolution of the company. A little later, the successor company, Richardson & Steirman, published the highly touted *A Time for Peace* by Mikhail Gorbachev, then premier of the U.S.S.R. This publishing coup, however, did not prevent this firm from also winding up its affairs in short order, as it seems to have disappeared after 1988.

In addition to its untimely status as an orphan book, there were a number of other factors that stunted the circulation of *The Mystery of Banking*. First, several reviewers of the original edition pointedly noted the lax, or nonexistent, copy editing and inferior production standards that disfigured its appearance. Second, in an important sense, the book was published "before its time." In 1983, its year of publication, the efforts of the Volcker Fed to rein in the double-digit price inflation of the late 1970s had just begun to show success. Price inflation was to remain at or below 5 percent for the rest of the decade. During the 1990s, inflation, as measured by the Consumer Price Index, declined even further and hovered between 2 and 3 percent. This led the Greenspan Fed and most professional monetary economists to triumphantly declare victory over the inflation foe and even to raise the possibility of a return of the deflation bogey.

Despite the adverse circumstances surrounding its publication, however, *The Mystery of Banking* has gone on to become a true underground classic. At the time of this writing, four used copies are for sale on Amazon.com for between $124.50 and $256.47. These prices are many times higher than the pennies asked for standard money-and-banking textbooks published in the 1980s and even exceed the wildly inflated prices of the latest editions of these textbooks that are extracted from captive audiences of college students. Such price discrepancies are a good indication that Rothbard's book is *very* different—in content, style, and organization—from standard treatments of the subject.

Rothbard's book is targeted at a readership actively interested in learning about the subject and not at indifferent students slouching in the 500-seat amphitheatres of our "research" universities. While it is therefore written in Rothbard's characteristically sparkling prose it does not shy away from a rigorous presentation of the basic theoretical principles that govern the operation of the monetary system. Indeed the book is peppered with diagrams, charts, and tables aplenty—and even a simple equation or two. But before you run for the hills, you should know that it is not a "textbook" in the conventional sense.

Conventional money-and-banking textbooks confront the hapless reader with a jumble of dumbed-down mainstream theories and models. Some of these have been discredited and most bear very little systematic relationship to one another or are in actual conflict. The Quantity Theory, in both its "classical" and monetarist versions, Keynes's liquidity preference theory of interest, the New Keynesian Aggregate Supply curve, the expectations-augmented Phillips curve–one after another, all make their dreary appearance on the scene. Worse yet, this theoretical hodgepodge is generally set out in the *last* four or five chapters of the textbook and is usually preceded by a bland recitation of random technical details and historical facts about monetary and financial institutions. Unfortunately, the befuddled reader cannot make heads or tails out of these facts without the guidance of a coherent theory. For the privilege of being bewildered, misled, and eventually bored to tears by this indigestible intellectual stew, students get to pay $100 or more for the textbook.

Rothbard will have none of this shabby and disrespectful treatment of his reader and of his science that is meted out by the typical textbook author. In sharp contrast, he begins by *first* clearly presenting the fundamental principles or "laws" that govern money and monetary institutions. These universal and immutable laws form a fully integrated system of sound monetary theory that has been painstakingly elaborated over the course of centuries by scores of writers and economists extending back at least to the sixteenth-century Spanish Scholastics of the School of Salamanca. As the leading authority in this tradition in the latter half of the twentieth century, Rothbard expounds its core principles in a logical, step-by-step manner, using plain and lucid prose and avoiding extraneous details. He supplements his verbal-logical analysis with graphs and charts to effectively illustrate the operation of these principles in various institutional contexts.

It is noteworthy that, despite the fact that this book was written twenty-five years ago, the theory Rothbard presents is up to date. One reason is that the advancement of knowledge in non-experimental or "aprioristic" sciences like economic theory, logic, and mathematics proceeds steadily but slowly. In the case of sound monetary theory, many of its fundamental principles had been firmly established during the nineteenth century. In the German edition of *The Theory of Money and Credit* published in 1912, Ludwig von Mises, Rothbard's mentor, integrated these principles with value and price theory to formulate the modern theory of money and prices. Rothbard elaborated upon and advanced Mises's theoretical system. Thus the second reason that the monetary theory presented in the book remains fresh and relevant is that Rothbard himself was the leading monetary economist in the sound money tradition in the second half of the twentieth century, contributing many of the building blocks to the theoretical structure that he lays out. These include: formulating the proper criteria for calculating the money supply in a fractional-reserve banking system; identifying the various components of the demand for money; refining and consistently applying the supply-and-demand apparatus to analyzing the value of money; drawing a categorical distinction between deposit banking and loan bank-ing; providing the first logical and coherent explanation of how fiat money came into being and displaced commodity money as a result of a series of political interventions. All these innovations and more were products of Rothbard's creative genius, and many of his theoretical breakthroughs have not yet been adequately rec-ognized by contemporary monetary theorists, even of the Aus-trian School.

Rothbard's presentation of the basic principles of money-and-banking theory in the first eleven chapters of the book guides the reader in unraveling the mystery of how the central bank operates to create money through the fractional-reserve banking system and how this leads to inflation of the money supply and a rise in overall prices in the economy. But he does not stop there. In the subsequent five chapters he resolves the historical mystery of how an inherently inflationary institution like central banking, which is destructive of the value of money and, in the extreme case of hyperinflation, of money itself, came into being and was accepted as essential to the operation of the market economy.

As in the case of his exposition of the theory, Rothbard's treatment of the history of the Fed is fundamentally at odds with that found in standard textbooks. In the latter, the history is shal-low and episodic. It is taken for granted that the Fed, like all cen-tral banks, was originally designed as an institution whose goal was to promote the public interest by operating as a "lender of last resort," providing "liquidity" to troubled banks during times of financial turbulence to prevent a collapse of the financial sys-tem. Later the Fed was given a second mandate, to maintain "sta-bility of the price level," a policy which was supposed to rid the economy of business cycles and therefore to preclude prolonged periods of recession and unemployment. Thus strewn throughout a typical textbook one will find accounts of how the Fed han-dled—usually, although not always, in an enlightened manner—various "shocks" to the monetary and financial system. Culpabil-ity for such shocks is almost invariably attributed to the unruly propensities or irrational expectations of business investors, consumers, or wage-earners. Even in the exceptional instances, such as the Great Depression, when inept Fed policy is blamed for making matters worse, the Fed's errors are ascribed to not yet having learned how to properly wield the "tools of monetary policy," the euphemism used to describe the various techniques the Fed uses in exercising its legal monopoly of counterfeiting money. Each new crisis, however, stimulates the public-spirited policymakers at the Fed by a trial-and-error process to eventually converge on the optimal monetary policy, which was supposedly hit upon in the heyday of the Greenspan Fed during 1990s.

Rothbard rejects such a superficial and naïve account of the Fed's origins and bolstering of the banking system development. Instead, he deftly uses sound monetary theory to beam a penetrating light through the thick fog of carefully cultivated myths that surround the operation of the Fed. Rather than recounting the Fed's response to isolated crises, he blends economic theory with historical insight to reveal the pecuniary and ideological motives of the specific individuals who played key roles in establishing, molding, and operating the Fed. Needless to say, Rothbard does not blithely accept the almost universal view that the Fed is the outcome of a public-spirited response to shocks and failures caused by unruly market forces. Rather he asks, and then answers, the incisive, and always disturbing, question, *"Cui bono?"* ("To whose benefit?"). In other words, which particular individuals and groups stood to benefit from the Fed's creation and its specific policies? In answering this question, Rothbard fearlessly names names and delves into the covert motives and goals of those named.

This constitutes yet another, and possibly the most important, reason why Rothbard's book had been ignored: for it is forbidden to even pose the question of "who benefits" with respect to the Fed and its legal monopoly of the money supply, lest one be smeared and marginalized as a "conspiracy theorist." Strangely, when a similar question is asked regarding the imposition of tariffs or government regulations of one sort or another, no one seems to bat an eye, and free-market economists even delight in and win plaudits for uncovering such "rent-seekers" in their popular and academic publications. Thus economists of the Chicago and Public Choice Schools have explained the origins and policies of Federal regulatory agencies such as the ICC, CAB, FDA, FTC, FCC, etc., as powerfully shaped by the interests of the industries that they regulated. Yet these same economists squirm in discomfort and seek a quick escape when confronted with the question of why this analysis does not apply to the Fed. Indeed, Rothbard does no more than portray the Fed as a cartelizing device that limits entry into and regulates competition within the lucrative fractional-reserve banking industry and stands ready to bail it out, thus guaranteeing its profits and socializing its losses. Rothbard further demonstrates, that not only bankers, but also incumbent politicians and their favored constituencies and special interest groups benefit from the Fed's power to create money at will. This power is routinely used in the service of vote-seeking politicians to surreptitiously tax money holders to promote the interests of groups that gain from artificially cheap interest rates and direct government subsidies. These beneficiaries include, among others, Wall Street financial institutions, manufacturing firms that produce capital goods, the military-industrial complex, the construction and auto industries, and labor unions.

With the U.S. housing crisis metamorphosing into a full-blown financial crisis in the U.S. and Europe and the specter of a global stagflation looming larger every day, the Fed's credibility and reputation is evaporating with the value of the U.S. dollar. The time is finally ripe to publish this new edition of the book that asked the forbidden question about the Fed and fractional-reserve banking when it was first published twenty-five years ago.

JOSEPH T. SALERNO
PACE UNIVERSITY
JULY 2008

I.

MONEY: ITS IMPORTANCE AND ORIGINS

1. THE IMPORTANCE OF MONEY

Today, money supply figures pervade the financial press. Every Friday, investors breathlessly watch for the latest money figures, and Wall Street often reacts at the opening on the following Monday. If the money supply has gone up sharply, interest rates may or may not move upward. The press is filled with ominous forecasts of Federal Reserve actions, or of regulations of banks and other financial institutions.

This close attention to the money supply is rather new. Until the 1970s, over the many decades of the Keynesian Era, talk of money and bank credit had dropped out of the financial pages. Rather, they emphasized the GNP and government's fiscal policy, expenditures, revenues, and deficits. Banks and the money supply were generally ignored. Yet after decades of chronic and accelerating inflation—which the Keynesians could not begin to cure—and after many bouts of "inflationary recession," it became obvious to all—even to Keynesians—that something was awry. The money supply therefore became a major object of concern.

But the average person may be confused by so many definitions of the money supply. What are all the Ms about, from M1-A and M1-B up to M-8? Which is the *true* money supply figure, if any single one can be? And perhaps most important of all, why are bank deposits included in all the various Ms as a crucial and dominant part of the money supply? Everyone knows that paper dollars, issued nowadays exclusively by the Federal Reserve Banks and imprinted with the words "this note is legal tender for all debts, public and private" constitute money. But why are checking accounts money, and where do they come from? Don't they have to be redeemed in cash on demand? So why are checking deposits considered money, and not just the paper dollars backing them?

One confusing implication of including checking deposits as a part of the money supply is that banks *create* money, that they are, in a sense, money-creating factories. But don't banks simply channel the savings we lend to them and relend them to productive investors or to borrowing consumers? Yet, if banks take our savings and lend them out, how can they *create* money? How can their liabilities become part of the money supply?

There is no reason for the layman to feel frustrated if he can't find coherence in all this. The best classical economists fought among themselves throughout the nineteenth century over whether or in what sense private bank notes (now illegal) or deposits should or should not be part of the money supply. Most economists, in fact, landed on what we now see to be the wrong side of the question. Economists in Britain, the great center of economic thought during the nineteenth century, were particularly at sea on this issue. The eminent David Ricardo and his successors in the Currency School, lost a great chance to establish truly hard money in England because they never grasped the fact that bank deposits are part of the supply of money. Oddly enough, it was in the United States, then considered a backwater of economic theory, that economists first insisted that bank deposits, like bank notes, were part of the money supply. Condy Raguet, of Philadelphia, first made this point in 1820. But English economists of the day paid scant attention to their American colleagues.

2. HOW MONEY BEGINS

Before examining what money *is*, we must deal with the importance of money, and, before we can do that, we have to understand how money arose. As Ludwig von Mises conclusively demonstrated in 1912, money does not and cannot originate by order of the State or by some sort of social contract agreed upon by all citizens; it must always originate in the processes of the free market.

Before coinage, there was *barter*. Goods were produced by those who were good at it, and their surpluses were exchanged for the products of others. Every product had its barter price in terms of all other products, and every person gained by exchanging something he needed less for a product he needed more. The voluntary market economy became a latticework of mutually beneficial exchanges.

In barter, there were severe limitations on the scope of exchange and therefore on production. In the first place, in order to buy something he wanted, each person had to find a seller who wanted precisely what he had available in exchange. In short, if an egg dealer wanted to buy a pair of shoes, he had to find a shoemaker who wanted, at that very moment, to buy eggs. Yet suppose that the shoemaker was sated with eggs. How was the egg dealer going to buy a pair of shoes? How could he be sure that he could find a shoemaker who liked eggs?

Or, to put the question in its starkest terms, I make a living as a professor of economics. If I wanted to buy a newspaper in a world of barter, I would have to wander around and find a newsdealer who wanted to hear, say, a 10-minute economics lecture from me in exchange. Knowing economists, how likely would I be to find an interested newsdealer?

This crucial element in barter is what is called the *double coincidence of wants*. A second problem is one of *indivisibilities*. We can see clearly how exchangers could adjust their supplies and sales of butter, or eggs, or fish, fairly precisely. But suppose that Jones owns a house, and would like to sell it and instead, purchase a car, a washing machine, or some horses? How could he do so? He could not chop his house into 20 different segments and exchange each one for other products. Clearly, since houses are *indivisible* and lose all of their value if they get chopped up, we face an insoluble problem. The same would be true of tractors, machines, and other large-sized products. If houses could not easily be bartered, not many would be produced in the first place.

Another problem with the barter system is what would happen to *business calculation*. Business firms must be able to calculate whether they are making or losing income or wealth in each of their transactions. Yet, in the barter system, profit or loss calculation would be a hopeless task.

Barter, therefore, could not possibly manage an advanced or modern industrial economy. Barter could not succeed beyond the needs of a primitive village.

But man is ingenious. He managed to find a way to overcome these obstacles and transcend the limiting system of barter. Trying to overcome the limitations of barter, he arrived, step by step, at one of man's most ingenious, important and productive inventions: *money*.

Take, for example, the egg dealer who is trying desperately to buy a pair of shoes. He thinks to himself: if the shoemaker is allergic to eggs and doesn't want to buy them, what *does* he want to buy? Necessity is the mother of invention, and so the egg man is impelled to try to find out what the shoemaker would like to obtain. Suppose he finds out that it's fish. And so the egg dealer goes out and buys fish, not because he wants to eat the fish himself (*he* might be allergic to fish), but because he wants it in order to *resell* it to the shoemaker. In the world of barter, everyone's purchases were purely for himself or for his family's direct use. But now, for the first time, a new element of demand has entered:

The egg man is buying fish not for its own sake, but instead to use it as an indispensable way of obtaining shoes. Fish is now being used as a *medium of exchange*, as an instrument of *indirect exchange*, as well as being purchased directly for its own sake.

Once a commodity begins to be used as a medium of exchange, when the word gets out it generates even further use of the commodity as a medium. In short, when the word gets around that commodity X is being used as a medium in a certain village, more people living in or trading with that village will purchase that commodity, since they know that it is being used there as a medium of exchange. In this way, a commodity used as a medium feeds upon itself, and its use spirals upward, until before long the commodity is in general use throughout the society or country as a medium of exchange. But when a commodity is used as a medium for most or all exchanges, that commodity is defined as being a *money*.

In this way money enters the free market, as market participants begin to select suitable commodities for use as the medium of exchange, with that use rapidly escalating until a general medium of exchange, or money, becomes established in the market.

Money was a leap forward in the history of civilization and in man's economic progress. Money—as an element in every exchange—permits man to overcome all the immense difficulties of barter. The egg dealer doesn't have to seek a shoemaker who enjoys eggs; and I don't have to find a newsdealer or a grocer who wants to hear some economics lectures. All we need do is exchange our goods or services for money, for the money commodity. We can do so in the confidence that we can take this universally desired commodity and exchange it for any goods that we need. Similarly, indivisibilities are overcome; a homeowner can sell his house for money, and then exchange that money for the various goods and services that he wishes to buy.

Similarly, business firms can now calculate, can figure out when they are making, or losing, money. Their income and their expenditures for all transactions can be expressed in terms of money. The firm took in, say, $10,000 last month, and spent

$9,000; clearly, there was a net profit of $1,000 for the month. No longer does a firm have to try to add or subtract in commensurable objects. A steel manufacturing firm does not have to pay its workers in steel bars useless to them or in myriad other physical commodities; it can pay them in money, and the workers can then use money to buy other desired products.

Furthermore, to know a good's "price," one no longer has to look at a virtually infinite array of relative quantities: the fish price of eggs, the beef price of string, the shoe price of flour, and so forth. Every commodity is priced in only one commodity: money, and so it becomes easy to compare these single money prices of eggs, shoes, beef, or whatever.

3. THE PROPER QUALITIES OF MONEY

Which commodities are picked as money on the market? Which commodities will be subject to a spiral of use as a medium? Clearly, it will be those commodities most useful as money in any given society. Through the centuries, many commodities have been selected as money on the market. Fish on the Atlantic seacoast of colonial North America, beaver in the Old Northwest, and tobacco in the Southern colonies were chosen as money. In other cultures, salt, sugar, cattle, iron hoes, tea, cowrie shells, and many other commodities have been chosen on the market. Many banks display money museums which exhibit various forms of money over the centuries.

Amid this variety of moneys, it is possible to analyze the qualities which led the market to choose that particular commodity as money. In the first place, individuals do not pick the medium of exchange out of thin air. They will overcome the double coincidence of wants of barter by picking a commodity which is *already* in widespread use for its own sake. In short, they will pick a commodity *in heavy demand*, which shoemakers and others will be likely to accept in exchange from the very start of the money-choosing process. Second, they will pick a commodity which is *highly divisible*, so that small chunks of other goods can be bought, and size of purchases can be flexible. For this they need a commodity which technologically does not lose its quotal value when divided into small pieces. For that reason a house or a tractor, being highly indivisible, is not likely to be chosen as money, whereas butter, for example, is highly divisible and at least scores heavily as a money for this particular quality.

Demand and divisibility are not the only criteria. It is also important for people to be able to carry the money commodity around in order to facilitate purchases. To be easily *portable*, then, a commodity must have *high value per unit weight*. To have high value per unit weight, however, requires a good which is not only in great demand but also relatively scarce, since an intense demand combined with a relatively scarce supply will yield a high price, or high value per unit weight.

Finally, the money commodity should be highly durable, so that it can serve as a store of value for a long time. The holder of money should not only be assured of being able to purchase other products right now, but also indefinitely into the future. Therefore, butter, fish, eggs, and so on fail on the question of durability.

A fascinating example of an unexpected development of a money commodity in modern times occurred in German POW camps during World War II. In these camps, supply of various goods was fixed by external conditions: CARE packages, rations, etc. But after receiving the rations, the prisoners began exchanging what they didn't want for what they particularly needed, until soon there was an elaborate price system for every product, each in terms of what had evolved as the money commodity: cigarettes. Prices in terms of cigarettes fluctuated in accordance with changing supply and demand.

Cigarettes were clearly the most "moneylike" products available in the camps. They were in high demand for their own sake, they were divisible, portable, and in high value per unit weight. They were not very durable, since they crumpled easily, but they could make do in the few years of the camps' existence.[1]

---

[1]See the justly famous article by R.A. Radford, "The Economic Organization of a P.O.W. Camp," *Economica* (November 1945): 189–201.

In all countries and all civilizations, two commodities have
been dominant whenever they were available to compete as moneys with other commodities: *gold* and *silver*.

At first, gold and silver were highly prized only for their lus-
ter and ornamental value. They were always in great demand.
Second, they were always relatively scarce, and hence valuable
per unit of weight. And for that reason they were portable as well.
They were also divisible, and could be sliced into thin segments
without losing their pro rata value. Finally, silver or gold were
blended with small amounts of alloy to harden them, and since
they did not corrode, they would last almost forever.

Thus, because gold and silver are supremely "moneylike"
commodities, they are selected by markets as money if they are
available. Proponents of the gold standard do not suffer from a
mysterious "gold fetish." They simply recognize that gold has
always been selected by the market as money throughout history.

Generally, gold and silver have both been moneys, side-by-
side. Since gold has always been far scarcer and also in greater
demand than silver, it has always commanded a higher price, and
tends to be money in larger transactions, while silver has been
used in smaller exchanges. Because of its higher price, gold has
often been selected as the unit of account, although this has not
always been true. The difficulties of mining gold, which makes its
production limited, make its long-term value relatively more stable than silver.

4. The Money Unit

We referred to *prices* without explaining what a price really is.
A price is simply the ratio of the two quantities exchanged in any
transaction. It should be no surprise that every monetary unit we
are now familiar with—the dollar, pound, mark, franc, et al.—
began on the market simply as names for different units of weight
of gold or silver. Thus the "pound sterling" in Britain, was exactly
that—one pound of silver.[2]

---

[2]At current writing, silver is approximately $13 an ounce, and the
pound is about $1.50, which means that the British "pound sterling," once

The "dollar" originated as the name generally applied to a
one-ounce silver coin minted by a Bohemian count named
Schlick, in the sixteenth century. Count Schlick lived in Joachims-
thal (Joachim's Valley). His coins, which enjoyed a great reputation for uniformity and fineness, were called *Joachimsthalers* and
finally, just *thalers*. The word *dollar* emerged from the pronunci-
ation of *thaler*.

Since gold or silver exchanges by weight, the various national
currency units, all defined as particular weights of a precious
metal, will be automatically fixed in terms of each other. Thus,
suppose that the dollar is defined as 1/20 of a gold ounce (as it
was in the nineteenth century in the United States), while the
pound sterling is defined as 1/4 of a gold ounce, and the French
franc is established at 1/100 of a gold ounce.[3] But in that case,
the *exchange rates* between the various currencies are automatically fixed by their respective quantities of gold. If a dollar is 1/20
of a gold ounce, and the pound is 1/4 of a gold ounce, then the
pound will automatically exchange for 5 dollars. And, in our
example, the pound will exchange for 25 francs and the dollar for
5 francs. The definitions of weight automatically set the exchange
rates between them.

Free market gold standard advocates have often been taunted
with the charge: "You are against the government fixing the price

---

proudly equal to one pound of silver, now equals only 1/8 of a silver ounce.
How this decline and fall happened is explained in the text.

[3]The proportions are changed slightly from their nineteenth century
definitions to illustrate the point more clearly. The "dollar" had moved
from Bohemia to Spain and from there to North America. After the Revolutionary War, the new United States changed its currency from the British
pound sterling to the Spanish-derived dollar. From this point on, we assume
gold as the only monetary metal, and omit silver, for purposes of simplifica-
tion. In fact, silver was a complicating force in all monetary discussions in
the nineteenth century. In a free market, gold and silver each would be free
to become money and would float freely in relation to each other ("parallel
standards"). Unfortunately, governments invariably tried to force a fixed
exchange rate between the two metals, a price control that always leads to
unwelcome and even disastrous results ("bimetallism").

of goods and services; why then do you make an exception for gold? Why do you call for the government fixing the price of gold and setting the exchange rates between the various currencies?"

The answer to this common complaint is that the question assumes the dollar to be an independent entity, a thing or commodity which should be allowed to fluctuate freely in relation to gold. But the rebuttal of the pro-gold forces points out that the dollar is *not* an independent entity, that it was originally simply a name for a certain weight of gold; the dollar, as well as the other currencies, is a unit of weight. But in that case, the pound, franc, dollar, and so on, are not exchanging as independent entities; they, too, are simply relative weights of gold. If 1/4 ounce of gold exchanges for 1/20 ounce of gold, how *else* would we expect them to trade than at 1:5?[4]

If the monetary unit is simply a unit of weight, then government's role in the area of money could well be confined to a simple Bureau of Weights and Measures, certifying this as well as other units of weight, length, or mass.[5] The problem is that governments have systematically betrayed their trust as guardians of the precisely defined weight of the money commodity.

If government sets itself up as the guardian of the international meter or the standard yard or pound, there is no economic incentive for it to betray its trust and change the definition. For the Bureau of Standards to announce suddenly that 1 pound is

---

[4]In older periods, foreign coins of gold and silver often circulated freely within a country, and there is, indeed, no economic reason why they should not do so. In the United States, as late as 1857, few bothered going to the U.S. Mint to obtain coins; the coins in general use were Spanish, English, and Austrian gold and silver pieces. Finally, Congress, perturbed at this slap to its sovereignty, outlawed the use of foreign coins within the U.S., forcing all foreign coinholders to go to the U.S. Mint and obtain American gold coins.

[5]Thus, Frederick Barnard's late nineteenth-century book on weights and measures has a discussion of coinage and the international monetary system in the appendix. Frederick A.P. Barnard, *The Metric System of Weights and Measures*, rev. ed. (New York: Columbia College, 1872).

now equal to 14 instead of 16 ounces would make no sense what-ever. There is, however, all too much of an economic incentive for governments to change, especially to lighten, the definition of the currency unit; say, to change the definition of the pound ster-ling from 16 to 14 ounces of silver. This profitable process of the government's repeatedly lightening the number of ounces or grams in the same monetary unit is called *debasement*.

How debasement profits the State can be seen from a hypo-thetical case: Say the *rur*, the currency of the mythical kingdom of Ruritania, is worth 20 grams of gold. A new king now ascends the throne, and, being chronically short of money, decides to take the debasement route to the acquisition of wealth. He announces a mammoth call-in of all the old gold coins of the realm, each now dirty with wear and with the picture of the previous king stamped on its face. In return he will supply brand new coins with his face stamped on them, and will return the same number of *rurs* paid in. Someone presenting 100 *rurs* in old coins will receive 100 *rurs* in the new.

Seemingly a bargain! Except for a slight hitch: During the course of this recoinage, the king changes the definition of the *rur* from 20 to 16 grams. He then pockets the extra 20 percent of gold, minting the gold for his own use and pouring the coins into circulation for his own expenses. In short, the number of grams of gold in the society remains the same, but since people are now accustomed to use the *name* rather than the weight in their money accounts and prices, the number of *rurs* will have increased by 20 percent. The money supply in *rurs*, therefore, has gone up by 20 percent, and, as we shall see later on, this will drive up prices in the economy in terms of *rurs*. *Debasement*, then, is the arbitrary redefining and lightening of the currency so as to add to the cof-fers of the State.[6]

The pound sterling has diminished from 16 ounces of silver to its present fractional state because of repeated debasements, or

---

[6]This enormous charge for recoinage is called "seigniorage," payment to the seignieur or sovereign, the monopoly minter of coins.

changes in definition, by the kings of England. Similarly, rapid and extensive debasement was a striking feature of the Middle Ages, in almost every country in Europe. Thus, in 1200, the French *livre tournois* was defined as 98 grams of fine silver; by 1600 it equaled only 11 grams.

A particularly striking case is the *dinar*, the coin of the Saracens in Spain. The *dinar*, when first coined at the end of the seventh century, consisted of 65 gold grains. The Saracens, notably sound in monetary matters, kept the dinar's weight relatively constant, and as late as the middle of the twelfth century, it still equaled 60 grains. At that point, the Christian kings conquered Spain, and by the early thirteenth century, the dinar (now called *maravedi*) had been reduced to 14 grains of gold. Soon the gold coin was too lightweight to circulate, and it was converted into a silver coin weighing 26 grains of silver. But this, too, was debased further, and by the mid-fifteenth century, the maravedi consisted of only 1½ silver grains, and was again too small to circulate.[7]

Where is the total money supply—that crucial concept—in all this? First, before debasement, when the regional or national currency unit simply stands for a certain unit of weight of gold, the total money supply is the aggregate of all the monetary gold in existence in that society, that is, all the gold ready to be used in exchange. In practice, this means the total stock of gold coin and gold bullion available. Since all property and therefore all money is owned by *someone*, this means that the total money stock in the society at any given time is the aggregate, the sum total, of all existing *cash balances*, or money stock, owned by each individual or group. Thus, if there is a village of 10 people, A, B, C, etc., the

---

[7]See Elgin Groseclose, *Money and Man* (New York: Frederick Ungar, 1961), pp. 57–76. Many of the European debasements were made under the guise of adjusting the always-distorted fixed bimetallic ratios between gold and silver. See Luigi Einaudi, "The Theory of Imaginary Money from Charlemagne to the French Revolution," in F.C. Lane and J.C. Riemersma, eds., *Enterprise and Secular Change* (Homewood, Ill.: Irwin, 1953), pp. 229–61.

total money stock in the village will equal the sum of all cash balances held by each of the 10 citizens. If we wish to put this in mathematical terms, we can say that

$$M = \Sigma \, m$$

where M is the total stock or supply of money in any given area or in society as a whole, m is the individual stock or cash balance owned by each individual, and Σ means the sum or aggregate of each of the ms.

After debasement, since the money unit is the *name* (dinar) rather than the actual weight (specific number of gold grams), the number of dinars or pounds or maravedis will increase, and thus increase the supply of money. M will be the sum of the individual dinars held by each person, and will increase by the extent of the debasement. As we will see later, this increased money supply will tend to raise prices throughout the economy.

II.

WHAT DETERMINES PRICES: SUPPLY AND DEMAND

What determines individual prices? Why is the price of eggs, or horseshoes, or steel rails, or bread, whatever it is? Is the market determination of prices arbitrary, chaotic, or anarchic?

Much of the past two centuries of economic analysis, or what is now unfortunately termed *microeconomics*, has been devoted to analyzing and answering this question. The answer is that any given price is always determined by two fundamental, underlying forces: supply and demand, or the supply of that product and the intensity of demand to purchase it.

Let us say that we are analyzing the determination of the price of any product, say, coffee, at any given moment, or "day," in time. At any time there is a stock of coffee, ready to be sold to the consumer. How that stock got there is not yet our concern. Let's say that, at a certain place or in an entire country, there are 10 million pounds of coffee available for consumption. We can then construct a diagram, of which the horizontal axis is units of quantity, in this case, millions of pounds of coffee. If 10 million pounds are now available, the stock, or supply, of coffee available is the vertical line at 10 million pounds, the line to be labeled S for supply.

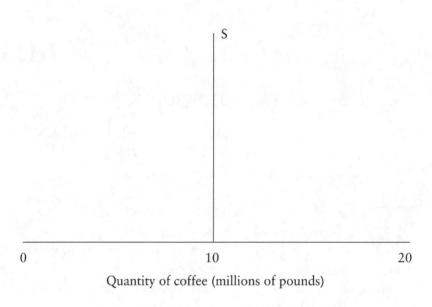

Quantity of coffee (millions of pounds)

FIGURE 2.1 — THE SUPPLY LINE

The *demand curve* for coffee is not objectively measurable as is supply, but there are several things that we can definitely say about it. For one, if we construct a hypothetical *demand schedule* for the market, we can conclude that, at any given time, and all other things remaining the same, the higher the price of a product the less will be purchased. Conversely, the lower the price the more will be purchased. Suppose, for example, that for some bizarre reason, the price of coffee should suddenly leap to $1,000 a pound. Very few people will be able to buy and consume coffee, and they will be confined to a few extremely wealthy coffee fanatics. Everyone else will shift to cocoa, tea, or other beverages. So if the coffee price becomes extremely high, few pounds of coffee will be purchased.

On the other hand, suppose again that, by some fluke, coffee prices suddenly drop to 1 cent a pound. At that point, everyone will rush out to consume coffee in large quantities, and they will forsake tea, cocoa or whatever. A very low price, then, will induce a willingness to buy a very large number of pounds of coffee.

A very high price means only a few purchases; a very low price means a large number of purchases. Similarly we can generalize on the range between. In fact we can conclude: The lower

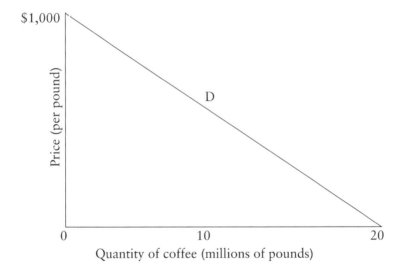

FIGURE 2.2 — THE DEMAND CURVE[1]

---

[1]Conventionally, and for convenience, economists for the past four decades have drawn the demand curves as falling straight lines. There is no particular reason to suppose, however, that the demand curves are straight lines, and no evidence to that effect. They might just as well be curved or jagged or anything else. The only thing we know with assurance is that they are falling, or negatively sloped. Unfortunately, economists have tended to forget this home truth, and have begun to manipulate these lines as if they actually existed in this shape. In that way, mathematical manipulation begins to crowd out the facts of economic reality.

the price of any product (other things being equal), the greater
the quantities that buyers will be willing to purchase. And vice
versa. For as the price of anything falls, it becomes less costly relative to the buyer's stock of money and to other competing uses
for the dollar; so that a fall in price will bring nonbuyers into the
market and cause the expansion of purchases by existing buyers.
Conversely, as the price of anything rises, the product becomes
more costly relative to the buyers' income and to other products,
and the amount they will purchase will fall. Buyers will leave the
market, and existing buyers will curtail their purchases.

The result is the "falling demand curve," which graphically
expresses this "law of demand" (Figure 2.2). We can see that the
quantity buyers will purchase ("the quantity demanded") varies
inversely with the price of the product. This line is labeled D for
demand. The vertical axis is P for price, in this case, dollars per
pound of coffee.

Supply, for any good, is the objective fact of how many goods
are available to the consumer. Demand is the result of the subjective values and demands of the individual buyers or consumers. S
tells us how many pounds of coffee, or loaves of bread or whatever are available; D tells us how many loaves would be purchased at different hypothetical prices. We never know the actual
demand curve: only that it is falling, in some way; with quantity
purchased increasing as prices fall and vice versa.

We come now to how prices are determined on the free market. What we shall demonstrate is that the price of any good or
service, at any given time, and on any given day, will tend to be
the price at which the S and D curves intersect (Figure 2.3).

In our example, the S and D curves intersect at the price of $3
a pound, and therefore that will be the price on the market.

To see why the coffee price will be $3 a pound, let us suppose
that, for some reason, the price is higher, say $5 (Figure 2.4). At
that point, the quantity supplied (10 million pounds) will be
greater than the quantity demanded, that is, the amount that consumers are willing to buy at that higher price. This leaves an

unsold surplus of coffee, coffee sitting on the shelves that cannot be sold because no one will buy it.

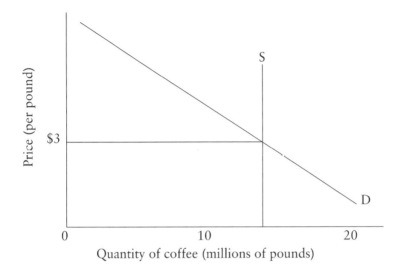

FIGURE 2.3 — SUPPLY AND DEMAND

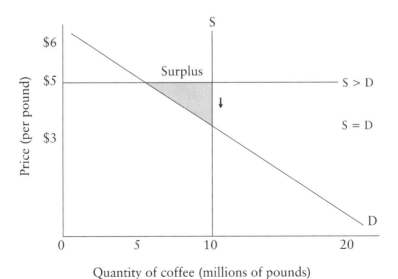

Quantity of coffee (millions of pounds)

FIGURE 2.4 — SURPLUS

At a price of $5 for coffee, only 6 million pounds are purchased, leaving 4 million pounds of unsold surplus. The pressure of the surplus, and the consequent losses, will induce sellers to lower their price, and as the price falls, the quantity purchased will increase. This pressure continues until the intersection price of $3 is reached, at which point the market is *cleared*, that is, there is no more unsold surplus, and supply is just equal to demand. People want to buy just the amount of coffee available, no more and no less.

At a price higher than the intersection, then, supply is greater than demand, and market forces will then impel a lowering of price until the unsold surplus is eliminated, and supply and demand are equilibrated. These market forces which lower the excessive price and clear the market are powerful and twofold: the desire of every businessman to increase profits and to avoid losses, and the free price system, which reflects economic changes and responds to underlying supply and demand changes. The profit motive and the free price system are the forces that equilibrate supply and demand, and make price responsive to underlying market forces.

On the other hand, suppose that the price, instead of being above the intersection, is below the intersection price. Suppose the price is at $1 a pound. In that case, the quantity demanded by consumers, the amount of coffee the consumers wish to purchase at that price, is much greater than the 10 million pounds that they would buy at $3. Suppose that quantity is 15 million pounds. But, since there are only 10 million pounds available to satisfy the 15 million pound demand at the low price, the coffee will then rapidly disappear from the shelves, and we would experience a *shortage* of coffee (shortage being present when something cannot be purchased at the existing price).

The coffee market would then be as shown in Figure 2.5.

Thus, at the price of $1, there is a shortage of 4 million pounds, that is, there are only 10 million pounds of coffee available to satisfy a demand for 14 million. Coffee will disappear quickly from the shelves, and then the retailers, emboldened by a

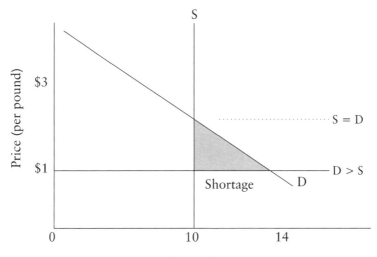

FIGURE 2.5 — SHORTAGE

desire for profit, will raise their prices. As the price rises, the shortage will begin to disappear, until it disappears completely when the price goes up to the intersection point of $3 a pound. Once again, free market action quickly eliminates shortages by raising prices to the point where the market is cleared, and demand and supply are again equilibrated.

Clearly then, the profit-loss motive and the free price system produce a built-in "feedback" or governor mechanism by which the market price of any good moves so as to clear the market, and to eliminate quickly any surpluses or shortages. For at the intersection point, which tends always to be the market price, supply and demand are finely and precisely attuned, and neither shortage nor surplus can exist (Figure 2.6).

Economists call the intersection price, the price which tends to be the daily market price, the "equilibrium price," for two reasons: (1) because this is the *only* price that equilibrates supply and demand, that equates the quantity available for sale with the quantity buyers wish to purchase; and (2) because, in an analogy with the physical sciences, the intersection price is the only price

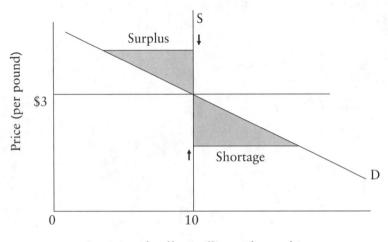

Quantity of coffee (millions of pounds)

FIGURE 2.6 — TOWARD EQUILIBRIUM

to which the market tends to move. And, if a price is displaced from equilibrium, it is quickly impelled by market forces to return to that point—just as an equilibrium point in physics is where something tends to stay and to return to if displaced.

If the price of a product is determined by its supply and demand and if, according to our example, the equilibrium price, where the price will move and remain, is $3 for a pound of coffee, why does any price ever *change*? We know, of course, that prices of all products are changing all the time. The price of coffee does not remain contentedly at $3 or any other figure. How and why does any price change ever take place?

Clearly, for one of two (more strictly, three) reasons: either D changes, or S changes, or both change at the same time. Suppose, for example, that S falls, say because a large proportion of the coffee crop freezes in Brazil, as it seems to do every few years. A drop in S is depicted in Figure 2.7.

Beginning with an equilibrium price of $3, the quantity of coffee produced and ready for sale on the market drops from 10 million to 6 million pounds. S changes to S′, the new vertical supply

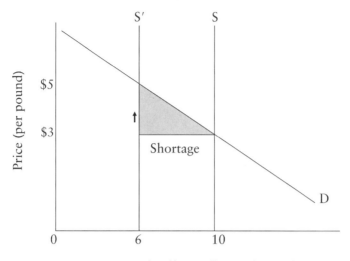

FIGURE 2.7 — DECLINE IN SUPPLY

line. But this means that at the new supply, S′, there is a shortage of coffee at the old price, amounting to 4 million pounds. The shortage impels coffee sellers to raise their prices, and, as they do so, the shortage begins to disappear, until the new equilibrium price is achieved at the $5 price.

To put it another way, all products are scarce in relation to their possible use, which is the reason they command a price on the market at all. Price, on the free market, performs a necessary *rationing* function, in which the available pounds or bushels or other units of a good are allocated freely and voluntarily to those who are most willing to purchase the product. If coffee becomes scarcer, then the price rises to perform an increased rationing function: to allocate the smaller supply of the product to the most eager purchasers. When the price rises to reflect the smaller supply, consumers cut their purchases and shift to other hot drinks or stimulants until the quantity demanded is small enough to equal the lower supply.

On the other hand, let us see what happens when the supply increases, say, because of better weather conditions or increased

productivity due to better methods of growing or manufacturing
the product. Figure 2.8 shows the result of an increase in S:

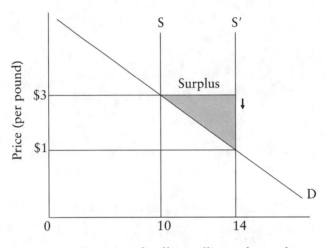

Quantity of coffee (millions of pounds)

FIGURE 2.8 — INCREASE OF SUPPLY

Supply increases from 10 to 14 million pounds or from S to
S'. But this means that at the old equilibrium price, $3, there is
now an excess of supply over demand, and 4 million pounds will
remain unsold at the old price. In order to sell the increased product, sellers will have to cut their prices, and as they do so, the
price of coffee will fall until the new equilibrium price is reached,
here at $1 a pound. Or, to put it another way, businessmen will
now have to cut prices in order to induce consumers to buy the
increased product, and will do so until the new equilibrium is
reached.

In short, price responds inversely to supply. If supply
increases, price will fall; if supply falls, price will rise.

The other factor that can and does change and thereby alters
equilibrium price is demand. Demand can change for various reasons. Given total consumer income, any increase in the demand
for one product necessarily reflects a fall in the demand for
another. For an increase in demand is defined as a willingness by

buyers to spend more money on—that is, to buy more—of a product at any given hypothetical price. In our diagrams, such an "increase in demand" is reflected in a shift of the entire demand curve upward and to the right. But given total income, if consumers are spending more on Product A, they must necessarily be spending less on Product B. The demand for Product B will decrease, that is, consumers will be willing to spend less on the product at any given hypothetical price. Graphically, the entire demand curve for B will shift downward and to the left. Suppose that we are now analyzing a shift in consumer tastes toward beef and away from pork. In that case, the respective markets may be analyzed as follows:

We have postulated an increase in consumer preference for beef, so that the demand curve for beef increases, that is, shifts upward and to the right, from D to D'. But the result of the increased demand is that there is now a shortage at the old equilibrium price, 0X, so that producers raise their prices until the shortage is eliminated and there is a new and higher equilibrium price, 0Y.

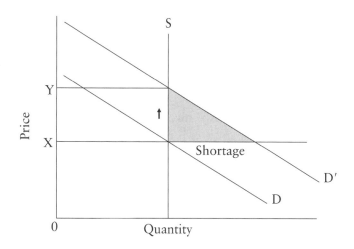

FIGURE 2.9 — THE BEEF MARKET: INCREASE IN DEMAND

On the other hand, suppose that there is a drop in preference, and therefore a fall in the demand for pork. This means that the demand curve for pork shifts downward and to the left, from D to D', as shown in Figure 2.10:

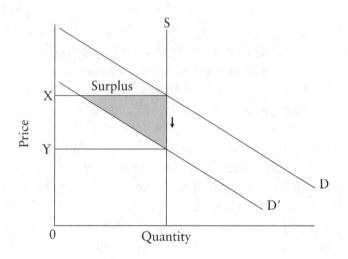

FIGURE 2.10 — THE PORK MARKET: DECLINE IN DEMAND

Here, the fall in demand from D to D' means that at the old equilibrium price for pork, 0X, there is now an unsold surplus because of the decline in demand. In order to sell the surplus, therefore, producers must cut the price until the surplus disappears and the market is cleared again, at the new equilibrium price 0Y.

In sum, price responds directly to changes in demand. If demand increases, price rises; if demand falls, the price drops.

We have been treating supply throughout as a given, which it always is at any one time. If, however, demand for a product increases, *and* that increase is perceived by the producers as lasting for a long period of time, future supply will increase. More beef, for example, will be grown in response to the greater demand and the higher price and profits. Similarly, producers will cut future supply if a fall in prices is thought to be permanent.

Supply, therefore, will respond over time to future demand as anticipated by producers. It is this response by supply to changes in expected future demand that gives us the familiar forward-sloping, or rising supply curves of the economics textbooks.

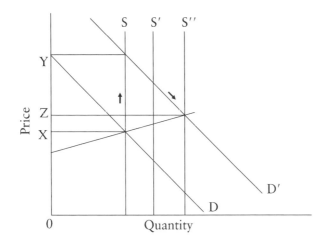

FIGURE 2.11 — THE BEEF MARKET: RESPONSE OF SUPPLY

As shown in Figure 2.9, demand increases from D to D′. This raises the equilibrium price of beef from 0X to 0Y, given the initial S curve, the initial supply of beef. But if this new higher price 0Y is considered permanent by the beef producers, supply will increase over time, until it reaches the new higher supply S″. Price will be driven back down by the increased supply to 0Z. In this way, higher demand pulls out more supply over time, which will lower the price.

To return to the original change in demand, on the free market a rise in the demand for and price of one product will necessarily be counterbalanced by a fall in the demand for another. The only way in which consumers, especially over a sustained period of time, can increase their demand for *all* products is if consumer incomes are increasing overall, that is, if consumers have more money in their pockets to spend on all products. But this can happen only if the stock or supply of money available increases; only in that case, with more money in consumer hands, can most or all demand curves rise, can shift upward and to the right, and prices can rise overall.

To put it another way: a continuing, sustained *inflation*—that is, a persistent rise in overall prices—can either be the result of a persistent, continuing fall in the supply of most or all goods and services, *or* of a continuing rise in the supply of money. Since we *know* that in today's world the supply of most goods and services rises rather than falls each year, and since we know, also, that the money supply keeps rising substantially every year, then it should be crystal clear that increases in the supply of money, *not* any sort of problems from the supply side, are the fundamental cause of our chronic and accelerating problem of inflation. Despite the currently fashionable supply-side economists, inflation is a demand-side (more specifically monetary or money supply) rather than a supply-side problem. Prices are continually being pulled up by increases in the quantity of money and hence of the monetary demand for products.

III.

Money and Overall Prices

1. The Supply and Demand for Money and Overall Prices

When economics students read textbooks, they learn, in the "micro" sections, how prices of specific goods are determined by supply and demand. But when they get to the "macro" chapters, lo and behold! supply and demand built on individual persons and their choices disappear, and they hear instead of such mysterious and ill-defined concepts as *velocity of circulation, total transactions,* and *gross national product*. Where are the supply-and-demand concepts when it comes to overall prices?

In truth, overall prices are determined by similar supply-and-demand forces that determine the prices of individual products. Let us reconsider the concept of *price*. If the price of bread is 70 cents a loaf, this means also that the *purchasing power* of a loaf of bread is 70 cents. A loaf of bread can command 70 cents in exchange on the market. The price and purchasing power of the unit of a product are one and the same. Therefore, we can construct a diagram for the determination of overall prices, with the price or the purchasing power of the money unit on the Y-axis.

While recognizing the extreme difficulty of arriving at a measure, it should be clear conceptually that the price or the purchasing power of the dollar is the inverse of whatever we can construct as the *price level*, or the level of overall prices. In mathematical terms,

$$PPM = \frac{1}{P}$$

where PPM is the purchasing power of the dollar, and P is the price level.

To take a highly simplified example, suppose that there are four commodities in the society and that their prices are as follows:

eggs	$	.50 dozen
butter	$	1 pound
shoes	$	20 pair
TV set	$	200 set

In this society, the PPM, or the purchasing power of the dollar, is an array of alternatives inverse to the above prices. In short, the purchasing power of the dollar is:

either	2 dozen eggs
or	1 pound butter
or	1/20 pair shoes
or	1/200 TV set

Suppose now that the price level doubles, in the easy sense that all prices double. Prices are now:

eggs	$	1 dozen
butter	$	2 pound
shoes	$	40 pair
TV set	$	400 set

In this case, PPM has been cut in half across the board. The purchasing power of the dollar is now:

either	1 dozen eggs
or	1/2 pound butter
or	1/40 pair shoes
or	1/400 TV set

Purchasing power of the dollar is therefore the inverse of the price level.

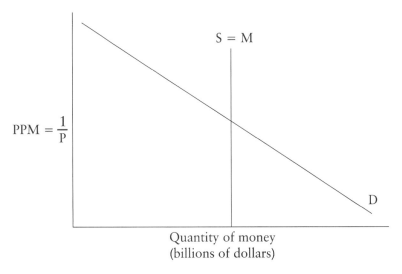

FIGURE 3.1 — SUPPLY OF AND DEMAND FOR MONEY

Let us now put PPM on the Y-axis and quantity of dollars on the X-axis. We contend that, on a complete analogy with supply, demand, and price above, the intersection of the vertical line indicating the supply of money in the country at any given time, with the falling demand curve for money, will yield the market equilibrium PPM and hence the equilibrium height of overall prices, at any given time.

Let us examine the diagram in Figure 3.1. The supply of money, M, is conceptually easy to figure: the total quantity of dollars at any given time. (What constitutes these dollars will be explained later.)

We contend that there is a falling demand curve for money in relation to hypothetical PPMs, just as there is one in relation to hypothetical individual prices. At first, the idea of a demand curve for money seems odd. Isn't the demand for money unlimited? Won't people take as much money as they can get? But this confuses what people would be willing to accept as a gift (which is indeed unlimited) with their *demand* in the sense of how much they would be willing to give up for the money. Or: how much money they would be willing to keep in their cash balances rather than spend. In this sense their demand for money is scarcely unlimited. If someone acquires money, he can do two things with it: either spend it on consumer goods or investments, or *else* hold on to it, and increase his individual money stock, his total cash balances. How much he wishes to hold on to is his demand for money.

Let us look at people's demand for cash balances. How much money people will keep in their cash balance is a function of the level of prices. Suppose, for example, that prices suddenly dropped to about a third of what they are now. People would need far less in their wallets, purses, and bank accounts to pay for daily transactions or to prepare for emergencies. Everyone need only carry around or have readily available only about a third the money that they keep now. The rest they can spend or invest. Hence, the total amount of money people would hold in their cash balances would be far less if prices were much lower than now. Contrarily, if prices were triple what they are today, people would need about three times as much in their wallets, purses, and bank accounts to handle their daily transactions and their emergency inventory. People would demand far greater cash balances than they do now to do the same "money work" if prices were much higher. The falling demand curve for money is shown in Figure 3.2.

Here we see that when the PPM is very high (i.e., prices overall are very low), the demand for cash balances is low; but when

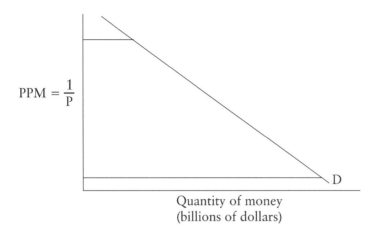

$$PPM = \frac{1}{P}$$

Quantity of money
(billions of dollars)

FIGURE 3.2 — DEMAND FOR MONEY

PPM is very low (prices are high), the demand for cash balances
is very high.

We will now see how the intersection of the falling demand
curve for money or cash balances, and the supply of money, determines the day-to-day equilibrium PPM or price level.

Suppose that PPM is suddenly very high, that is, prices are
very low. M, the money stock, is given, at $100 billion. As we see
in Figure 3.3, at a high PPM, the supply of total cash balances, M,
is greater than the demand for money. The difference is surplus
cash balances—money, in the old phrase, that is burning a hole in
people's pockets. People find that they are suffering from a monetary imbalance: their cash balances are greater than they need at
that price level. And so people start trying to get rid of their cash
balances by spending money on various goods and services.

But while people can get rid of money individually, by buying
things with it, they can't get rid of money in the aggregate,
because the $100 billion still exists, and they can't get rid of it
short of burning it up. But as people spend more, this drives up
demand curves for most or all goods and services. As the demand
curves shift upward and to the right, prices rise. But as prices overall rise further and further, PPM begins to fall, as the downward

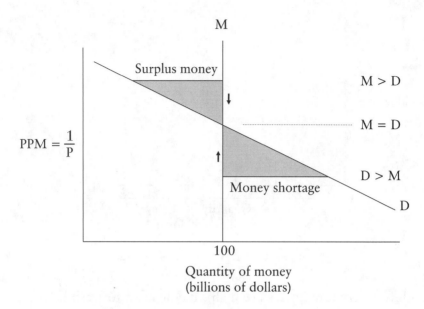

FIGURE 3.3 —DETERMINATION OF THE PURCHASING
POWER OF MONEY

arrow indicates. And as the PPM begins to fall, the surplus of cash balances begins to disappear until finally, prices have risen so much that the $100 billion no longer burns a hole in anyone's pocket. At the higher price level, people are now willing to keep the exact amount of $100 billion that is available in the economy. The market is at last cleared, and people now wish to hold no more and no less than the $100 billion available. The demand for money has been brought into equilibrium with the supply of money, and the PPM and price level are in equilibrium. People were not able to get rid of money in the aggregate, but they were able to drive up prices so as to end the surplus of cash balances.

Conversely, suppose that prices were suddenly three times as high and PPM therefore much lower. In that case, people would need far more cash balances to finance their daily lives, and there would be a shortage of cash balances compared to the supply of money available. The demand for cash balances would be greater than the total supply. People would then try to alleviate this imbalance, this shortage, by adding to their cash balances. They can only do so by spending less of their income and adding the remainder to their cash balance. When they do so, the demand curves for most or all products will shift downward and to the left, and prices will generally fall. As prices fall, PPM *ipso facto* rises, as the upward arrow shows. The process will continue until prices fall enough and PPM rises, so that the $100 billion is no longer less than the total amount of cash balances desired.

Once again, market action works to equilibrate supply and demand for money or cash balances, and demand for money will adjust to the total supply available. Individuals tried to scramble to add to their cash balances by spending less; in the aggregate, they could not add to the money supply, since that is given at $100 billion. But in the process of spending less, prices overall fell until the $100 billion became an adequate total cash balance once again.

The price level, then, and the purchasing power of the dollar, are determined by the same sort of supply-and-demand feedback mechanism that determines individual prices. The price level tends to be at the intersection of the supply of and demand for money, and tends to return to that point when displaced.

As in individual markets, then, the price or purchasing power of the dollar varies directly with the demand for money and inversely with the supply. Or, to turn it around, the price level varies directly with the supply of money and inversely with the demand.

2. Why Overall Prices Change

Why does the price level ever change, if the supply of money and the demand for money determine the height of overall prices? If, and only if, one or both of these basic factors—the supply of or demand for money—changes. Let us see what happens when the supply of money changes, that is, in the modern world, when the supply of nominal units changes rather than the actual weight of gold or silver they used to represent. Let us assume, then, that the supply of dollars, pounds, or francs increases, without yet

examining how the increase occurs or *how* the new money gets
injected into the economy.

Figure 3.4 shows what happens when M, the supply of dollars, of total cash balances of dollars in the economy, increases.

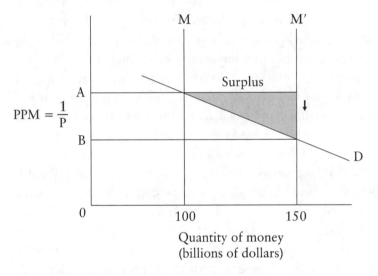

FIGURE 3.4 — INCREASE IN THE SUPPLY OF MONEY

The original supply of money, M, intersects with the demand
for money and establishes the PPM (purchasing power of the dollar) and the price level at distance 0A. Now, in whatever way, the
supply of money increases to M'. This means that the aggregate
total of cash balances in the economy has increased from M, say
$100 billion, to M', $150 billion. But now people have $50 bil-
lion surplus in their cash balances, $50 billion of excess money
over the amount needed in their cash balances at the previous 0A
prices level. Having too much money burning a hole in their
pockets, people spend the cash balances, thereby raising individual demand curves and driving up prices. But as prices rise, people find that their increased aggregate of cash balances is getting
less and less excessive, since more and more cash is now needed
to accommodate the higher price levels. Finally, prices rise until
PPM has fallen from 0A to 0B. At these new, higher price levels,

the M'—the new aggregate cash balances—is no longer excessive, and the demand for money has become equilibrated by market forces to the new supply. The *money market*—the intersection of the demand and supply of money—is once again cleared, and a new and higher equilibrium price level has been reached.

Note that when people find their cash balances excessive, they try to get rid of them, but since all the money stock is owned by *someone*, the new M' cannot be gotten rid of in the aggregate; by driving prices up, however, the demand for money becomes equilibrated to the new supply. Just as an increased supply of pork drives down prices so as to induce people to buy the new pork production, so an increased supply of dollars drives down the purchasing power of the dollar until people are willing to hold the new dollars in their cash balances.

What if the supply of money, M, *decreases*, admittedly an occurrence all too rare in the modern world? The effect can be seen in Figure 3.5.

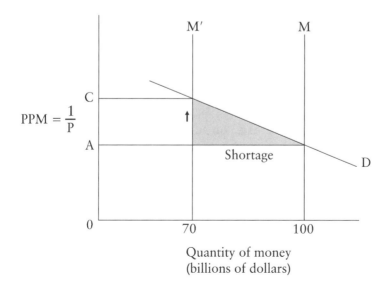

FIGURE 3.5 — A FALL IN THE SUPPLY OF MONEY

In the unusual case of a fall in the supply of money, then, total cash balances fall, say, from $100 billion (M) to $70 billion (M'). When this happens, the people find out that at the old equilibrium price level 0A, aggregate cash balances are not enough to satisfy their cash balance needs. They experience, therefore, a cash balance shortage. Trying to increase his cash balance, then, each individual spends less and saves in order to accumulate a larger balance. As this occurs, demand curves for specific goods fall downward and to the left, and prices therefore fall. As this happens, the cash balance shortage is alleviated, until finally prices fall low enough until a new and lower equilibrium price level (0C) is established. Or, alternatively, the PPM is at a new and higher level. At the new price level of PPM, 0C, the demand for cash balances is equilibrated with the new and decreased supply M'. The demand and supply of money is once again cleared. At the new equilibrium, the decreased money supply is once again just sufficient to perform the cash balance function.

Or, put another way, at the lower money supply people scramble to increase cash balances. But since the money supply is set and outside their control, they cannot increase the supply of cash balances in the aggregate.[1] But by spending less and driving down the price level, they increase the value or purchasing power of each dollar, so that real cash balances (total money supply corrected for changes in purchasing power) have gone up to offset the drop in the total supply of money. M might have fallen by $30 billion, but the $70 billion is now as good as the previous total because each dollar is worth more in *real*, or purchasing power, terms.

An increase in the supply of money, then, will lower the price or purchasing power of the dollar, and thereby increase the level of prices. A fall in the money supply will do the opposite, lowering prices and thereby increasing the purchasing power of each dollar.

---

[1]Why doesn't an excess demand for cash balances increase the money supply, as it would in the case of beef, in the long run? For a discussion of the determinants of the supply of money, see chapter IV.

The other factor of change in the price level is the demand for money. Figures 3.6 and 3.7 depict what happens when the demand for money changes.

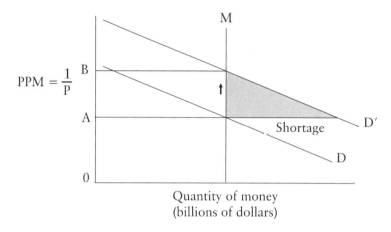

$$\text{PPM} = \frac{1}{P}$$

FIGURE 3.6 — AN INCREASE IN THE DEMAND FOR MONEY

The demand for money, for whatever reason, increases from D to D′. This means that, whatever the price level, the amount of money that people in the aggregate wish to keep in their cash balances will increase. At the old equilibrium price level, 0A, a PPM that previously kept the demand and supply of money equal and cleared the market, the demand for money has now increased and become greater than the supply. There is now an excess demand for money, or shortage of cash balances, at the old price level. Since the supply of money is given, the scramble for greater cash balances begins. People will spend less and save more to add to their cash holdings. In the aggregate, M, or the total supply of cash balances, is fixed and cannot increase. But the fall in prices resulting from the decreased spending will alleviate the shortage. Finally, prices fall (or PPM rises) to 0B. At this new equilibrium price, 0B, there is no longer a shortage of cash balances. Because of the increased PPM, the old money supply, M, is now enough to satisfy the increased demand for cash balances. Total cash balances have remained the same in nominal terms, but in *real* terms, in terms of purchasing power, the $100 billion is now worth more and will perform more of the cash balance function. The market is again cleared, and the money supply and demand brought once more into equilibrium.

Figure 3.7 shows what happens when the demand for money falls.

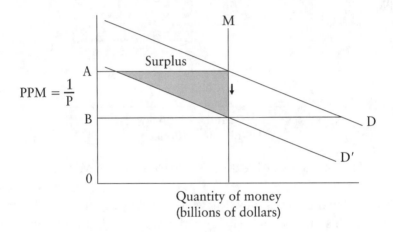

FIGURE 3.7 — A FALL IN THE DEMAND FOR MONEY

The demand for money falls from D to D'. In other words, whatever the price level, people are now, for whatever reason, willing to hold lower cash balances than they did before. At the old equilibrium price level, 0A, people now find that they have a surplus of cash balances burning a hole in their pockets. As they spend the surplus, demand curves for goods rise, driving up prices. But as prices rise, the total supply of cash balances, M, becomes no longer surplus, for it now must do cash balance work at a higher price level. Finally, when prices rise (PPM falls) to 0B, the surplus of cash balance has disappeared and the demand and supply of money has been equilibrated. The same money supply, M, is once again satisfactory despite the fall in the demand for money, because the same M must do more cash balance work at the new, higher price level.

So prices, overall, can change for only two reasons: If the supply of money increases, prices will rise; if the supply falls, prices will fall. If the demand for money increases, prices will fall (PPM rises); if the demand for money declines, prices will rise (PPM falls). The purchasing power of the dollar varies inversely with the supply of dollars, and directly with the demand. Overall prices are determined by the same supply-and-demand forces we are all familiar with in individual prices. *Micro* and *macro* are not mysteriously separate worlds; they are both plain economics and governed by the same laws.

IV.

THE SUPPLY OF MONEY

To understand chronic inflation and, in general, to learn what determines prices and why they change, we must now focus on the behavior of the two basic causal factors: the supply of and the demand for money.

The supply of money is the total number of currency units in the economy. Originally, when each currency unit was defined strictly as a certain weight of gold or silver, the name and the weight were simply interchangeable. Thus, if there are $100 billion in the economy, and the dollar is defined as 1/20 of a gold ounce, then M can be equally considered to be $100 billion or 5 billion gold ounces. As monetary standards became lightened and debased by governments, however, the money supply increased as the same number of gold ounces were represented by an increased supply of francs, marks, or dollars.

Debasement was a relatively slow process. Kings could not easily have explained continuous changes in their solemnly defined standards. Traditionally, a new king ordered a recoinage with his own likeness stamped on the coins and, in the process, often redefined the unit so as to divert some much needed revenue into his own coffers. But this variety of increased money supply did not usually occur more than once in a generation.

Since paper currency did not yet exist, kings had to be content with debasement and its hidden taxation of their subjects.

1. What Should the Supply of Money Be?

What should the supply of money be? What is the "optimal" supply of money? Should M increase, decrease, or remain constant, and why?

This may strike you as a curious question, even though economists discuss it all the time. After all, economists would never ask the question: What should the supply of biscuits, or shoes, or titanium, be? On the free market, businessmen invest in and produce supplies in whatever ways they can best satisfy the demands of the consumers. All products and resources are scarce, and no outsider, including economists, can know *a priori* what products should be worked on by the scarce labor, savings, and energy in society. All this is best left to the profit-and-loss motive of earning money and avoiding losses in the service of consumers. So if economists are willing to leave the "problem" of the "optimal supply of shoes" to the free market, why not do the same for the optimal supply of money?

In a sense, this might answer the question and dispose of the entire argument. But it is true that money is different. For while money, as we have seen, was an indispensable discovery of civilization, it does not in the least follow that the more money the better.

Consider the following: Apart from questions of distribution, an increase of consumer goods, or of productive resources, clearly confers a net social benefit. For consumer goods are consumed, used up, in the process of consumption, while capital and natural resources are used up in the process of production. Overall, then, the more consumer goods or capital goods or natural resources the better.

But money is uniquely different. For money is never used up, in consumption or production, despite the fact that it is indispensable to the production and exchange of goods. Money is simply transferred from one person's assets to another.[1] Unlike consumer or capital goods, we cannot say that the more money in circulation the better. In fact, since money only performs an exchange function, we can assert with the Ricardians and with Ludwig von Mises that *any* supply of money will be equally optimal with any other.[2] In short, *it doesn't matter* what the money supply may be; every M will be just as good as any other for performing its cash balance exchange function.

Let us hark back to Figure 3.4. We saw that, with an M equal to $100 billion, the price level adjusted itself to the height 0A. What happens when $50 billion of new money is injected into the economy? After all the adjustments are made, we find that prices have risen (or PPM fallen) to 0B. In short, although more consumer goods or capital goods will increase the general standard of living, *all* that an increase in M accomplishes is to dilute the purchasing power of each dollar. One hundred fifty billion dollars is no better at performing monetary functions than $100 billion. No overall social benefit has been accomplished by increasing the money supply by $50 billion; all that has happened is the dilution of the purchasing power of each of the $100 billion. The increase of the money supply was socially useless; any M is as good at performing monetary functions as any other.[3]

To show why an increase in the money supply confers no social benefits, let us picture to ourselves what I call the "Angel

---

[1]A minor exception for small transactions is the eroding of coins after lengthy use, although this can be guarded against by mixing small parts of an alloy with gold.

[2]See Ludwig von Mises, *The Theory of Money and Credit* (Indianapolis: Liberty Classics, 1981), p. 165 and passim.

[3]Similarly, the fall in M depicted in Figure 3.4 also confers no overall social benefit. All that happens is that each dollar now increases in purchasing power to compensate for the smaller number of dollars. There is no need to stress this point, however, since there are no social pressures agitating for *declines* in the supply of money.

Gabriel" model.[4] The Angel Gabriel is a benevolent spirit who wishes only the best for mankind, but unfortunately knows nothing about economics. He hears mankind constantly complaining about a lack of money, so he decides to intervene and do something about it. And so overnight, while all of us are sleeping, the Angel Gabriel descends and magically doubles everyone's stock of money. In the morning, when we all wake up, we find that the amount of money we had in our wallets, purses, safes, and bank accounts has doubled.

What will be the reaction? Everyone knows it will be instant hoopla and joyous bewilderment. Every person will consider that he is now twice as well off, since his money stock has doubled. In terms of our Figure 3.4, everyone's cash balance, and therefore total M, has doubled to $200 billion. Everyone rushes out to spend their new surplus cash balances. But, as they rush to spend the money, all that happens is that demand curves for all goods and services rise. Society is no better off than before, since real resources, labor, capital, goods, natural resources, productivity, have not changed at all. And so prices will, overall, approximately double, and people will find that they are not really any better off than they were before. Their cash balances have doubled, but so have prices, and so their purchasing power remains the same. Because he knew no economics, the Angel Gabriel's gift to mankind has turned to ashes.

But let us note something important for our later analysis of the real world processes of inflation and monetary expansion. It is not true that *no one* is better off from the Angel Gabriel's doubling of the supply of money. Those lucky folks who rushed out the next morning, just as the stores were opening, managed to spend their increased cash *before* prices had a chance to rise; *they* certainly benefited. Those people, on the other hand, who decided to wait a few days or weeks before they spent their money, *lost* by the deal, for they found that their buying prices

---

[4]With apologies to David Hume and Ludwig von Mises, who employed similar models, though without using this name.

rose before they had the chance to spend the increased amounts of money. In short, society did not gain overall, but the early spenders benefited *at the expense* of the late spenders. The profligate gained at the expense of the cautious and thrifty: another joke at the expense of the good Angel.[5]

The fact that every supply of M is equally optimal has some startling implications. First, it means that no one—whether government official or economist—need concern himself with the money supply or worry about its optimal amount. Like shoes, butter, or hi-fi sets, the supply of money can readily be left to the marketplace. There is no need to have the government as an allegedly benevolent uncle, standing ready to pump in more money for allegedly beneficial economic purposes. The market is perfectly able to decide on its own money supply.

But isn't it necessary, one might ask, to make sure that more money is supplied in order to "keep up" with population growth? Bluntly, the answer is No. There is no need to provide every citizen with some per capita quota of money, at birth or at any other time. If M remains the same, and population increases, then presumably this would increase the demand for cash balances, and the increased D would, as we have seen in Figure 3.6, simply lead to a new equilibrium of lower prices, where the existing M could satisfy the increased demand because *real* cash balances would be higher. Falling prices would respond to increased demand and thereby keep the monetary functions of the cash balance-exchange at its optimum. There is no need for government to intervene in money and prices because of changing population or for any other reason. The "problem" of the proper supply of money is not a problem at all.

2. THE SUPPLY OF GOLD AND THE COUNTERFEITING PROCESS

Under a gold standard, where the supply of money is the total weight of available gold coin or bullion, there is only one way to

---

[5]Mises, *Money and Credit*, pp. 163 ff.

increase the supply of money: digging gold out of the ground. An individual, of course, who is not a gold miner can only acquire more gold by *buying* it on the market in exchange for a good or service; but that would simply shift existing gold from seller to buyer.

How much gold will be mined at any time will be a market choice determined as in the case of any other product: by estimating the expected profit. That profit will depend on the monetary value of the product compared to its cost. Since gold *is* money, how much will be mined will depend on its cost of production, which in turn will be partly determined by the general level of prices. If overall prices rise, costs of gold mining will rise as well, and the production of gold will decline or perhaps disappear altogether. If, on the other hand, the price level falls, the consequent drop in costs will make gold mining more profitable and increase supply.

It might be objected that even a small annual increase in gold production is an example of free market failure. For if any M is as good as any other, isn't it wasteful and even inflationary for the market to produce gold, however small the quantity?

But this charge ignores a crucial point about gold (or any other money-commodity). While any increase in gold is indeed useless from a monetary point of view, it will confer a nonmonetary social benefit. For an increase in the supply of gold or silver will raise its supply, and lower its price, for consumption or industrial uses, and in that sense will confer a net benefit to society.

There is, however, another way to obtain money than by buying or mining it: *counterfeiting*. The counterfeiter mints or produces an inferior object, say brass or plastic, which he tries to palm off as gold.[6] That is a cheap, though fraudulent and illegal way of producing "gold" without having to mine it out of the earth.

---

[6]One reason for gold's universal acceptance as money on the free market is that gold is very difficult to counterfeit: Its look, its sound as a coin, are easily recognizable, and its purity can be readily tested.

Counterfeiting is of course *fraud*. When the counterfeiter mints brass coins and passes them off as gold, he cheats the seller of whatever goods he purchases with the brass. And every subsequent buyer and holder of the brass is cheated in turn. But it will be instructive to examine the precise process of the fraud, and see how not only the purchasers of the brass but *everyone else* is defrauded and loses by the counterfeit.

Let us compare and contrast the motives and actions of our counterfeiter with those of our good Angel Gabriel. For the Angel was also a counterfeiter, creating money out of thin air, but since his motives were the purest, he showered his misconceived largess equally (or equi-proportionately) on one and all. But our real-world counterfeiter is all too different. His motives are the reverse of altruistic, and he is not worried about overall social benefits.

The counterfeiter produces his new coins, and spends them on various goods and services. A *New Yorker* cartoon of many years ago highlighted the process very well. A group of counterfeiters are eagerly surrounding a printing press in their basement when the first $10 bill comes off the press. One counterfeiter says to his colleagues: "Boy, retail spending in the neighborhood is sure in for a shot in the arm." As indeed it was.

Let us assume that the counterfeiting process is so good that it goes undetected, and the cheaper coins pass easily as gold. What happens? The money supply in terms of dollars has gone up, and therefore the price level will rise. The value of each existing dollar has been diluted by the new dollars, thereby diminishing the purchasing power of each old dollar. So we see right away that the *inflation process*—which is what counterfeiting is— injures all the legitimate, existing dollar-holders by having their purchasing power diluted. In short, counterfeiting defrauds and injures not only the specific holders of the new coins but all holders of old dollars—meaning, everyone else in society.

But this is not all: for the fall in PPM does not take place over-all and all at once, as it tends to do in the Angel Gabriel model. The money supply is not benevolently but foolishly showered on all alike. On the contrary, the new money is injected *at a specific point* in the economy and then ripples through the economy in a step-by-step process.

Let us see how the process works. Roscoe, a counterfeiter, produces $10,000 of fake gold coins, worth only a fraction of that amount, but impossible to detect. He spends the $10,000 on a Chevrolet. The new money was first added to Roscoe's money stock, and then was transferred to the Chevy dealer. The dealer then takes the money and hires an assistant, the new money stock now being transferred from the dealer to the assistant. The assistant buys household appliances and furniture, thereby transferring the new money to those sellers, and so forth. In this way, new money ripples through the economy, raising demand curves as it goes, and thereby raising individual prices. If there is a vast counterfeiting operation in Brooklyn, then the money supply in Brooklyn will rise first, raising demand curves and prices for the products there. Then, as the money ripples outward, other money stocks, demand curves, and prices will rise.

Thus, in contrast to the Angel Gabriel, there is no single overall expansion of money, and hence no uniform monetary and price inflation. Instead, as we saw in the case of the early spenders, those who get the money early in this ripple process *benefit at the expense of* those who get it late or not at all. The first producers or holders of the new money will find their stock increasing before very many of their buying prices have risen. But, as we go down the list, and more and more prices rise, the people who get the money at the end of the process find that they lose from the inflation. Their buying prices have all risen before their own incomes have had a chance to benefit from the new money. And some people will never get the new money at all: either because the ripple stopped, or because they have fixed incomes—from salaries or bond yields, or as pensioners or holders of annuities.

Counterfeiting, and the resulting inflation, is therefore a process by which some people—the early holders of the new money—benefit at the expense of (i.e., they expropriate) the late receivers. The first, earliest and largest net gainers are, of course, the counterfeiters themselves.

Thus, we see that when new money comes into the economy as counterfeiting, it is a method of fraudulent gain at the expense of the rest of society and especially of relatively fixed income groups. Inflation is a process of subtle expropriation, where the victims understand that prices have gone up but not why this has happened. And the inflation of counterfeiting does not even confer the benefit of adding to the *non*monetary uses of the money commodity.

Government is supposed to apprehend counterfeiters and duly break up and punish their operations. But what if government *itself* turns counterfeiter? In that case, there is no hope of combating this activity by inventing superior detection devices. The difficulty is far greater than that.

The governmental counterfeiting process did not really hit its stride until the invention of paper money.

3. GOVERNMENT PAPER MONEY

The inventions of paper and printing gave enterprising governments, always looking for new sources of revenue, an "Open Sesame" to previously unimagined sources of wealth. The kings had long since granted to themselves the monopoly of minting coins in their kingdoms, calling such a monopoly crucial to their "sovereignty," and then charging high seigniorage prices for coining gold or silver bullion. But this was piddling, and occasional debasements were not fast enough for the kings' insatiable need for revenue. But if the kings could obtain a monopoly right to print paper tickets, and *call them* the equivalent of gold coins, then there was an unlimited potential for acquiring wealth. In short, if the king could become a legalized monopoly counterfeiter, and simply issue "gold coins" by printing paper tickets with the same names on them, the king could inflate the money supply indefinitely and pay for his unlimited needs.

If the money unit had remained as a standard unit of weight, such as "gold ounce" or "gold grain," then getting away with this act of legerdemain would have been far more difficult. But the public had already gotten used to pure *name* as the currency unit, an habituation that enabled the kings to get away with debasing the definition of the money name. The next fatal step on the road to chronic inflation was for the government to print paper tickets and, using impressive designs and royal seals, *call* the cheap paper the gold unit and use it as such. Thus, if the dollar is defined as 1/20 gold ounce, paper money comes into being when the government prints a paper ticket and *calls* it "a dollar," treating it as the equivalent of a gold dollar or 1/20 gold ounce.

If the public will accept the paper dollar as equivalent to gold, then the government may become a legalized counterfeiter, and the counterfeiting process comes into play. Suppose, in a certain year, the government takes in $250 billion in taxes, and spends $300 billion. It then has a budget deficit of $50 billion.

How does it finance its deficit? *Individuals*, or business firms, can finance their own deficits in two ways: (a) borrowing money from people who have savings; and/or (b) drawing down their cash balances to pay for it. The government also can employ these two ways but, if people will accept the paper money, it now has a way of acquiring money not available to anyone else: It can print $50 billion and spend it!

A crucial problem for government as legalized counterfeiter and issuer of paper money is that, at first, no one will be found to take it in exchange. If the kings want to print money in order to build pyramids, for example, there will at first be few or no pyramid contractors willing to accept these curious-looking pieces of paper. They will want the *real thing*: gold or silver. To this day, "primitive tribes" will not accept paper money, even with their alleged sovereign's face printed on it with elaborate decoration. Healthily skeptical, they demand *"real"* money in the form of gold or silver. It takes centuries of propaganda and cultivated trust for these suspicions to fade away.

At first, then, the government must guarantee that these paper tickets will be redeemable, on demand, in their equivalent in gold coin or bullion. In other words, if a government paper ticket says "ten dollars" on it, the government itself must pledge to redeem that sum in a "real" ten-dollar gold coin. But even then, the government must overcome the healthy suspicion: If the government has the coin to back up its paper, why does it have to issue paper in the first place? The government also generally tries to back up its paper with coercive legislation, either compelling the public to accept it at par with gold (the paper dollar equal to the gold dollar), or compelling all creditors to accept paper money as equivalent to gold ("legal tender laws"). At the very least, of course, the government must agree to accept its own paper in taxes. If it is not careful, however, the government might find its issued paper bouncing right back to it in taxes and used for little else. For coercion by itself is not going to do the trick without public trust (misguided, to be sure) to back it up.

Once the paper money becomes generally accepted, however, the government can then inflate the money supply to finance its needs. If it prints $50 billion to spend on pyramids, then it—the government—gets the new money first and spends it. The pyramid contractors are the second to receive the new money. They will then spend the $50 billion on construction equipment and hiring new workers; these in turn will spend the money. In this way, the new $50 billion ripples out into the system, raising demand curves and individual prices, and hence the *level* of prices, as it goes.

It should be clear that by printing new money to finance its deficits, the government and the early receivers of the new money benefit at the expense of those who receive the new money last or not at all: pensioners, fixed-income groups, or people who live in areas remote from pyramid construction. The expansion of the money supply has caused inflation; but, more than that, the essence of inflation is the process by which a large and hidden tax is imposed on much of society for the benefit of government and the early receivers of the new money. Inflationary increases of the money supply are pernicious forms of tax because they are covert, and few people are able to understand why prices are rising. Direct, overt taxation raises hackles and can cause revolution; inflationary increases of the money supply can fool the public— its victims—for centuries.

Only when its paper money has been accepted for a long while is the government ready to take the final inflationary step: making it irredeemable, cutting the link with the gold. After calling its dollar bills equivalent to 1/20 gold ounce for many years, and having built up the customary usage of the paper dollar as money, the government can then boldly and brazenly sever the link with gold, and then simply start referring to the dollar bill *as* money itself. Gold then becomes a mere commodity, and the only money is paper tickets issued by the government. The gold standard has become an arbitrary fiat standard.[7]

The government, of course, is now in seventh heaven. So long as paper money was redeemable in gold, the government had to be careful how many dollars it printed. If, for example, the government has a stock of $30 billion in gold, and keeps issuing more paper dollars redeemable in that gold, at a certain point, the public might start getting worried and call upon the government for redemption. If it wants to stay on the gold standard, the embarrassed government might have to contract the number of dollars in circulation: by spending less than it receives, and buying back and burning the paper notes. No government wants to do anything like *that*.

So the threat of gold redeemability imposes a constant check and limit on inflationary issues of government paper. If the government can remove the threat, it can expand and inflate without cease. And so it begins to emit propaganda, trying to persuade the public not to use gold coins in their daily lives. Gold is

---

[7]Often, even irredeemable paper is only accepted at first because the government promises, or the public expects, that the paper after a few years, and whenever the current "emergency" is over, will become redeemable in gold once more. More years of habituation are generally necessary before the public will accept a frankly permanent fiat standard.

"old-fashioned," outdated, "a barbarous relic" in J.M. Keynes's famous dictum, and something that only hicks and hillbillies would wish to use as money. Sophisticates use paper. In this way, by 1933, very few Americans were actually using gold coin in their daily lives; gold was virtually confined to Christmas presents for children. For that reason, the public was ready to accept the confiscation of their gold by the Roosevelt administration in 1933 with barely a murmur.

4. The Origins of Government Paper Money

Three times before in American history, since the end of the colonial period, Americans had suffered under an irredeemable fiat money system. Once was during the American Revolution, when, to finance the war effort, the central government issued vast quantities of paper money, or "Continentals." So rapidly did they depreciate in value, in terms of goods and in terms of gold and silver moneys, that long before the end of the war they had become literally worthless. Hence, the well-known and lasting motto: "Not Worth a Continental." The second brief period was during the War of 1812, when the U.S. went off the gold standard by the end of the war, and returned over two years later. The third was during the Civil War, when the North, as well as the South, printed *greenbacks*, irredeemable paper notes, to pay for the war effort. Greenbacks had fallen to half their value by the end of the war, and it took many struggles and 14 years for the U.S. to return to the gold standard.[8]

During the Revolutionary and Civil War periods, Americans had an important option: they could still use gold and silver coins. As a result, there was not only price inflation in irredeemable paper money; there was also inflation in the price of gold and silver in relation to paper. Thus, a paper dollar might start as equivalent to a gold dollar, but, as mammoth numbers of

---

[8]During World War I, the U.S. Government, in effect, suspended redeemability of the dollar in gold.

paper dollars were printed by the government, they depreciated in value, so that one gold dollar would soon be worth two paper dollars, then three, five, and finally 100 or more paper dollars.

Allowing gold and paper dollars to circulate side-by-side meant that people could stop using paper and shift into gold. Also, it became clear to everyone that the cause of inflation was *not* speculators, workers, consumer greed, "structural" features or other straw men. For how could such forces be at work only with *paper*, and not with *gold*, money? In short, if a sack of flour was originally worth $3, and is now worth the same $3 in gold, but $100 in paper, it becomes clear to the least sophisticated that something about *paper* is at fault, since workers, speculators, businessmen, greed, and so on, are always at work whether gold or paper is being used.

Printing was first invented in ancient China and so it is not surprising that government paper money began there as well. It emerged from the government's seeking a way to avoid physically transporting gold collected in taxes from the provinces to the capital at Peking. As a result, in the mid-eighth century, provincial governments began to set up offices in the capital selling paper drafts which could be collected in gold in the provincial capitals. In 811–812, the central government outlawed the private firms involved in this business and established its own system of drafts on provincial governments (called "flying money").[9]

The first government paper money in the Western world was issued in the British American province of Massachusetts in 1690.[10] Massachusetts was accustomed to engaging in periodic

---

[9]Gordon Tullock, "Paper Money—A Cycle in Cathay," *Economic History Review* 9, no. 3 (1957): 396.

[10]Strictly speaking, the first paper money was issued five years earlier in the French province of Quebec, to be known as Card Money. In 1685, the governing *intendant* of Quebec, Monsieur Meules, had the idea of dividing some playing cards into quarters, marking them with various monetary denominations, and then issuing them to pay for wages and materials. He ordered the public to accept the cards as legal tender and they were later

plunder expeditions against prosperous French Quebec. The successful plunderers would then return to Boston and sell their loot, paying off the soldiers with the booty thus amassed. This time, however, the expedition was beaten back decisively, and the soldiers returned to Boston in ill humor, grumbling for their pay. Discontented soldiers are liable to become unruly, and so the Massachusetts government looked around for a way to pay them off.

It tried to borrow 3 to 4 thousand pounds sterling from Boston merchants, but the Massachusetts credit rating was evidently not the best. Consequently, Massachusetts decided in December 1690 to print £7,000 in paper notes, and use them to pay the soldiers. The government was shrewd enough to realize that it could not simply print irredeemable paper, for no one would have accepted the money, and its value would have dropped in relation to sterling. It therefore made a twofold pledge when it issued the notes: It would redeem the notes in gold or silver out of tax revenues in a few years, and that absolutely no further paper notes would be issued. Characteristically, however, both parts of the pledge quickly went by the board: the issue limit disappeared in a few months, and the bills continued unredeemed for nearly 40 years. As early as February 1691, the Massachusetts government proclaimed that its issue had fallen "far short," and so it proceeded to emit £40,000 more to repay all of its outstanding debt, again pledging falsely that this would be the absolutely final note issue.

The typical cycle of broken pledges, inflationary paper issues, price increases, depreciation, and compulsory par and legal tender laws had begun—in colonial America and in the Western world.[11]

So far, we have seen that M, the supply of money, consists of two elements: (a) the stock of gold bullion and coin, a supply produced on the market; and (b) government paper tickets issued in

---

redeemed in specie sent from France. See Murray N. Rothbard, *Conceived in Liberty* (New Rochelle, N.Y.: Arlington House, 1975), vol. II, p. 130n.

[11]See ibid., pp. 123–40.

the same denominations—a supply issued and clearly determined by the government. While the production and supply of gold is therefore "endogenous to" (produced from within) the market, the supply of paper dollars—being determined by the government—is "exogenous to" (comes from outside) the market. It is an artificial intervention into the market imposed by government.

It should be noted that, because of its great durability, it is almost impossible for the stock of gold and silver actually to *decline*. Government paper money, on the other hand, can decline either (a) if government retires money out of a budget surplus or (b) if inflation or loss of confidence causes it to depreciate or disappear from circulation.

We have not yet come to *banking*, and how that affects the supply of money. But before we do so, let us examine the demand for money, and see how it is determined, and what affects its height and intensity.

V.

THE DEMAND FOR MONEY

L et's analyze the various elements that constitute the public's demand for money. We have already seen that the demand curve for money will be falling in relation to the purchasing power of money; what we want to look at now is the cause of upward or downward shifts in that demand curve.

1. THE SUPPLY OF GOODS AND SERVICES

Before money can be *held* in one's cash balance, it must be obtained in exchange. That is, we must sell goods and services we produce in order to "buy" money. However, if the supply of goods and services increases in the economy (i.e., supply curves shift to the right), the demand for money in exchange will also increase. An increased supply of goods produced will raise the demand for money and also therefore lower the overall level of prices. As we can see in Figure 3.6, as the demand for money rises, a shortage of cash balances develops at the old equilibrium price level, and prices fall until a new equilibrium, PPM, is achieved.

Historically, the supply of goods and services has usually increased every year. To the extent it does so, this increase in the demand for money will tend to lower prices over a period of time. Indeed, so powerful has this force been for lowering prices, that they fell from the mid-eighteenth century until 1940, with the only exception being during periods of major wars: the Napoleonic Wars, War of 1812, the Civil War, and World War I. Paper money was increasing the money supply during this era, but increases in M were more than offset by the enormous increases in the supply of goods produced during the Industrial Revolution in an unprecedented period of economic growth. Only during wartime, when the governments ran the printing presses at full blast to pay for the war effort, did the money supply overcome the effects of increasing production and cause price levels to zoom upward.[1]

2. Frequency of Payment

The demand for money is also affected by the frequency with which people are paid their wages or salaries. Suppose, for example, that Mr. Jones and Mr. Smith are each paid an income of $12,000 a year, or $1,000 per month. But there is a difference: Jones is paid every week, and Smith every month. Does this make any difference to their economic situation? Let us first take Smith, and find out what his cash balance is on each day. Let us assume, to keep things simple, that each man is paid on the first day of the wage period, and then spends money at an even rate until the last day, when his money is exhausted (and we assume that each man's income equals his expenditures for the relevant time periods).

Smith receives $1,000 on the first of the month, and then draws down his $1,000 cash balance at an even rate until the end of the month by a bit more than $33 a day.

---

[1]The only exception was the period 1896–1914, when new gold discoveries caused moderate increases in the price level.

Smith: Income and Cash Balance

	Income	Cash Balance
Day 1	$1,000	$1,000
Day 2	0	967
Day 3	0	934
. . .		
Day 30	0	0
Day 1	$1,000	$1,000

FIGURE 5.1 — CASH BALANCE: MONTHLY INCOME

What is Smith's *average* cash balance for the month? We can find out by simply adding $1,000 on Day 1, and 0 on Day 30, and dividing by 2: the answer is $500.

Let us now compare Smith to Jones, who has the same total income, but receives his paycheck once a week. Figuring four weeks to the month to simplify matters, this means that Jones gets a check of $250 at the beginning of each week and then draws it down steadily until he reaches a cash balance of zero at the end of the week. His monetary picture will be as follows:

Jones: Income and Cash Balance

	Income	Cash Balance
Day 1	$250	$250
Day 2	0	215
Day 3	0	180
. . .		
Day 7	0	0
Day 1	$250	$250

FIGURE 5.2 — CASH BALANCE: WEEKLY INCOME

Jones gets a check for $250 at the beginning of each week, and then draws down his cash balance each day by approximately $35 until he reaches zero at the end of the week. His income is the same as Smith's; but what is his *average* cash balance? Again, we can arrive at this figure by adding $250, at the beginning of each week, and 0 and dividing by 2: the result is $125.

In short, even though their incomes are identical, Smith, who gets paid less frequently, has to keep an average cash balance four times that of Jones. Jones is paid four times as frequently as Smith, and hence has to keep a cash balance of only 1/4 the amount.

Cash balances, therefore, do not only do work in relation to the level of prices. They also perform work in relation to the frequency of income. The less frequent the payment, the higher the average cash balance, and therefore the *greater* the demand for money, the greater the amount, at any price level, that a person will seek to keep in his cash balance. The same cash balances can do more money work the greater the frequency of payment.

In my salad days, I experienced the problem of frequency of payment firsthand. I was working on a foundation grant. My income was fairly high, but I was getting paid only twice a year. The result was that the benefits of my respectable income were partially offset by the necessity of keeping an enormous cash balance in the bank, just to finance my daily expenditures. In many painful ways, I was far worse off than I would have been with the same income with more frequent checks coming in.

What effect might this have on the price level? If the general frequency of payment changes in a society, this will shift the demand for money and raise or lower the price level. Thus, if people suddenly stop being paid once a month, and instead get paid twice a month, this will lower everyone's demand for money. They will keep a lower cash balance for their existing income and price level, and so the demand for money will shift downward, as in Figure 3.7. People will try to get rid of their surplus cash balances and, as they do so by spending money on goods and services, prices will be driven upward until a new higher equilibrium price level will clear the market and equilibrate the existing supply to the decreased demand.

On the other hand, if frequency of payment of salaries should shift generally from once a week to twice a month, the reverse will happen. People will now need to carry a higher average cash balance for their given incomes. In their scramble for higher cash balances, their demand for money rises, as in Figure 3.6 above. They can only raise their cash balances by cutting back their spending, which in turn will lower prices of goods and thereby relieve the "shortage" of cash balances.

Realistically, however, frequency of payment does not change very often, if at all. Any marked change, furthermore, will only be one-shot, and certainly will not be continuous. Frequency of payment is not going to go up or down every year. Changes in frequency, therefore, could scarcely account for our contemporary problems of chronic inflation. If anything, the general shift from blue-collar to white-collar jobs in recent decades has probably reduced the frequency of payment a bit, and therefore had a slight price-lowering effect. But we can safely ignore this factor if we are looking for important causal factors.

3. CLEARING SYSTEMS

On the other hand, there is another causal factor which can only *lower* the demand for money over time: new methods of economizing the need for cash balances. These are technological innovations like any other, and will result in a lower demand for money for each successful innovation.

An example is the development of more efficient "clearing systems," that is, institutions for the clearing of debt. My eighth-grade teacher, perhaps unwittingly, once illustrated the effect of clearing systems on reducing average cash balances. In effect he said to the class: Suppose that each of you owes $10 that will be due on the first day of next month. If there are, say, 30 kids in each class, each will need to come up with $10 to pay their debt, so that a total cash balance of $300 will be demanded by the class in order to pay their various debts.

But now, my teacher pointed out, suppose that each of you still owes $10 due on the first day of next month. But each of you owes $10 to the boy or girl on your left. More precisely: The teacher owes $10 to the first kid in the front of the class, then each kid in turn owes $10 to the kid on his left, until finally the last person at the end of the line, in turn, owes $10 to the teacher. Each of these debts is due on the first of the month. But in that case, each of us can wipe out his or her debt all at once, at a single blow, without using any cash balance at all. Presto chango! The class's demand for cash balance for repaying debt has been reduced as if by magic, from $300 to zero. If there were an institutional mechanism for finding and clearing these debts, we could dramatically and drastically reduce our need for accumulating and keeping cash balances, at least for the payment of debt.

Any devices for economizing cash balances will do as well as clearing systems in reducing the public's demand for money. *Credit cards* are an excellent current example. Contrary to some views, credit cards are *not* in themselves money and therefore do not add to the money supply. Suppose, for example, that I eat dinner in a restaurant, run up a $20 bill, and pay by American Express card rather than by cash. The American Express card is *not* money. One way to see that is to note whether using the card constitutes *final payment* for the dinner. One crucial feature of money is that using it constitutes final payment; there is no need for any more. If I pay for the dinner with a $20 bill, for example, that's it; my debt has been canceled finally and completely. Hence the $20 was truly money. But handing the restaurant my American Express card hardly completes the matter; on the contrary, I then have to pay American Express $20, plus interest at some later date.

In fact, when a credit card is used, *two* credit transactions are taking place at once. In the above example, American Express lends me the money by paying the restaurant on my behalf; at the same time, I pledge to pay American Express $20 plus interest. In other words, American Express picks up my tab and then I owe it money.

Credit cards, then, are *not* part of the money supply. But carrying them enables me to walk around with a far lower cash balance, for they provide me with the ability to borrow instantly from the credit card companies. Credit cards permit me to economize on cash.

The development of credit cards, clearing systems, and other devices to economize cash, will therefore cause the demand for money to be reduced, and prices to increase. Again, however, these effects are one-shot, as the new device is invented and spreads throughout the economy, and its impact is probably not very important quantitatively. These new devices cannot begin to account for the chronic, let alone the accelerating, inflation that plagues the modern world.

4. Confidence in the Money

An intangible, but highly important determinant of the demand for money, is the basic confidence that the public or market has in the money itself. Thus, an attempt by the Mongols to introduce paper money in Persia in the twelfth and thirteenth centuries flopped, because no one would accept it. The public had no confidence in the paper money, despite the awesomely coercive decrees that always marked Mongol rule. Hence, the public's demand for the money was zero. It takes many years—in China it took two to three centuries—for the public to gain enough confidence in the money, so that its demand for the money will rise from near zero to a degree great enough to circulate throughout the kingdom.

Public confidence in the country's money can be lost as well as gained. Thus, suppose that a money is King Henry's paper, and King Henry has entered a war with another state which he seems about to lose. King Henry's money is going to drop in public esteem and its demand can suddenly collapse.

It should be clear then, that the demand for paper money, in contrast to gold, is potentially highly volatile. Gold and silver are always in demand, regardless of clime, century, or government in power. But public confidence in, and hence demand for, paper money depends on the ultimate confidence—or lack thereof—of the public in the viability of the issuing government. Admittedly, however, this influence on the demand for money will only take effect in moments of severe crisis for the ruling regime. In the usual course of events, the public's demand for the government's money will likely be sustained.

5. INFLATIONARY OR DEFLATIONARY EXPECTATIONS

We have dealt so far with influences on the demand for money that have been either one-shot (frequency of payment and clearing systems), remote (confidence in the money), or gradual (supply of good and services). We come now to the most important single influence on the demand for money: This is the public's expectation of what will happen to prices in the near, or foreseeable, future. Public expectation of future price levels is far and away the most important determinant of the demand for money.

But expectations do not arise out of thin air; generally, they are related to the immediate past record of the economy. If prices, for example, have been more or less stable for decades, it is very likely that the public will expect prices to continue on a similar path. There is no absolute necessity for this, of course; if conditions are changing swiftly, or are expected to change quickly, then people will take the changes into account.

If prices are generally expected to remain the same, then the demand for money, at least from the point of view of expectations, will remain constant, and the demand for money curve will remain in place. But suppose that, as was the case during the relatively free-market and hard-money nineteenth century, prices fell gradually from year to year. In that case, when people knew in their hearts that prices would be, say, 3 percent lower next year, the tendency would be to hold on to their money and to postpone purchase of the house or washing machine, or whatever, until next year, when prices would be lower. Because of these *deflationary expectations*, then, the demand for money will rise, since people will hold on to more of their money at any given price level, as they are expecting prices to fall shortly. This rise in the demand for money (shown in Figure 3.6) would cause prices to fall immediately. In a sense, the market, by expecting a fall in prices, *discounts* that fall, and makes it happen right away instead of later. Expectations speed up future price reactions.

On the other hand, suppose that people anticipate a large increase in the money supply and hence a large future increase in prices. Their deflationary expectations have now been replaced by *inflationary expectations*. People now know in their hearts that prices will *rise* substantially in the near future. As a result, they decide to buy now—to buy the car, the house, or the washing machine—instead of waiting for a year or two when they know full well that prices will be higher. In response to inflationary expectations, then, people will draw down their cash balances, and their demand for money curve will shift downward (shown in Figure 3.7). But as people act on their expectations of rising prices, their lowered demand for cash pushes up the prices now rather than later. The more people anticipate future price increases, the faster will those increases occur.

Deflationary price expectations, then, will lower prices, and inflationary expectations will raise them. It should also be clear that the greater the spread and the intensity of these expectations, the bigger the shift in the public's demand for money, and the greater the effect in changing prices.

While important, however, the expectations component of the demand for money is speculative and reactive rather than an independent force. Generally, the public does not change its expectations suddenly or arbitrarily; they are usually based on the record of the immediate past. Generally, too, expectations are sluggish in revising themselves to adapt to new conditions; expectations, in short, tend to be conservative and dependent on the record of the recent past. The independent force is changes in the money supply; the demand for money reacts sluggishly and reactively to the money supply factor, which in turn is largely

determined by government, that is, by forces and institutions outside the market economy.

During the 1920s, Ludwig von Mises outlined a typical inflation process from his analysis of the catastrophic hyperinflation in
Germany in 1923—the first runaway inflation in a modern,
industrialized country. The German inflation had begun during
World War I, when the Germans, like most of the warring
nations, inflated their money supply to pay for the war effort, and
found themselves forced to go off the gold standard and to make
their paper currency irredeemable. The money supply in the warring countries would double or triple. But in what Mises saw to
be Phase I of a typical inflation, prices did not rise nearly proportionately to the money supply. If M in a country triples, why
would prices go up by much less? Because of the psychology of
the average German, who thought to himself as follows: "I know
that prices are much higher now than they were in the good old
days before 1914. But that's because of wartime, and because all
goods are scarce due to diversion of resources to the war effort.
When the war is over, things will get back to normal, and prices
will fall back to 1914 levels." In other words, the German public originally had strong deflationary expectations. Much of the
new money was therefore added to cash balances and the Germans' demand for money rose. In short, while M increased a
great deal, the demand for money also rose and thereby offset
some of the inflationary impact on prices. This process can be
seen in Figure 5.3.

In Phase I of inflation, the government pumps a great deal of
new money into the system, so that M increases sharply to M'.
Ordinarily, prices would have risen greatly (or PPM fallen
sharply) from 0A to 0C. But deflationary expectations by the public have intervened and have increased the demand for money
from D to D', so that prices will rise and PPM falls much less substantially, from 0A to 0B.

Unfortunately, the relatively small price rise often acts as
heady wine to government. Suddenly, the government officials
see a new Santa Claus, a cornucopia, a magic elixir. They can

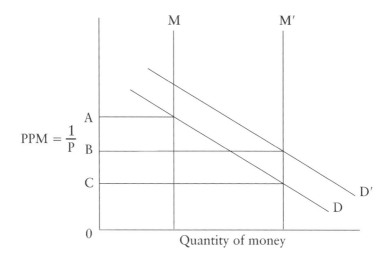

FIGURE 5.3 — PHASE I OF INFLATION

increase the money supply to a fare-thee-well, finance their deficits and subsidize favored political groups with cheap credit, and prices will rise only by a little bit!

It is human nature that when you see something work well, you do more of it. If, in its ceaseless quest for revenue, government sees a seemingly harmless method of raising funds without causing much inflation, it will grab on to it. It will continue to pump new money into the system, and, given a high or increasing demand for money, prices, at first, might rise by only a little.

But let the process continue for a length of time, and the public's response will gradually, but inevitably, change. In Germany, after the war was over, prices still kept rising; and then the postwar years went by, and inflation continued in force. Slowly, but surely, the public began to realize: "We have been waiting for a return to the good old days and a fall of prices back to 1914. But prices have been steadily *increasing*. So it looks as if there will be no return to the good old days. Prices will not fall; in fact, they will probably keep going up." As this psychology takes hold, the public's thinking in Phase I changes into that of Phase II: "Prices will keep going up, instead of going down. Therefore, I know in my heart that prices will be *higher* next year." The public's *deflationary* expectations have been superseded by *inflationary* ones. Rather than hold on to its money to wait for price declines, the public will spend its money faster, will draw down cash balances to make purchases ahead of price increases. In Phase II of inflation, instead of a rising demand for money moderating price increases, a falling demand for money will *intensify* the inflation (Figure 5.4).

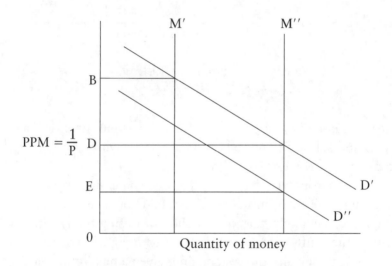

FIGURE 5.4 — PHASE II OF INFLATION

Here, in Phase II of the inflation, the money supply increases again, from M′ to M′′. But now the psychology of the public changes, from deflationary to inflationary expectations. And so, instead of prices rising (PPM falling) from 0B to 0D, the falling demand for money, from D′ to D′′, raises prices from 0D to 0E. Expectations, having caught up with the inflationary reality, now accelerate the inflation instead of moderating it.

Both these phases of a typical inflation can be combined as shown in Figure 5.5.

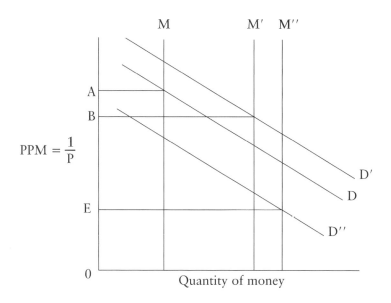

FIGURE 5.5 — COMBINED INFLATION: PHASES I AND II

There is no scientific way to predict at what point in any inflation expectations will reverse from deflationary to inflationary. The answer will differ from one country to another, and from one epoch to another, and will depend on many subtle cultural factors, such as trust in government, speed of communication, and many others. In Germany, this transition took four wartime years and one or two postwar years. In the United States, after World War II, it took about two decades for the message to slowly seep in that inflation was going to be a permanent fact of the American way of life.

When expectations tip decisively over from deflationary, or steady, to inflationary, the economy enters a danger zone. The crucial question is how the government and its monetary authorities are going to react to the new situation. When prices are going up faster than the money supply, the people begin to experience a severe *shortage* of money, for they now face a shortage of cash balances relative to the much higher price levels. Total cash balances are no longer sufficient to carry transactions at the higher price. The people will then clamor for the government to issue more money to catch up to the higher price. If the government tightens its own belt and stops printing (or otherwise creating) new money, then inflationary expectations will eventually be reversed, and prices will fall once more—thus relieving the money shortage by lowering prices. But if government follows its own inherent inclination to counterfeit and appeases the clamor by printing more money so as to allow the public's cash balances to "catch up" to prices, then the country is off to the races. Money and prices will follow each other upward in an ever-accelerating spiral, until finally prices "run away," doing something like tripling every hour. Chaos ensues, for now the psychology of the public is not merely inflationary, but *hyper*inflationary, and Phase III's runaway psychology is as follows: "The value of money is disappearing even as I sit here and contemplate it. I must get rid of money right away, and buy *anything*, it matters not what, so long as it isn't money." A frantic rush ensues to get rid of money at all costs and to buy *anything* else. In Germany, this was called a "flight into real values." The demand for money falls precipitously almost to zero, and prices skyrocket upward virtually to infinity. The money collapses in a wild "crack-up boom." In the German hyperinflation of 1923, workers were paid twice a day, and the housewife would stand at the factory gate and rush with wheelbarrows full of million mark notes to buy anything at all for money. Production fell, as people became more interested in speculating than in real production or in working for wages. Germans began to use foreign currencies or to barter in commodities. The once-proud mark collapsed.

The absurd and disastrous way in which the Reichsbank—the German Central Bank—met the crucial clamor for more money to spend immediately in the hyperinflation of the early 1920s is revealed in a notorious speech delivered by Rudolf Havenstein, the head of the Reichsbank, in August 1923. The Reichsbank was the sole source of paper money, and Havenstein made clear that the bank would meet its responsibilities by fulfilling the increased demand for paper money. Denominations of the notes would be multiplied, and the Reichsbank would stand ready to keep its printing presses open all night to fill the demand. As Havenstein put it:

> The wholly extraordinary depreciation of the mark has naturally created a rapidly increasing demand for additional currency, which the Reichsbank has not always been able fully to satisfy. A simplified production of notes of large denominations enabled us to bring ever greater amounts into circulation. But these enormous sums are barely adequate to cover the vastly increased demand for the means of payment, which has just recently attained an absolutely fantastic level, especially as a result of the extraordinary increases in wages and salaries.
>
> The running of the Reichsbank's note-printing organization, which has become absolutely enormous, is making the most extreme demands on our personnel.[2]

During the later months of 1923, the German mark suffered from an accelerating spiral of hyperinflation: the German government (Reichsbank) poured out ever-greater quantifies of paper money which the public got rid of as fast as possible. In July 1914, the German mark had been worth approximately 25 cents. By November 1923, the mark had depreciated so terrifyingly that it took 4.2 trillion marks to purchase one dollar (in contrast to 25.3 billion marks to the dollar only the month before).

And yet, despite the chaos and devastation, which wiped out the middle class, pensioners and fixed-income groups, and the emergence of a form of barter (often employing foreign currency as money), the mark continued to be used. How did Germany get out of its runaway inflation? Only when the government resolved to *stop* monetary inflation, and to take steps dramatic enough to convince the inflation-wracked German public that it was serious about it. The German government brought an end to the crack-up boom by the "miracle of the *Rentenmark*." The mark was

---

[2]In Fritz K. Ringer, ed., *The German Inflation of 1923* (New York: Oxford University Press, 1969), p. 96.

scrapped, or rather, a new currency, the *Rentenmark*, was issued, valued at 1 trillion old marks, which were convertible into the new currency. The government pledged that the quantity of *Rentenmarks* issued would be strictly limited to a fixed amount (a pledge that was kept for some time), and the Reichsbank was prohibited from printing any further notes to finance the formerly enormous government deficit. Once these stern measures had been put into effect, the hyperinflation was brought to an end. The German economy rapidly recovered. Yet, it must be pointed out that the German economy did not escape a posthyperinflation recession, called a "stabilization crisis," in which the swollen and unsound investments of the inflationary period were rapidly liquidated. No one complained bitterly; the lessons of the monstrous inflation were burned into everyone's heart.[3]

Only a clear and dramatic cessation of the spiraling expansion of the money supply can turn off the money tap and thereby reverse the accelerating inflationary expectations of the public. Only such a dramatic end to monetary inflation can induce the public to start holding cash balances once again.

Thus we see that price levels are determined by the supply and the demand for money, and that expansion of the money supply—a function solely of government—is the prime active force in inflation.

---

[3]For a good overview of the German economy, see Gustav Stolper, *The German Economy, 1870 to the Present* (New York: Harcourt, Brace & World, 1967); for an excellent history and analysis of the German hyperinflation, see Costantino Bresciani-Turroni, *The Economics of Inflation* (London: George Allen & Unwin, 1937).

VI.

LOAN BANKING

We have so far seen how price levels are determined, showing how they are set by the interaction of the supply of and demand for money. We have seen that the money supply is generally the dominant force in changing prices, while the demand for money is reactive either to long-term conditions or to changes in supply. We have seen, too, that the cause of our chronic inflation is continuing increases in the supply of money, which eventually generate inflationary expectations that aggravate and accelerate the inflation. Eventually, if unchecked, the inflation runs away into a crack-up boom and destruction of the currency. In recent decades, absolute control over the supply of money has been in the hands, not of private enterprise or the free market, but of government.

How does *banking* fit into all this? In what way does banking generate part of the supply of money? Is banking inflationary, and if so, in what sense? How does banking work?

When one speaks of *banks*, there is a semantic problem, since the word bank covers several very different functions and activities. In particular, modern banking mixes and confuses two different operations with very different effects: loans and deposits. Let

75

us first see how what we might call *loan banking* originated and what its relationship might be to the money supply and to inflation.

Most people *think* of banks as institutions which channel their savings into productive loans and investments. *Loan* banking is essentially that healthy and productive process in operation.

Let's see how it works. Suppose that I have saved $10,000 and have decided to set up a loan business, or what we might call a loan bank.[1] I set up the Rothbard Loan Company.

A *must* in making any sense whatever out of the banking system is to become familiar with the common accounting device of the *T-account*, or balance sheet. The balance sheet is a product of one of the most important inventions of modern civilization: double-entry bookkeeping, which came to Renaissance Italy from the Arab civilization of North Africa. Before double-entry bookkeeping, business firms kept single-entry books, which were simply running accounts of expenditures, income, and so on. They found it impossible to know where they had made mistakes, and therefore could not try to correct them. Double-entry bookkeeping, on the other hand, often means that any entry on one side of the ledger must immediately, and automatically, be balanced by an entry on the other side, the totals of which must be identical. It then becomes relatively easy to find out where the totals do not balance, and therefore where the error has occurred.

While the concept of double-entry bookkeeping was established during the Renaissance, the familiar T-account balance sheet was formalized only at the start of the "classical" period of modern accounting, that is, the late nineteenth century.[2]

---

[1]We are using "dollars" instead of "gold ounces," because this process is the same whether we are on a gold or a fiat standard.

[2]In particular, the originator of the Assets = Liability + Equity equation was the distinguished American accountant, Charles E. Sprague, who conceived the idea in 1880 and continued to advance the idea until after the turn of the century. See Gary J. Previts and Barbara D. Merino, *A History of Accounting in America* (New York: Ronald Press, 1979), pp. 107–13.

On the T-account balance sheet, the left side is the monetary valuation, at any given time, of the total assets of the business firm. This side is, appropriately enough, labeled "Assets." On the right side we have the total amount of assets owned by one or more owners. In short, any and all assets must be owned by *some-one*, so that if we add up the assets owned by A, B, C . . . etc., they should yield a total identical to the total sum of the assets. Some assets are owned in fact by the owner or owners of the firm (Equity Capital). Others are owed to, and therefore in an economic sense claimed or owned by, various creditors of the firm (Liabilities). So that, as total assets are apportioned among the various owners or claimants, the total of the right column, "Equity plus Liabilities," must precisely equal the total assets on the left side.

Let us now return to the Rothbard Loan Company. I have saved $10,000 in cash, and place it in my firm's account. The balance sheet of the new company is now as follows:

Assets		Equity & Liabilities	
Cash	$10,000		
		Equity	
		Rothbard	$10,000
Total	$10,000	Total	$10,000

FIGURE 6.1 — STARTING THE LOAN BANK

The T-account shows that the assets of the Rothbard Loan Company are now $10,000 in cash, and that I own these assets. Total assets are precisely equal to total assets owned.

The purpose of forming the Rothbard Loan Company is, of course, to lend money out and to earn interest. Suppose that I now lend $9,000 to Joe's Diner for a new counter, keeping

$1,000 as a cash reserve. Joe borrows $9,000 at 10 percent interest, promising to pay me back $9,900 in one year's time. In short, I give Joe $9,000, in return for which he gives me an IOU for $9,900 for one year in the future. My asset is now an IOU from Joe to be realized in the future. The balance sheet of the Rothbard Loan Company is now as follows:

Assets		Equity & Liabilities	
Cash	$1,000		
IOU from Joe	9,900		
		Equity	
		Rothbard	$10,900
Total	$10,900	Total	$10,900

FIGURE 6.2 — MAKING A LOAN

My assets have now happily grown, at least in anticipation. Total assets and equity are now $10,900. What, in all of this, has happened to the total supply of money so far? The answer is, nothing. Let us say that there was at the onset of the Rothbard Loan Company, $10,000 in circulation. I saved $10,000, and then loaned $9,000 to Joe. The money supply has in no sense increased; some of mine has simply been saved (that is, not spent on consumer goods), and loaned to someone who will spend it, in this case on productive investment.

Let us now see what happens one year later when Joe repays the $9,900. The IOU is canceled, and I now have in cash the loan paid back plus interest (Figure 6.3).

The loan is repaid, and my firm, and therefore myself, is $900 richer. But, once again, there has been no increase in society's stock of money. For in order to pay back the loan, Joe had to save $900 out of profits. Again, Joe and I are transferring to each

Assets		Equity & Liabilities	
Cash	$10,900		
		Equity	
		Rothbard	$10,900
Total	$10,900	Total	$10,900

FIGURE 6.3 — THE LOAN AS PAID

other the ownership of existing cash balances which we have saved by not consuming. My loan bank has channeled savings into loans, the loans have been repaid, and at no point has the money supply increased. Loan banking is a productive, noninflationary institution.

The loan to Joe did not have to be made for business investment. It could have been a loan for consumption purposes, say, to enable him to buy a new car. Joe anticipates having higher income or lower expenditures next year, enabling him to pay back the loan with interest. In this case, he is not so much making a monetary profit from the loan as rearranging the time pattern of his expenditures, paying a premium for the use of money now rather than having to wait to buy the car. Once again, the total money supply has not changed; money is being saved by me and my firm, and loaned to Joe, who then saves enough of the existing money supply to fulfill his contractual obligations. Credit, and loan banking, is productive, benefits both the saver and the borrower, and causes no inflationary increase in the money supply.

Suppose now that my loan bank is flourishing and I expand the firm by taking in a partner, my brother-in-law, who contributes another $10,900 in cash to the firm. The Rothbard Loan Bank now looks as follows:

Assets		Equity & Liabilities	
Cash	$21,800		
		Equity	
		Rothbard	$10,900
		Brother-in-law	10,900
Total	$21,800	Total	$21,800

FIGURE 6.4 — EXPANDING BANK EQUITY

The firm has now expanded, and the increased assets are owned equally by my brother-in-law and me. Total assets, and total assets owned, have grown equally and accordingly. Once again, there has been no increase in the stock of money, for my brother-in-law has simply saved $10,900 from the existing supply, and invested it. Then, when more loans are made, cash shifts into IOUs and interest receipts eventually add to cash, total assets, and equity.

As the loan bank expands, we might decide to keep raising capital by expanding the number of partners, or perhaps by converting to a joint-stock company (legally, a corporation), which issues low-denomination stock and can thereby tap the savings of small investors. Thus, we might set up the Rothbard Loan Bank Corporation, which sells 10,000 shares at $10 apiece, and thereby accumulates $100,000 for making loans. Assume that $95,000 is loaned out and $5,000 kept in cash. The balance sheet of the Rothbard Loan Bank Corporation would now be as shown in Figure 6.5.

We could list the shareholders, and how many shares thus owned in proportion to the total assets of the newly-expanded Rothbard Loan Corporation. We won't, because the important point is that more savings have been channeled into productive credit, to earn an interest return. Note that there has been no increase in the supply of money, and therefore no impetus toward inflation.

Assets		Equity & Liabilities	
Cash	$ 5,000		
IOUs	$ 95,000		
		Equity	
		Shareholders	$100,000
Total	$100,000	Total	$21,800

FIGURE 6.5 — BANK GOING PUBLIC

Let us now expand the bank further. In addition to shareholders, the Rothbard Bank now decides to float bonds or other debentures, and thereby borrow from some people in order to lend to others. Let us assume that the Rothbard Bank issues $50,000 worth of bonds, and sells them on the bond market. The bonds are to be repaid in 20 years, paying 10 percent per year on their face value. Now $50,000 in cash is added to the bank's coffers. We can also sell certificates of deposit, a relatively new banking instrument in which the owner of the certificate, Jones, buys a certificate worth $20,000 for six months, at 10 percent interest. In effect, Jones lends the Rothbard bank $20,000 in exchange for the bank's IOU that it will repay Jones $21,000 in six months' time. The Rothbard Bank borrows these moneys because it expects to be able to lend the new cash at a greater than 10 percent rate, thus earning a profit differential between the interest it pays out and the interest it earns. Suppose it is able to lend the new money at 15 percent interest, thereby making a profit of 5 percent on these transactions. If its administrative expenses of operation are, say, 2 percent, it is able to make a 3 percent profit on the entire transaction.

The new balance sheet of the Rothbard Bank, after it has issued $50,000 worth of long-term bonds, and sold a $20,000 short-term certificate of deposit to Jones, looks like this:

Assets		Equity & Liabilities	
		Liabilities	
Cash	$75,000	Bonds	$50,000
IOUs	$95,000	Certificate of deposit	
		to Jones	$20,000
		Total	$70,000
		Equity	
		Shareholders	$100,000
Total	$170,000	Total	$170,000

FIGURE 6.6 — BANK ISSUING DEBENTURES

The balance sheet of the Rothbard Bank has now become far more complex. The assets, cash and IOUs are owned or claimed by a combination of people: by the legal owners, or equity, and by those who have money claims on the bank. In the economic sense, the legal owners and the creditors jointly *own* part of the Rothbard Bank, because they have joint claims on the bank's assets. To the shareholders' invested $100,000 are now added $50,000 borrowed from bondholders and a $20,000 CD (certificate of deposit) sold to Jones. Once again, of course, the Rothbard Bank takes the newly acquired cash and lends it for further IOUs, so that the balance sheet now looks like Figure 6.7.

The Rothbard Bank is now doing exactly what most people think banks always do: borrowing money from some (in addition to investing the savings of the owners) and lending money to others. The bank makes money on the interest differential because it

Assets		Equity & Liabilities	
		Liabilities	
Cash	$5,000	Bonds	$50,000
IOUs	$165,000	CD	$20,000
		Total	$70,000
		Equity	
		Shareholders	$100,000
Total	$170,000	Total	$170,000

FIGURE 6.7 — BANK LENDING BORROWED FUNDS

is performing the important social service of channeling the borrowed savings of many people into productive loans and investments. The bank is expert on where its loans should be made and to whom, and reaps the reward for this service.

Note that there has still been no inflationary action by the loan bank. No matter how large it grows, it is still only tapping savings from the existing money stock and lending that money to others.

If the bank makes unsound loans and goes bankrupt, then, as in *any* kind of insolvency, its shareholders and creditors will suffer losses. This sort of bankruptcy is little different from any other: unwise management or poor entrepreneurship will have caused harm to owners and creditors.

Factors, investment banks, finance companies, and moneylenders are just some of the institutions that have engaged in loan banking. In the ancient world, and in medieval and pre-modern Europe, most of these institutions were forms of "moneylending proper," in which owners loaned out their own saved money. Loan banks, in the sense of intermediaries, borrowing from savers to lend to borrowers, began only in Venice in the late Middle Ages. In England, intermediary-banking began only with the "scriveners" of the early seventeenth century.[3] The scriveners were clerks who wrote contracts and bonds, and were therefore often in a position to learn of mercantile transactions and engage in moneylending and borrowing. By the beginning of the eighteenth century, scriveners had been replaced by more advanced forms of banking.

---

[3]During the sixteenth century, most English moneylending was conducted, not by specialized firms, but by wealthy merchants in the clothing and woolen industries, as an outlet for their surplus capital. See J. Milnes Holden, *The History of Negotiable Instruments in English Law* (London: The Athlone Press, 1955), pp. 205–06.

VII.

DEPOSIT BANKING

1. WAREHOUSE RECEIPTS

Deposit banking began as a totally different institution from loan banking. Hence it was unfortunate that the same name, *bank*, became attached to both. If loan banking was a way of channeling savings into productive loans to earn interest, deposit banking arose to serve the convenience of the holders of gold and silver. Owners of gold bullion did not wish to keep it at home or office and suffer the risk of theft; far better to store the gold in a safe place. Similarly, holders of gold coin found the metal often heavy and inconvenient to carry, and needed a place for safekeeping. These deposit banks functioned very much as safe-deposit boxes do today: as safe "money warehouses." As in the case of any warehouse, the *depositor* placed his goods *on deposit* or in trust at the warehouse, and in return received a ticket (or warehouse receipt) stating that he could redeem his goods whenever he presented the ticket at the warehouse. In short, his ticket or receipt or claim check was to be instantly redeemable *on demand* at the warehouse.

Money in a warehouse can be distinguished from other deposited goods, such as wheat, furniture, jewelry, or whatever. All of these goods are likely to be redeemed fairly soon after storage, and then revert to their regular use as a consumer or capital good. But gold, apart from jewelry or industrial use, largely serves as money, that is, it is only *exchanged* rather than used in consumption or production. Originally, in order to use his gold for exchange, the depositor would have to redeem his deposit and then turn the gold over to someone else in exchange for a good or service. But over the decades, one or more money warehouses, or deposit banks, gained a reputation for probity and honesty. Their warehouse receipts then began to be transferred directly as a surrogate for the gold coin itself. The warehouse receipts were scrip for the real thing, in which metal they could be redeemed. They functioned as "gold certificates."[1] In this situation, note that the total money supply in the economy has not changed; only its *form* has altered. Suppose, for example, that the initial money supply in a country, when money is only gold, is $100 million. Suppose now that $80 million in gold is deposited in deposit banks, and the warehouse receipts are now used as proxies, as substitutes, for gold. In the meanwhile, $20 million in gold coin and bullion are left outside the banks in circulation. In this case, the total money supply is still $100 million, except that now the money in circulation consists of $20 million in gold coin and $80 million in gold certificates standing in for the actual $80 million of gold in bank vaults. Deposit banking, when the banks really act as genuine money warehouses, is still eminently productive and noninflationary.

How can deposit banks charge for this important service? In the same way as any warehouse or safe-deposit box: by charging a fee in proportion to the time that the deposit remains in the

---

[1]Dobie writes: "a transfer of the warehouse receipt, in general confers the same measure of title that an actual delivery of the goods which it represents would confer." Armistead M. Dobie, *Handbook on the Law of Bailments and Carriers* (St. Paul, Minn.: West Publishing Co., 1914), p. 163.

bank vaults. There should be no mystery or puzzlement about *this* part of the banking process.

How do these warehouse receipt transactions relate to the T-account balance sheets of the deposit banks? In simple justice, not at all. When I store a piece of furniture worth $5,000 in a warehouse, in law and in justice the furniture does *not* show up as an asset of the warehouse during the time that I keep it there.

The warehouse does not add $5,000 to both its assets and liabilities because it in no sense *owns* the furniture; neither can we say that I have *loaned* the warehouse the furniture for some indefinite time period. The furniture is mine and remains mine; I am only keeping it there for safekeeping and therefore I am legally and morally entitled to redeem it any time I please. I am not therefore the bank's "creditor"; it doesn't *owe* me money which I may some day collect. Hence, there is no debt to show up on the Equity + Liability side of the ledger. Legally, the entire transaction is not a loan but a *bailment*, hiring someone for the safekeeping of valuables.

Let us see why we are dealing with a bailment, not a loan. In a loan, or a *credit transaction*, the creditor exchanges a *present good*—that is, a good available for use at any time in the present—for a *future good,* an IOU redeemable at some date in the future. Since present goods are more valuable than future goods, the creditor will invariably charge, and the debtor pay, an interest premium for the loan.

The hallmark of a loan, then, is that the money is due at some future date and that the debtor pays the creditor interest. But the deposit, or *claim transaction*, is precisely the opposite. The money must be paid by the bank *at any time* the depositor presents the ticket, and not at some precise date in the future. And the bank—the alleged "borrower" of the money—generally does not pay the depositor for making the loan. Often, it is the depositor who pays the bank for the service of safeguarding his valuables.

Deposit banking, or money warehousing, was known in ancient Greece and Egypt, and appeared in Damascus in the early thirteenth century, and in Venice a century later. It was prominent in Amsterdam and Hamburg in the seventeenth and eighteenth centuries.

In England, there were no banks of deposit until the Civil War in the mid-seventeenth century. Merchants were in the habit of keeping their surplus gold in the king's mint in the Tower of London—an institution which of course was accustomed to storing gold. The habit proved to be an unfortunate one, for when Charles I needed money in 1638 shortly before the outbreak of the Civil War, he simply confiscated a large sum of gold, amounting to £200,000, calling it a "loan" from the depositors. Although the merchants finally got their money back, they were understandably shaken by the experience, and forsook the mint, instead depositing their gold in the coffers of private goldsmiths, who were also accustomed to the storing and safekeeping of the valuable metal.[2] The goldsmith's warehouse receipts then came to be used as a surrogate for the gold money itself.[3]

All men are subject to the temptation to commit theft or fraud, and the warehousing profession is no exception. In warehousing, one form of this temptation is to steal the stored products outright—to skip the country, so to speak, with the stored gold and jewels. Short of this thievery, the warehouse man is subject to a more subtle form of the same temptation: to steal or "borrow" the valuables "temporarily" and to profit by speculation or whatever, returning the valuables before they are redeemed so that no one will be the wiser. This form of theft is known as *embezzlement*,

---

[2]The business of the goldsmiths was to manufacture gold and silver plate and jewelry, and to purchase, mount and sell jewels. See J. Milnes Holden, *The History of Negotiable Instruments in English Law* (London: The Athlone Press, 1955), pp. 70–71.

[3]These were two other reasons for the emergence of the goldsmiths as money warehouses during the Civil War. Apprentices, who had previously been entrusted with merchants' cash, were now running off to the army, so that merchants now turned to the goldsmiths. At the same time, the gold plate business had fallen off, for impoverished aristocrats were melting down their gold plate for ready cash instead of buying new products. Hence, the goldsmiths were happy to turn to this new form of business. Ibid.

which the dictionary defines as "appropriating fraudulently to one's own use, as money or property entrusted to one's care."

But the speculating warehouseman is always in trouble, for the depositor can come and present his claim check *at any time,* and he is legally bound to redeem the claim, to return the valuables instantly on demand. Ordinarily, then, the warehousing business provides little or no room for this subtle form of theft. If I deposit a gold watch or a chair in a warehouse, I want the object when I call for it, and if it isn't there, the warehouseman will be on a trip to the local prison.

In some forms of warehousing, the temptation to embezzle is particularly heady. The depositor is here not so much interested in getting back the *specific* object as he is in receiving the *same kind* of product. This will occur in the case of *fungible* commodities such as grain, where each unit of the product is identical to every other. Such a deposit is a "general" rather than a "specific" deposit warrant. It now becomes more convenient for the warehouseman to mix all bushels of grain of the same type into a common bin, so that anyone redeeming his grain receives bushels from the same bin. But now the temptation to embezzle has increased enormously. All the warehouseman need do is arrive at a workable estimate of what *percentage* of the grain will probably be redeemed in the next month or year, and then he can lend out or speculate on the rest.

In sophisticated transactions, however, the warehouseman is not likely physically to remove the grain. Since warehouse receipts serve as surrogates for the grain itself, the warehouseman will instead print fake, or *counterfeit,* warehouse receipts, which will look exactly like the others.

But, it might be asked, what about the severe legal penalties for embezzlement? Isn't the threat of criminal charges and a jail term enough to deter all but the most dedicated warehouse embezzlers? Perhaps, except for the critical fact that bailment law scarcely existed until the eighteenth century. It was only by the twentieth century that the courts finally decided that the grain warehouseman was truly a bailee and not simply a debtor.

2. Deposit Banking and Embezzlement

Gold coin and bullion—money—provides an even greater temptation for embezzlement to the deposit banker than grain to the warehouseman. Gold coin and bullion are fully as fungible as wheat; the gold depositor, too, unless he is a collector or numismatist, doesn't care about receiving the identical gold coins he once deposited, so long as they are of the same mark and weight. But the temptation is even greater in the case of money, for while people *do* use up wheat from time to time, and transform it into flour and bread, gold as money *does not have to be used at all*. It is only employed in exchange and, so long as the bank continues its reputation for integrity, its warehouse receipts can function very well as a surrogate for gold itself. So that if there are few banks in the society and banks maintain a high reputation for integrity, there need be little redemption at all. The confident banker can then estimate that a smaller part of his receipts will be redeemed next year, say 15 percent, while fake warehouse receipts for the other 85 percent can be printed and loaned out without much fear of discovery or retribution.

The English goldsmiths discovered and fell prey to this temptation in a very short time, in fact by the end of the Civil War. So eager were they to make profits in this basically fraudulent enterprise, that they even offered to pay interest to depositors so that they could then "lend out" the money. The "lending out," however, was duplicitous, since the depositors, possessing their warehouse receipts, were under the impression that their money was safe in the goldsmiths' vaults, and so exchanged them as equivalent to gold. Thus, gold in the goldsmiths' vaults was covered by two or more receipts. A genuine receipt originated in an actual deposit of gold stored in the vaults, while counterfeit ones, masquerading as genuine receipts, had been printed and loaned out by goldsmiths and were now floating around the country as surrogates for the same ounces of gold.[4]

---

[4]See ibid., p. 72.

The same process of defrauding took place in one of the earliest instances of deposit banking: ancient China. Deposit banking began in the eighth century, when shops accepted valuables and received a fee for safekeeping. After a while, the deposit receipts of these shops began to circulate as money. Finally, after two centuries, the shops began to issue and hand out more printed receipts than they had on deposit; they had caught onto the deposit banking scam.[5] Venice, from the fourteenth to the sixteenth centuries, struggled with the same kind of bank fraud.

Why, then, were the banks and goldsmiths not cracked down on as defrauders and embezzlers? Because deposit banking law was in even worse shape than overall warehouse law and moved in the opposite direction to declare money deposits not a bailment but a debt.

Thus, in England, the goldsmiths, and the deposit banks which developed subsequently, boldly printed counterfeit warehouse receipts, confident that the law would not deal harshly with them. Oddly enough, no one tested the matter in the courts during the late seventeenth or eighteenth centuries. The first fateful case was decided in 1811, in *Carr v. Carr*. The court had to decide whether the term "debts" mentioned in a will included a cash balance in a bank deposit account. Unfortunately, Master of the Rolls Sir William Grant ruled that it did. Grant maintained that since the money had been paid generally into the bank, and was not earmarked in a sealed bag, it had become a loan rather than

---

[5]By A.D. 700–800 there were shops in China which would accept valuables and, for a fee, keep them safe. They would honour drafts drawn on the items in deposit, and, as with the goldsmith's shops in Europe, their deposit receipts gradually began to circulate as money. It is not known how rapidly this process developed, but by A.D. 1000 there were apparently a number of firms in China which issued regular printed notes and which had discovered that they could circulate more notes than the amount of valuables they had on deposit.

Tullock, "Paper Money: A Cycle in Cathay," *Economic History Review* 9 (August 1957): 396.

a bailment.[6] Five years later, in the key follow-up case of
Devaynes v. Noble, one of the counsel argued, correctly, that "a
banker is rather a bailee of his customer's funds than his debtor . . .
because the money in . . . [his] hands is rather a deposit than a
debt, and may therefore be instantly demanded and taken up."
But the same Judge Grant again insisted—in contrast to what
would be happening later in grain warehouse law—that "money
paid into a banker's becomes immediately a part of his general
assets; and he is merely a debtor for the amount."[7]

The classic case occurred in 1848 in the House of Lords, in
Foley v. Hill and Others. Asserting that the bank customer is only
its creditor, "with a superadded obligation arising out of the custom (sic?) of the bankers to honour the customer's cheques,"
Lord Cottenham made his decision, lucidly if incorrectly and
even disastrously:

> Money, when paid into a bank, ceases altogether to be the
> money of the principal; it is then the money of the banker,
> who is bound to an equivalent by paying a similar sum to
> that deposited with him when he is asked for it. . . . The
> money placed in the custody of a banker is, to all intents and
> purposes, the money of the banker, to do with it as he
> pleases; he is guilty of no breach of trust in employing it; he
> is not answerable to the principal if he puts it into jeopardy,
> if he engages in a hazardous speculation; he is not bound to
> keep it or deal with it as the property of his principal; but
> he is, of course, answerable for the amount, because he has
> contracted.[8]

Thus, the banks, in this astonishing decision, were given *carte
blanche*. Despite the fact that the money, as Lord Cottenham

---

[6]*Carr v. Carr* (1811) 1 Mer. 543. In J. Milnes Holden, *The Law and
Practice of Banking*, vol. I, *Banker and Customer* (London: Pitman Publishing, 1970), p. 31.

[7]*Devaynes v. Noble* (1816) 1 Met. 529; in ibid.

[8]*Foley v. Hill and Others* (1848) 2. H.L.C., pp. 36–37; in ibid., p. 32.

conceded, was "placed in the custody of the banker," he can do virtually anything with it, and if he cannot meet his contractual obligations he is only a legitimate insolvent instead of an embezzler and a thief who has been caught red-handed. To *Foley* and the previous decisions must be ascribed the major share of the blame for our fraudulent system of *fractional reserve banking* and for the disastrous inflations of the past two centuries.

Even though American banking law has been built squarely on the *Foley* concept, there are intriguing anomalies and inconsistencies. While the courts have insisted that the bank deposit is only a debt contract, they still try to meld in something more. And the courts remain in a state of confusion about whether or not a deposit—the "placing of money in a bank for safekeeping"—constitutes an *investment* (the "placing of money in some form of property for income or profit"). For if it is purely safekeeping and not investment, then the courts might one day be forced to concede, after all, that a bank deposit is a bailment; but if an investment, then how do safekeeping and redemption on demand fit into the picture?[9]

Furthermore, if only *special bank* deposits where the identical object must be returned (e.g., in one's safe-deposit box) are to be considered bailments, and general bank deposits are debt, then why doesn't the same reasoning apply to other fungible, general deposits such as wheat? Why aren't wheat warehouse receipts

---

[9]See *Michie on Banks and Banking*, rev. ed. (Charlottesville, Va.: Michie Co., 1973), vol. 5A, p. 20. Also see pp. 1–13, 27–31, and ibid., *1979 Cumulative Supplement*, pp. 3–4, 7–9. Thus, Michie states that a "bank deposit is more than an ordinary debt, and the depositor's relation to the bank is not identical with that of an ordinary creditor." Citing a Pennsylvania case, Michie adds that "a bank deposit is different from an ordinary debt in this, that from its very nature it is constantly subject to the check of the depositor, and is always payable on demand". *People's Bank v. Legrand*, 103 Penn.309, 49 Am.R.126. Michie, *Banks and Banking*, p. 13n. Also, despite the laws insistence that a bank "becomes the absolute owner of money deposited with it," a bank still "cannot speculate with its depositors' money." *Banks and Banking*, pp. 28, 30–31.

only a debt? Why is this inconsistent law, as the law concedes, "peculiar to the banking business"?[10,11]

3. FRACTIONAL RESERVE BANKING

The carte blanche for deposit banks to issue counterfeit warehouse receipts for gold had many fateful consequences. In the first place, it meant that any deposit of money *could* now take its place in the balance sheet of the bank. For the duration of the deposit, the gold or silver now became an owned asset of the bank, with redemption due as a supposed *debt*, albeit instantly on demand. Let us assume we now have a Rothbard Deposit Bank. It opens for business and receives a deposit of $50,000 of gold from Jones, for which Jones receives a warehouse receipt which he may redeem on demand at any time. The balance sheet of the Rothbard Deposit Bank is now as shown in Figure 7.1.

Although the first step has begun on the slippery slope to fraudulent and deeply inflationary banking, the Rothbard Bank has not yet committed fraud or generated inflation. Apart from a general deposit now being considered a debt rather than bailment,

---

[10]Michie, *Banks and Banking*, p. 20. The answer of the distinguished legal historian Arthur Nussbaum is that the "contrary view" (that a bank deposit is a bailment not a debt) "would lay an unbearable burden upon banking business." No doubt exuberant bank profits from issue of fraudulent warehouse receipts would come to an end. But grain elevators and other warehouses, after all, remain in business successfully; why not genuine safekeeping places for money? Arthur Nussbaum, *Money in the Law: National and International* (Brooklyn: Foundation Press, 1950), p. 105.

[11]The economist, Jevons, in a cry from the heart, lamented the existence of the general deposit, since it has "become possible to create a fictitious supply of a commodity, that is, to make people believe that a supply exists which does not exist . . ." On the other hand, special deposits, such as "bills of lading, pawn-tickets, dock-warrants, or certificates which establish ownership to a definite object," are superior because "they cannot possibly be issued in excess of the good actually deposited, unless by distinct fraud." He concluded wistfully that "it used to be held as a general rule of law, that a present grant or assignment of goods not in existence is without operation." William Stanley Jevons, *Money and the Mechanism of Exchange*, 15th ed. (London: Kegan Paul, 1905), pp. 206–12, 221.

The Rothbard Deposit Bank

Assets		Equity & Liabilities	
Gold coin or bullion	$50,000	Warehouse receipts for gold	$50,000
Total Assets	$50,000	Total Liabilities	$50,000

FIGURE 7.1 — A DEPOSIT BANK

nothing exceptionable has happened. Fifty thousand dollars' worth of gold has simply been deposited in a bank, after which the warehouse receipts circulate from hand to hand or from bank to bank as a surrogate for the gold in question. No fraud has been committed and no inflationary impetus has occurred, because the Rothbard Bank is still backing all of its warehouse receipts by gold or cash in its vaults.

The amount of cash kept in the bank's vaults ready for instant redemption is called its *reserves*. Hence, this form of honest, non-inflationary deposit banking is called "100 percent reserve banking," because the bank keeps all of its receipts backed fully by gold or cash. The fraction to be considered is

$$\frac{\text{Reserves}}{\text{Warehouse Receipts}}$$

and in our example the fraction is

$$\frac{\$50,000}{\$50,000}$$

or 100 percent. Note, too, that regardless of how much gold is deposited in the banks, the total money supply remains precisely the same so long as each bank observes the 100 percent rule. Only the *form* of the money will change, not its total amount or its significance. Thus, suppose that the total money supply of a country is $100,000,000 in gold coin and bullion, of which $70,000,000 is deposited in banks, the warehouse receipts being fully backed by gold and used as a substitute for gold in making monetary exchanges. The total money supply of the country (that is, money actually used in making exchanges) would be:

$30,000,000 (gold) + $70,000,000 (warehouse receipts for gold)

The total amount of money would remain the same at $100,000,000; its form would be changed to mainly warehouse receipts for gold rather than gold itself.

The irresistible temptation now emerges for the goldsmith or other deposit banker to commit fraud and inflation: to engage, in short, in *fractional reserve banking*, where total cash reserves are *lower*, by some fraction, than the warehouse receipts outstanding. It is unlikely that the banker will simply abstract the gold and use it for his own consumption; there is then no likelihood of *ever* getting the money should depositors ask to redeem it, and this act *would* run the risk of being considered embezzlement. Instead, the banker will either lend out the *gold*, or far more likely, will issue fake warehouse receipts for gold and lend them out, eventually getting repaid the principal plus interest. In short, *the deposit banker has suddenly become a loan banker*; the difference is that he is not taking his own savings or borrowing in order to lend to consumers or investors. Instead he is taking someone else's money and lending it out *at the same time* that the depositor thinks his money is still available for him to redeem. Or rather, and even worse, the banker issues fake warehouse receipts and lends them out as if they were real warehouse receipts represented by cash. At the same time, the original depositor thinks that his warehouse receipts are represented by money available at any time he wishes to cash them in. Here we have the system of *fractional reserve banking*, in which more than one warehouse receipt is backed by the same amount of gold or other cash in the bank's vaults.

It should be clear that modern fractional reserve banking is a shell game, a Ponzi scheme, a fraud in which fake warehouse receipts are issued and circulate as equivalent to the cash supposedly represented by the receipts.

Let us see how this works in our T-accounts.

The Rothbard Bank, having had $50,000 of gold coin deposited in it, now issues $80,000 of fraudulent warehouse receipts and lends them to Smith, expecting to be repaid the $80,000 plus interest.

The Rothbard Bank

Assets		Equity & Liabilities	
Gold coin	$50,000	Warehouse receipts	
IOU from Smith	$80,000	for gold	$130,000
Total Assets	$130,000	Total Liabilities	$130,000

Figure 7.2 — Fractional Reserve Banking

The Rothbard Bank has issued $80,000 of fake warehouse receipts which it lends to Smith, thus increasing the total money supply from $50,000 to $130,000. The money supply has increased by the precise *amount of the credit*—$80,000— expanded by the fractional reserve bank. One hundred percent reserve banking has been replaced by fractional reserves, the fraction being

$$\frac{\$50,000}{\$130,000}$$

or 5/13.

Thus, fractional reserve banking is at one and the same time fraudulent and inflationary; it generates an increase in the money supply by issuing fake warehouse receipts for money. Money in circulation has increased by the amount of warehouse receipts issued beyond the supply of gold in the bank.

The form of the money supply in circulation has again shifted, as in the case of 100 percent reserve banking: A greater proportion of warehouse receipts to gold is now in circulation. But something new has now been added: The total amount of money in circulation has now been increased by the new warehouse receipts issued. Gold coin in the amount of $50,000 formerly in circulation has now been replaced by $130,000 of warehouse receipts. The lower the fraction of the reserve, the greater the amount of new money issued, pyramiding on top of a given total of reserves.

Where did the money come from? It came—and this is the most important single thing to know about modern banking—it came out of thin air. *Commercial banks—that is, fractional reserve banks—create money out of thin air*. Essentially they do it in the same way as *counterfeiters*. Counterfeiters, too, create money out of thin air by printing something masquerading as money or as a warehouse receipt for money. In this way, they fraudulently extract resources from the public, from the people who have genuinely earned their money. In the same way, fractional reserve banks counterfeit warehouse receipts for money, which then circulate as equivalent to money among the public. There is one exception to the equivalence: The law fails to treat the receipts as counterfeit.

Another way of looking at the essential and inherent unsoundness of fractional reserve banking is to note a crucial rule of sound financial management—one that is observed everywhere *except* in the banking business. Namely, *that the time structure of the firm's assets should be no longer than the time structure of its liabilities*. In short, suppose that a firm has a note of $1 million due to creditors next January 1, and $5 million due the following January 1. If it knows what is good for it, it will arrange to have assets of the same amount falling due on these dates or a bit earlier. That is, it will have $1 million coming due to it before or on January 1, and $5 million by the year following. Its time structure of assets is no longer, and preferably a bit shorter, than its liabilities coming due. But deposit banks do not and *cannot* observe this rule. On the contrary, its liabilities—its warehouse receipts—are due instantly, on demand, while its outstanding loans to debtors are inevitably available only after some time period, short or long as the case may be. A bank's assets are always "longer" than its liabilities, which are instantaneous. Put another way, *a bank is always inherently bankrupt*, and would actually become so if its depositors all woke up to the fact that the money they believe to be available on demand is actually not there.[12]

One attempted justification of fractional reserve banking, often employed by the late Professor Walter E. Spahr, maintains that the banker operates somewhat like a bridge builder. The builder of a bridge estimates approximately how many people will be using it from day to day; he doesn't attempt the absurd task of building a bridge big enough to accommodate every resident of the area should he or she wish to travel on the bridge at the same time. But if the bridge builder may act on estimates of the small fraction of citizens who will use the bridge at any one time, why may not a banker likewise estimate what percentage of his deposits will be redeemed at any one time, and keep no more than the required fraction? The problem with this analogy is that citizens in no sense have a legal claim to be able to cross the bridge at any given time. But holders of warehouse receipts to money emphatically *do have* such a claim, even in modern banking law, to their own property any time they choose to redeem it. But the legal claims issued by the bank must then be fraudulent, since the bank could not possibly meet them all.[13]

---

[12]Cf. Elgin Groseclose, *Money and Man*, pp. 178–79.

[13]See Murray N. Rothbard, *The Case for a 100 Percent Gold Dollar* (Washington, D.C.: Libertarian Review Press, November 1974), p. 25. Mises trenchantly distinguishes between a "credit transaction," where a present good is exchanged for a future good (or IOU due in the future), and a *claim transaction,* such as a warehouse receipt, where the depositor or claimant does not give up any of the present good (e.g., wheat, or money). On the contrary, he retains his claim to the deposited good, since he can redeem it at any time. As Mises states:

It should be clear that for the purpose of analyzing fractional reserve banking, it doesn't make any difference what is considered money or cash in the society, whether it be gold, tobacco, or even government fiat paper money. The technique of pyramiding by the banks remains the same. Thus, suppose that now gold has been outlawed, and cash or legal tender money consists of *dollars* printed by the central government. The process of pyramiding remains the same, except that the base of the pyramid is paper dollars instead of gold coin.[14]

Our Rothbard Bank which receives $50,000 of government paper money on deposit, then proceeds to pyramid $80,000 on top of it by issuing fake warehouse receipts.

The Rothbard Bank

Assets		Equity & Liabilities	
Gold coin	$50,000	Warehouse receipts	
IOU from Smith	$80,000	to cash	$130,000
Total Assets	$130,000	Total Liabilities	$130,000

FIGURE 7.3 — FRACTIONAL RESERVE BANKING (PAPER)

A depositor of a sum of money who acquires in exchange for it a claim convertible into money at any time which will perform exactly the same service for him as the sum it refers to has exchanged no present good for a future good. The claim that he has acquired by his deposit is also a present good for him. The depositing of money in no way means that he has renounced immediate disposal over the utility it commands.

Ludwig von Mises, *The Theory of Money and Credit*, 2nd ed. (New Haven: Yale University Press, 1953), p. 268.

[14]As we shall see later, while the *pyramiding process* remains the same, the opportunity for inflating the base is much greater under fiat paper than with gold.

Just as in the gold case, the total money supply has increased from $50,000 to $130,000, consisting precisely in the issue of new warehouse receipts, and in the credit expanded by the fractional reserve bank.

Just as in the case of outright counterfeiting, the new money—this time in the form of new warehouse receipts—does not shower upon everyone alike. The new money is injected *at some particular point* in the economic system—in this case, the Rothbard Bank issues it and it is immediately loaned to Smith—and the new money then ripples out into the economy. Smith, let us say, uses the $80,000 of new money to buy more equipment, the equipment manufacturer buys raw materials and pays more for labor, and so on. As the new money pours into the system and ripples outward, demand curves for particular goods or services are increased along the way, and prices are increased as well. The more extensive the spread of bank credit, and the more new money is pumped out, the greater will be its effect in raising prices. Once again, the early receivers from the new money benefit at the expense of the late receivers—and still more, of those who never receive the new money at all. The earliest receivers—the bank and Smith—benefit most, and, like a hidden tax or tribute, the late receivers are fraudulently despoiled of their rightful resources.

Thus, fractional reserve banking, like government fiat paper or technical counterfeiting, is inflationary, and aids some at the expense of others. But there are even more problems here. Because unlike government paper and unlike counterfeiting (unless the counterfeit is detected), the bank credit is subject to contraction as well as expansion. In the case of bank credit, what comes up, can later come down, and generally does. The expansion of bank credit makes the banks shaky and leaves them open, in various ways, to a contraction of their credit.

Thus, let us consider the Rothbard Bank again. Suppose that the loan to Smith of $80,000 was for a two-year period. At the end of the two years, Smith is supposed to return the $80,000 plus interest. But when Smith pays the $80,000 (forgetting about the interest payment to keep things simple), he will very likely pay in Rothbard Bank warehouse receipts, which are then canceled. The repayment of the $80,000 loan means that $80,000 in fake warehouse receipts has been canceled, and the money supply has now contracted back to the original $50,000. After the repayment, the balance sheet of the Rothbard Bank will be as follows:

The Rothbard Bank

Assets		Equity & Liabilities	
Cash	$50,000	Warehouse receipts to cash	$50,000
Total Assets	$50,000	Total Liabilities	$50,000

FIGURE 7.4 — REPAYMENT OF BANK LOANS

We are back to the pre-expansion figures of our original example (Figure 7.1).

But if the money supply contracts, this means that there is deflationary pressure on prices, and prices will contract, in a similar kind of ripple effect as in the preceding expansion. Ordinarily, of course, the Rothbard Bank, or any other fractional reserve bank, will not passively sit back and see its loans and credit contract. Why should it, when the bank makes its money by inflationary lending? But, the important point is that fractional reserve banks are sitting ducks, and are always subject to contraction. When the banks' state of inherent bankruptcy is discovered, for example, people will tend to cash in their deposits, and the contractionary, deflationary pressure could be severe. If banks have to contract suddenly, they will put pressure on their borrowers, try to call in or will refuse to renew their loans, and the deflationary pressure will bring about a recession—the successor to the inflationary boom.

Note the contrast between fractional reserve banking and the pure gold coin standard. Under the pure gold standard, there is virtually no way that the money supply can actually *decline*, since gold is a highly durable commodity. Nor will it be likely that government fiat paper will decline in circulation; the only rare example would be a budget surplus where the government burned the paper money returning to it in taxes. But fractional reserve bank credit expansion is always shaky, for the more extensive its inflationary creation of new money, the more likely it will be to suffer contraction and subsequent deflation. We already see here the outlines of the basic model of the famous and seemingly mysterious business cycle, which has plagued the Western world since the middle or late eighteenth century. For every business cycle is marked, and even ignited, by inflationary expansions of bank credit. The basic model of the business cycle then becomes evident: bank credit expansion raises prices and causes a seeming boom situation, but a boom based on a hidden fraudulent tax on the late receivers of money. The greater the inflation, the more the banks will be sitting ducks, and the more likely will there be a subsequent credit contraction touching off liquidation of credit and investments, bankruptcies, and deflationary price declines. This is only a crude outline of the business cycle, but its relevance to the modern world of the business cycle should already be evident.

Establishing oneself as a fractional reserve bank, however, is not as easy as it seems, despite the law unfortunately looking the other way at systemic fraud. For the Rothbard Bank, or any other bank, to have its warehouse receipts functioning in lieu of gold or government paper requires a long initial buildup of trust on the part of the public. The Rothbard Bank must first build up a reputation over the decades as a bank of safety, probity, and honesty, and as always ready and able to redeem its liabilities on demand. This cannot be achieved overnight.

4. Bank Notes and Deposits

Through the centuries, there have been two basic forms of money warehouse receipts. The first, the most obvious, is the written receipt, a piece of paper on which the deposit bank promises to pay to the bearer a certain amount of cash in gold or silver (or in government paper money). This written form of warehouse receipt is called the *bank note*. Thus, in the United States before the Civil War, hundreds if not thousands of banks issued their own notes, some in response to gold deposited, others in the course of extending fractional reserve loans. At any rate, if someone comes into the possession (either by depositing gold or by selling a product in exchange) of, say, a $100 note from the Bank of New Haven, it will function as part of the money supply so long as people accept the $100 note as a substitute, a surrogate, for the gold. If someone uses the $100 note of the Bank of New Haven to buy a product sold by another person who is a customer of the Bank of Hartford, the latter will go to his bank and exchange the $100 New Haven note for a similar note from the Bank of Hartford.

The bank note has always been the basic form of warehouse receipt used by the mass of the public. Later, however, there emerged another form of warehouse receipt used by large merchants and other sophisticated depositors. Instead of a tangible receipt, the bank simply opened a deposit account on its books. Thus, if Jones deposited $10,000 in a bank, he received, if he wished, not tangible bank notes, but an open book account or deposit account for $10,000 on the bank's books. The bank's demand debt to Jones was not in the form of a piece of paper but of an intangible book account which could be redeemed at any time in cash. Confusingly, these open book accounts came to be called *demand deposits,* even though the tangible bank note was just as much a demand deposit from an economic or a legal point of view. When used in exchange, instead of being transferred physically as in the case of a bank note, the depositor, Jones, would write out an order, directing the bank to transfer his book account to, say, Brown. Thus, suppose that Jones has a deposit account of $10,000 at the Rothbard Bank.

Suppose now that Jones buys a hi-fi set from Brown for $3,000. Jones writes out an order to the bank, directing it to transfer $3,000 from his open book account to that of Brown. The order will appear somewhat as follows:

> *Rothbard Bank*
> Pay to the order of John Brown $3,000
> Three thousand and 00/000
> (signed)
> Robert Jones

This written instrument is, of course, called a *check*. Note that the check *itself* is not functioning as a money surrogate here. The check is simply a written order transferring the demand deposit from one person to another. The demand deposit, not the check, functions as money, for the former is a warehouse receipt (albeit unwritten) for money or cash.

The Rothbard Bank's balance sheet is now as follows:

The Rothbard Bank

Assets		Equity & Liabilities	
Gold	$10,000	Demand deposits	
		to Jones	$7,000
		to Brown	$3,000
Total Assets	$10,000	Total Liabilities	$10,000

FIGURE 7.5 — TRANSFERRING DEMAND DEPOSITS

Note that from this purchase of a hi-fi set, nothing has changed in the total money supply in the country. The bank was and still is pursuing a 100 percent reserve policy; all of its demand liabilities are still covered or backed 100 percent by cash in its vaults. There is no fraud and no inflation.

Economically, then, the demand deposit and the tangible bank note are simply different technological forms of the same thing: a demand receipt for cash at the money warehouse. Their economic consequences are the same and there is no reason for the legal system to treat them differently. Each form will tend to have its own technological advantages and disadvantages on the market. The bank note is simpler and more tangible, and doesn't require quite the same degree of sophistication or trust by the holders of the receipt. It also involves less work for the bank, since it doesn't have to change the names on its books; all it needs to know is that a certain quantity of bank notes is out in circulation. If Jones buys a hi-fi set from Brown, the bank note changes hands without anyone having to report the change at the bank, since the bank is liable to the note-holder in any case. For small transactions—purchase of a newspaper or ham sandwich—it is difficult to visualize having to write out a check in payment. On the other hand, demand deposits have the advantage of allowing one to write out checks for exact amounts. If, for example, the hi-fi set costs some nonrounded amount, such as $3,168.57, it may well be easier to simply write out the check than trying to find notes and coins for the exact amount—since notes will generally be in fixed denominations ($1, $5, $10, etc.).[15] Also, it will often be more convenient to use demand deposits for large transactions, when amassing cash can be cumbersome and inconvenient. Moreover, there is far greater danger of loss from theft or accident when carrying cash than when having a certain known amount on a bank's books.

---

[15]Bank notes, however, were made more flexible in seventeenth-century England by the banks allowing *part* payment of a note, with the payment deducted from the original face value of the note. Holden, *Negotiable Instruments,* p. 91n.

All of these factors will tend, on the free market, to limit the use of bank deposits to large users and for large transactions.[16] As late as World War I, the general public in the Western world rarely used bank deposits. Most transactions were effected in cash, and workers received cash rather than bank checks for wages and salaries. It was only after World War II, under the impetus of decades of special support and privilege by government, that checking accounts became nearly universal.

A bank can issue fraudulent and inflationary warehouse receipts just as easily in the form of open book deposits as it can in bank notes. To return to our earlier example, the Rothbard Bank, instead of printing fraudulent, uncovered bank notes worth $80,000 and lending them to Smith, can simply open up a new or larger book account for Smith, and credit him with $80,000, thereby, at the stroke of a pen and as if by magic, increasing the money supply in the country by $80,000.

In the real world, as fractional reserve banking was allowed to develop, the rigid separation between deposit banking and loan banking was no longer maintained in what came to be known as *commercial banks*.[17] The bank accepted deposits, loaned out its

---

[16] . . . banking in general only became important with the development of the issue of notes. People would deposit coin and bullion with a bank more readily when they received something in exchange such as a banknote, originally in the form of a mere receipt, which could be passed from hand-to-hand. And it was only after the bankers had won the public over to confidence in the banks by circulating their notes, that the public was persuaded to leave large sums on deposit on the security of a mere book-entry.

Vera C. Smith, *The Rationale of Central Banking* (London: P.S. King & Son, 1936), p. 6.

[17]The later institution of the "investment bank," in contrast, lends out saved or borrowed funds, generally in the underwriting of industrial or government securities. In contrast to the commercial bank, whose deposit liabilities exchange as equivalent to money and hence add to the money supply, the liabilities of the investment bank are simply debts which are not "monetized" by being a demand claim on money.

equity and the money it borrowed, and also created notes or deposits out of thin air which it loaned out to its own borrowers. On the balance sheet, all these items and activities were jumbled together. Part of a bank's activity was the legitimate and productive lending of saved or borrowed funds; but most of it was the fraudulent and inflationary creation of a fraudulent warehouse receipt, and hence a money surrogate out of thin air, to be loaned out at interest.

Let us take a hypothetical mixed bank, and see how its balance sheet might look, so that we can analyze the various items.

Jones Bank

Assets		Equity & Liabilities	
IOUs from		Demand Liabilities:	
borrowers	$1,700,000	Notes	$1,000,000
Cash	$300,000	Deposits	$800,000
		Total	$1,800,000
		Equity	$200,000
Total Assets	$2,000,000	Total Liabilities	$2,000,000

FIGURE 7.6 — MIXED LOAN AND DEPOSIT BANK

Our hypothetical Jones Bank has a stockholders' equity of $200,000, warehouse receipts of $1.8 million distributed as $1 million of bank notes and $800,000 of demand deposits, cash in the vault of $300,000, and IOUs outstanding from borrowers of $1.7 million. Total assets, and total equity and liabilities, each equal $2 million.

We are now equipped to analyze the balance sheet of the bank from the point of view of economic and monetary importance. The crucial point is that the Jones Bank has demand liabilities, instantly payable on presentation of the note or deposit, totaling

$1.8 million, whereas cash in the vault ready to meet these obligations is only $300,000.[18] The Jones Bank is engaging in fractional reserve banking, with the fraction being

$$\frac{\$300,000}{\$1,800,000}$$

or 1/6. Or, looking at it another way, we can say that the invested stockholder equity of $200,000 is invested in loans, while the other $1.5 million of assets have been loaned out by the creation of fraudulent warehouse receipts for money.

The Jones Bank could increase its equity by a certain amount, or borrow money by issuing bonds, and then invest them in extra loans, but these legitimate loan operations would not affect the 1/6 fraction, or the amount of fraudulent warehouse receipts outstanding. Suppose, for example, that stockholders invest another $500,000 in the Jones Bank, and that this cash is then loaned to various borrowers. The balance sheet of the Jones Bank would now appear as shown in Figure 7.7.

Thus, while the Jones Bank has extended its credit, and its new extension of $500,000 of assets and liabilities is legitimate, productive and noninflationary, its inflationary issue of $1,500,000 continues in place, as does its fractional reserve of 1/6.

A requirement that banks act as any other warehouse, and that they keep their demand liabilities fully covered, that is, that they engage only in 100 percent banking, would quickly and completely put an end to the fraud as well as the inflationary impetus of modern banking. Banks could no longer add to the money supply, since they would no longer be engaged in what is tantamount

---

[18]We should note, however, that if they wanted to, the holders of $800,000 of the bank's demand deposits could cash them in for the notes of the Jones Bank, as well as for gold or government paper money. In fact, the notes and deposits of the Jones Bank are interchangeable for each other, one for one: deposits could, if the owner wished, be exchanged for newly-printed notes, while notes could be handed in and exchanged for newly-credited deposits.

Jones Bank

Assets		Equity & Liabilities	
IOUs from		Demand Liabilities:	
borrowers	$2,200,000	Notes	$1,000,000
Cash	$300,000	Deposits	$800,000
		Total	$1,800,000
		Equity	$700,000
Total Assets	$2,500,000	Total Liabilities	$2,500,000

FIGURE 7.7 — FRACTIONAL RESERVE IN A MIXED BANK

to counterfeiting. But suppose that we don't have a legal requirement for 100 percent banking. How inflationary would be a system of free and unrestricted banking, with no government intervention? Is it true, as is generally believed, that a system of free banking would lead to an orgy of unrestricted money creation and inflation?

VIII.

FREE BANKING AND THE LIMITS ON BANK CREDIT INFLATION

Let us assume now that banks are not required to act as genuine money warehouses, and are unfortunately allowed to act as debtors to their depositors and noteholders rather than as bailees retaining someone else's property for safekeeping. Let us also define a system of *free banking* as one where banks are treated like any other business on the free market. Hence, they are not subjected to any government control or regulation, and entry into the banking business is completely free. There is one and only one government "regulation": that they, like any other business, must pay their debts promptly or else be declared insolvent and be put out of business.[1] In short, under free banking, banks are totally free, even to engage in fractional reserve banking, but they must redeem their notes or demand deposits on demand, promptly and without cavil, or otherwise be forced to close their doors and liquidate their assets.

---

[1]This is not the place to investigate the problem whether bankruptcy laws confer a special privilege on the debtor to weasel out of his debts.

Propagandists for central banking have managed to convince most people that free banking would be banking out of control, subject to wild inflationary bursts in which the supply of money would soar almost to infinity. Let us examine whether there are any strong checks, under free banking, on inflationary credit expansion.

In fact, there are several strict and important limits on inflationary credit expansion under free banking. One we have already alluded to. If I set up a new Rothbard Bank and start printing bank notes and issuing bank deposits out of thin air, why should anyone accept these notes or deposits? Why should anyone trust a new and fledgling Rothbard Bank? Any bank would have to build up trust over the years, with a record of prompt redemption of its debts to depositors and noteholders before customers and others on the market will take the new bank seriously. The buildup of trust is a prerequisite for any bank to be able to function, and it takes a long record of prompt payment and therefore of noninflationary banking, for that trust to develop.

There are other severe limits, moreover, upon inflationary monetary expansion under free banking. One is the extent to which people are willing to use bank notes and deposits. If creditors and vendors insist on selling their goods or making loans in gold or government paper and refuse to use banks, the extent of bank credit will be extremely limited. If people in general have the wise and prudent attitudes of many "primitive" tribesmen and refuse to accept anything but hard gold coin in exchange, bank money will not get under way or wreak inflationary havoc on the economy.

But the extent of banking is a general background restraint that does precious little good once banks have become established. A more pertinent and magnificently powerful weapon against the banks is the dread *bank run*—a weapon that has brought many thousands of banks to their knees. A bank run occurs when the clients of a bank—its depositors or noteholders—lose confidence in their bank, and begin to fear that the bank does not really have the ability to redeem their money on demand.

Then, depositors and noteholders begin to rush to their bank to cash in their receipts, other clients find out about it, the run intensifies and, of course, since a fractional reserve bank is *indeed* inherently bankrupt—a run will close a bank's door quickly and efficiently.[2]

Various movies of the early 1930s have depicted a bank run in action. Rumors spread throughout a town that the bank is really insolvent—that it doesn't have the money to redeem its deposits. Depositors form lines at 6:00 A.M. waiting to take their money out of the bank. Hearing of the rumors and seeing the lines, more depositors rush to "take their money out of the bank" (money, of course, which is not really there). The suave and authoritative bank manager tries to assure the depositors that the rumors are all nonsense and that the excited and deluded people should return quietly to their homes. But the bank clients cannot be mollified. And then, since of course the hysterical and deluded folk are really quite right and the money is of course *not* there to cover their demands, the bank in fact *does* go bankrupt, and is out of business in a few hours.

The bank run is a marvelously effective weapon because (a) it is irresistible, since once it gets going it cannot be stopped, and (b) it serves as a dramatic device for calling everyone's attention to the inherent unsoundness and insolvency of fractional reserve banking. Hence, bank runs feed on one another, and can induce other bank runs to follow. Bank runs instruct the public in the essential fraudulence of fractional reserve banking, in its essence as a giant Ponzi scheme in which a few people can redeem their deposits *only* because most depositors do not follow suit.

When a bank run will occur cannot be determined, since, at least in theory, clients can lose confidence in their banks at any time. In practice, of course, loss of confidence does not come out of thin air. It will happen, say, after an inflationary boom has been

---

[2]From 1929 to 1933, the last year when runs were permitted to do their work of cleansing the economy of unsound and inflationary banks, 9,200 banks failed in the United States.

underway for some time, and the fraction of reserves/demand liabilities has been lowered through credit expansion. A rash of bank
runs will bring the insolvency of many banks and deflationary
contraction of credit and the money supply.

In chapter VII, we saw that fractional reserve banking
expands money and credit, but that this can be reversed on a dime
by enforced credit contraction and deflation of the money supply.
Now we see one way this can occur. The banks pyramid notes and
deposits on top of a certain amount of cash (gold and government
paper); the ever-lower fractional reserve ratio weakens the confidence of customers in their banks; the weakened confidence
causes demands for redemption culminating in a run on banks;
and bank runs stimulate similar bank runs until a cycle of deflation and bank collapse is underway. Fractional reserve banking
has given rise to a boom and bust business cycle.

But the bank run, too, is a cataclysmic meat axe event that
occurs only after a considerable inflation of bank credit. It is true
that continuing, never-ending *fear* of a bank run will provide a
healthy check on inflationary bank operations. But still the bank
run allows for a considerable amount of credit expansion and
bank inflation before retribution arrives. It is not a continuing,
day-to-day restraint; it happens only as a one-shot phenomenon,
long after inflation has caught hold and taken its toll.

Fortunately, the market *does* provide a superb, day-to-day
grinding type of severe restraint on credit expansion under free
banking. It operates *even* while confidence in banks by their customers is as buoyant as ever. It does not depend, therefore, on a
psychological loss of faith in the banks. This vital restraint is simply the *limited clientele of each bank*. In short, the Rothbard Bank
(or the Jones Bank) is constrained, first, by the fear of a bank run
(loss of confidence in the bank by its own customers); but it is
also, and even more effectively, constrained by the very fact that,
in the free market, the clientele of the Rothbard Bank is extremely
limited. The day-to-day constraint on banks under free banking is
the fact that nonclients will, by definition, call upon the bank for
redemption.

Let us see how this process works. Let us hark back to Figures 7.2 and 7.3 where the Rothbard Bank has had $50,000 of gold coin or government paper deposited in it, and then proceeded to pyramid on top of that $50,000 by issuing $80,000 more of fake warehouse receipts and lending them out to Smith. The Rothbard Bank has thereby increased the money supply in its own bailiwick from $50,000 to $130,000, and its fractional reserve has fallen from 100 percent to 5/13. But the important point to note now is that this process *does not stop there*. For what does Smith do with his $80,000 of new money? We have already mentioned that new money ripples out from its point of injection: Smith clearly does not sit on the money. He spends it on more equipment or labor or on more consumer goods. In any case, he *spends* it. But what happens to the credit status of the money? That depends crucially on whether or not the person Smith spends the money on is *himself* a customer of the Rothbard Bank.

Let us assume, as in Figure 8.1, that Smith takes the new receipts and spends them on equipment made by Jones, *and* that Jones, too, is a client of the Rothbard Bank. In that case, there is no pressure on the Rothbard Bank, and the inflationary credit expansion proceeds without difficulty. Figure 8.1 shows what happens to the Rothbard Bank's balance sheet (to simplify, let us assume that the loan to Smith was in the form of demand deposits).

The Rothbard Bank

Assets		Equity & Liabilities	
Gold	$50,000	Demand deposits:	
IOU from Smith	$80,000	to Smith	$0
		to Jones	$80,000
		to Others	$50,000
Total Assets	$130,000	Total demand deposits	$130,000

FIGURE 8.1 — A BANK WITH MANY CLIENTS

Thus, total liabilities, or demand deposits, remain what they were after the immediate loan to Smith. Fifty thousand dollars is owed to the original depositors of gold (and/or to people who sold goods or services to the original depositors for gold); Smith has written a check for his $80,000 for the purchase of equipment from Jones, and Jones is now the claimant for the $80,000 of demand deposits. Total demand deposits for the Rothbard Bank have remained the same. Moreover, all that has happened, from the Rothbard Bank's point of view, is that deposits have been shuffled around from one of its clients to another. So long, then, as *confidence is retained* by its depositors in the Rothbard Bank, it can continue to expand its operations and its part of the money supply with impunity.

But—and here is the rub—suppose that Jones is *not* a client of the Rothbard Bank. After all, when Smith borrows money from that bank he has no interest in patronizing only fellow clients of his bank. He wants to invest or spend the money in ways most desirable or profitable to himself. In a freely competitive banking system, there is no guarantee—indeed not even a likelihood—that Jones, or the person whom *Jones* will spend the money on, will himself be a client of the Rothbard Bank.

Suppose, then, that Jones is *not* a client of the Rothbard Bank. What then? Smith gives a check (or a note) to Jones for the equipment for $80,000. Jones, not being a client of the Rothbard Bank, will therefore call upon the Rothbard Bank for redemption. But the Rothbard Bank doesn't have the money; it has only $50,000; it is $30,000 short, and therefore the Rothbard Bank is now bankrupt, out of business.

The beauty and power of this restraint on the banks is that it does not depend on loss of confidence in the banks. Smith, Jones, and everyone else can go on being blithely ignorant and trusting of the fractional reserve banking system. And yet the redemption weapon does its important work. For Jones calls on the Rothbard Bank for redemption, *not* because he doesn't trust the bank or thinks it is going to fail, but simply because he patronizes another bank and wants to shift his account to his preferred bank. The mere existence of bank competition will provide a powerful, continuing, day-to-day constraint on fractional reserve credit expansion. Free banking, even where fractional reserve banking is legal and not punished as fraud, will scarcely permit fractional reserve inflation to exist, much less to flourish and proliferate. Free banking, far from leading to inflationary chaos, will insure almost as hard and noninflationary a money as 100 percent reserve banking itself.

In practice, the concrete method by which Jones insists on redemption in order to shift his account from the Rothbard Bank to his own can take several forms, each of which have the same economic effects. Jones can refuse to take Smith's check, insisting on cash, so that Smith becomes the redeemer of his own deposits. Jones—if the Rothbard Bank could supply him with the gold—could then deposit the gold in his own bank. Or Jones himself could arrive at the Rothbard Bank and demand redemption. In practice, of course, Jones would not bother, and would leave these financial affairs to his own bank, which would demand redemption. In short, Jones would take Smith's check, made out to him on the account of the Rothbard Bank, and deposit it in his own bank, getting a demand deposit there for the amount deposited. Jones's bank would take the check and demand redemption from the Rothbard Bank. The Rothbard Bank would then have to confess it could not pay, and would hence go out of business.

Figure 8.2 shows how this process works. We assume that Jones's account is in the Boonville Bank. We do not bother showing the complete balance sheet of the Boonville Bank because it is irrelevant to our concerns, as is the soundness of the bank.

Thus, we see that dynamically from this transaction, the Boonville Bank finds itself with an increased demand deposit owed to Jones of $80,000, balanced by a check on the Rothbard Bank for $80,000. When it cashes the check for redemption, it puts such a severe redemption pressure on the Rothbard Bank that the latter goes bankrupt.

Rothbard Bank			*Boonville Bank*	
Assets	Equity & Liabilities		Assets	Equity & Liabilities
Gold $50,000	Demand			Demand
IOU from	deposits to			deposit to
Smith $80,000	Boonville $80,000			Jones + $80,000
	to Others $50,000			
Total Assets	Total demand		Due from	
	deposits		Rothbard Bank	
	$130,000		$130,000	+ $80,000

FIGURE 8.2 — REDEMPTION BY ANOTHER BANK

Why should the Boonville Bank call upon the Rothbard Bank for redemption? Why should it do anything else? The banks are competitors, not allies. The banks either pay no interest on their demand deposits—the usual situation—or else the interest will be far lower than the interest they themselves can earn on their loans. The longer the Boonville Bank holds off on redemption the more money it loses. Furthermore, as soon as it obtains the gold, it can try to pyramid bank credit on top of it. Banks therefore have everything to lose and nothing to gain by holding up on redeeming notes or demand deposits from other banks.

It should be clear that the sooner the borrowers from an expanding bank spend money on products of clients of *other* banks—in short, as soon as the new money ripples out to *other* banks—the issuing bank is in big trouble. For the sooner and the more intensely clients of *other* banks come into the picture, the sooner will severe redemption pressure, even unto bankruptcy, hit the expanding bank. Thus, from the point of view of checking inflation, the more banks there are in a country, and therefore *the smaller the clientele of each bank,* the better. If each bank has only a few customers, any expanded warehouse receipts will pass over to nonclients very quickly, with devastating effect and rapid bankruptcy. On the other hand, if there are only a few banks in a country, and the clientele of each is extensive, then the expansionary process could go on a long time, with clients shuffling notes and deposits to one another within the same bank, and the inflationary process continuing at great length. The more banks, and the fewer the clientele of each, then, the less room there will be for fractional reserve inflation under free banking. If there are a myriad of banks, there may be no room at all to inflate; if there are a considerable but not great number, there will be more room for inflation, but followed fairly quickly by severe redemption pressure and enforced contraction of loans and bank credit in order to save the banks. The wider the number of clients, the more time it will take for the money to ripple out to other banks; on the other hand, the greater the degree of inflationary credit expansion, the faster the rippling out and hence the swifter the inevitable redemption, monetary contraction, and bank failures.

Thus, we may consider a spectrum of possibilities, depending on how many competing banks there are in a country. At one admittedly absurd pole, we may think of each bank as having only one client; in that case, of course, there would be no room whatever for any fractional reserve credit. For the borrowing client would immediately spend the money on somebody who would by definition be a client of another bank. Relaxing the limits a bit to provide a myriad of banks with only a few clients each would scarcely allow much more room for bank inflation. But then, as we assume fewer and fewer banks, each with a more and more extensive clientele, there will be increasing room for credit expansion until a rippling out process enforces contraction, deflation, and bank failures. Then, if there are only a few banks in a country, the limits on inflation will be increasingly relaxed, and there will be more room for inflation, and for a subsequent business cycle of contraction, deflation, and bank failures following an inflationary boom.

Finally, we come to the case of one bank, in which we assume that for some reason, everyone in the country is the client of a single bank, say the "Bank of the United States." In that case, our limit disappears altogether, for then all payments by check or bank note take place between clients of the *same* bank. There is therefore no day-to-day clientele limit from the existence of other banks, and the only limit to *this* bank's expansion of inflationary credit is a general loss of confidence that it can pay in cash. For it, too, is subject to the overall constraint of fear of a bank run.

Of course we have been abstracting from the existence of other countries. There may be no clientele limits within a country to its monopoly bank's expansion of money and credit. But of course there is trade and flows of money between countries. Since there is international trade and money flows between countries, attenuated limits on inflationary bank credit still exist.

Let us see what happens when one country, say France, has a monopoly bank and it begins merrily to expand the number of demand deposits and bank notes in francs. We assume that every country is on the gold standard, that is, every country defines its currency as some unit of weight of gold. As the number of francs in circulation increases, and as the French inflationary process continues, francs begin to ripple out abroad. That is, Frenchmen will purchase more products or invest more in other countries. But this means that claims on the Bank of France will pile up in the banks of other countries. As the claims pile up, the foreign banks will call upon the Bank of France to redeem its warehouse receipts in gold, since, in the regular course of events, German, Swiss, or Ceylonese citizens or banks have no interest whatever in piling up claims to francs. What they want is gold so they can invest or spend on what they like or pyramid on top of their own gold reserves. But this means that gold will increasingly flow out of France to other countries, and pressure on the Bank of France will be aggravated. For not only has its fractional reserve already declined from the pyramiding of more and more notes and deposits on top of a given amount of gold, but now the fraction is declining even more alarmingly because gold is unexpectedly and increasingly flowing out of the coffers of the Bank of France. Note again, that the gold is flowing out not from any loss of confidence in the Bank of France by Frenchmen or even by foreigners, but simply that in the natural course of trade and in response to the inflation of francs, gold is flowing out of the French bank and into the banks of other countries.

Eventually, the pressure of the gold outflow will force the Bank of France to contract its loans and deposits, and deflation of the money supply and of bank credit will hit the French economy.

There is another aspect of this monetary boom-and-bust process. For with only one, or even merely a few banks in a country, there is ample room for a considerable amount of monetary inflation. This means of course that during the boom period, the banks expand the money supply and prices increase. In our current case, prices of French products rise because of the monetary inflation and this will intensify the speed of the gold outflow. For French prices have risen while prices in other countries have remained the same, since bank credit expansion has not occurred there. But a rise in French prices means that French products become less attractive both to Frenchmen and to foreigners. Therefore, foreigners will spend less on French products, so that exports from France will fall, and French citizens will tend to shift their purchases from dearer domestic products to relatively cheaper imports. Hence, imports into France will rise. Exports falling and imports rising means of course a dread *deficit in the balance of payments*. This deficit is embodied in an outflow of gold, since gold, as we have seen, is needed to pay for the rising imports. Specifically, gold pays for the increased gap between rising imports and falling exports, since ordinarily exports provide sufficient foreign currency to pay for imports.

Thus for all these reasons, inflationary bank credit expansion in one country causes prices to rise in that country, as well as an outflow of gold and a deficit in the balance of payments to other countries. Eventually, the outflow of gold and increasing demands on the French bank for redemption force the bank to contract credit and deflate the money supply, with a resulting fall in French prices. In this *recession* or bust period, gold flows back in again, for two interconnected reasons. One, the contraction of credit means that there are fewer francs available to purchase domestic or foreign products. Hence imports will fall. Second, the fall of prices at home stimulates foreigners to buy more French goods, and Frenchmen to shift their purchase from foreign to domestic products. Hence, French exports will rise and imports fall, and gold will flow back in, strengthening the position of the Bank of France.

We have of course been describing the essence of the famous Hume-Ricardo "specie flow price mechanism," which explains how international trade and money payments work on the "classical gold standard." In particular, it explains the mechanism that places at least some limit on inflation, through price and money changes and flows of gold, and that tends to keep international prices and the balance of payments of each country in long-run equilibrium. This is a famous textbook analysis. But there are two vitally important aspects of this analysis that have gone unnoticed, except by Ludwig von Mises. First, we have here not only a theory of international money flows but also a rudimentary theory of the business cycle as a phenomenon sparked by inflation and contraction of money and credit by the fractional reserve banking system.

Second, we should now be able to see that the Ricardian specie flow price process is one and the same mechanism by which *one* bank is unable to inflate much if at all in a free banking system. For note what happens when, say, the Rothbard Bank expands its credit and demand liabilities. If there is any room for expansion at all, money and prices among Rothbard Bank clients rise; this brings about increased demands for redemption among clients of other banks who receive the increased money. Gold outflows to other banks from their pressure for redemption forces the Rothbard Bank to contract and deflate in order to try to save its own solvency.

The Ricardian specie flow price mechanism, therefore, is simply a special case of a general phenomenon: When one or more banks expand their credit and demand liabilities, they will lose gold (or, in the case of banks *within* a country, government paper) to other banks, thereby cutting short the inflationary process and leading to deflation and credit contraction. The Ricardian analysis is simply the polar case where all banks within a country can expand together (if there is only one monopoly bank in the country), and so the redemption constraint on inflation only comes, relatively weakly, from the banks of other countries.

But couldn't the banks within a country form a cartel, where each could support the others in holding checks or notes on other banks without redeeming them? In that way, if banks could agree not to redeem each other's liabilities, all banks could inflate together, and act as *if* only one bank existed in a country. Wouldn't a system of free banking give rise to unlimited bank inflation through the formation of voluntary bank cartels?

Such bank cartels could be formed legally under free banking, but there would be every economic incentive working against their success. No cartels in other industries have ever been able to succeed for any length of time on the free market; they have only succeeded—in raising prices and restricting production—when government has stepped in to enforce their decrees and restrict entry into the field. Similarly in banking. Banks, after all, are competing with each other, and the tendency on the market will be for inflating banks to lose gold to sounder, noninflating banks, with the former going out of business. The economic incentives would cut against any cartel, for without it, the sounder, less inflated banks could break their inflated competitors. A cartel would yoke these sounder banks to the fate of their shakier, more inflated colleagues. Furthermore, as bank credit inflation proceeds, incentives would increase for the sound banks to break out of the cartel and call for the redemption of the plethora of warehouse receipts pouring into their vaults. Why should the sounder banks wait and go down with an eventually sinking ship, as fractional reserves become lower and lower? Second, an inflationary bank cartel would induce new, sound, near-100 percent reserve banks to enter the industry, advertising to one and all their noninflationary operations, and happily earning money and breaking their competitors by calling on them to redeem their inflated notes and deposits. So that, while a bank cartel is logically possible under free banking, it is in fact highly unlikely to succeed.

We conclude that, contrary to propaganda and myth, free banking would lead to hard money and allow very little bank credit expansion and fractional reserve banking. The hard rigor of redemption by one bank upon another will keep any one bank's expansion severely limited.

Thus, Mises was highly perceptive when he concluded that

> It is a mistake to associate with the notion of free banking the image of a state of affairs under which everybody is free to issue bank notes and to cheat the public *ad libitum*. People often refer to the dictum of an anonymous American quoted by (Thomas) Tooke: "free trade in banking is free trade in swindling." However, freedom in the issuance of banknotes would have narrowed down the use of banknotes considerably if it had not entirely suppressed it. It was this idea which (Henri) Cernuschi advanced in the hearings of the French Banking Inquiry on October 24, 1865: "I believe that what is called freedom of banking would result in a total suppression of banknotes in France. I want to give everybody the right to issue banknotes so that nobody should take any banknotes any longer."[3]

---

[3]Ludwig von Mises, *Human Action* (New Haven, Conn.: Yale University Press, 1949), p. 443; *Human Action*, Scholar's Edition (Auburn, Ala.: Ludwig von Mises Institute, 1998), p. 443.

IX.

CENTRAL BANKING: REMOVING THE LIMITS

Free banking, then, will inevitably be a regime of hard money and virtually no inflation. In contrast, the essential purpose of central banking is to use government privilege to remove the limitations placed by free banking on monetary and bank credit inflation. The Central Bank is either government-owned and operated, or else especially privileged by the central government. In any case, the Central Bank receives from the government the monopoly privilege for issuing bank notes or cash, while other, privately-owned commercial banks are only permitted to issue demand liabilities in the form of checking deposits. In some cases, the government treasury itself continues to issue paper money as well, but classically the Central Bank is given the sole privilege of issuing paper money in the form of bank notes—Bank of England notes, Federal Reserve Notes, and so forth. If the client of a commercial bank wants to cash in his deposits for paper money, he cannot then obtain notes from his own bank, for that bank is not permitted to issue them. His bank would have to obtain the paper money from the Central Bank. The bank could only obtain such

Central Bank cash by *buying* it, that is, either by selling the Central Bank various assets it agrees to buy, or by drawing down its own checking account with the Central Bank.

For we have to realize that the Central Bank is a bankers' bank. Just as the public keeps checking accounts with commercial banks, so all or at least most of them keep checking accounts with the Central Bank. These checking accounts, or "demand deposits at the Central Bank," are drawn down to buy cash when the banks' own depositors demand redemption in cash.

To see how this process works, let us take a commercial bank, the Martin Bank, which has an account at the Central Bank (Figure 9.1).

Martin Bank

Assets		Equity & Liabilities	
IOUs	$4 million	Demand deposits	$5 million
Reserves = Demand deposits at Central Bank	$1 million		
Total Assets	$5 million		

FIGURE 9.1 — CENTRAL BANKING

We are ignoring Central Bank notes kept for daily transactions in the Martin Bank's vault, which will be a small fraction of its account with the Central Bank. Also, we see that the Martin Bank holds little or no gold. A vital feature of classical central banking is that even when the banking system remains on the gold standard, virtually all bank holdings of gold are centralized into the Central Bank.

In Figure 9.1, the Martin Bank is practicing fractional reserve banking. It has pyramided $5 million of warehouse receipts on top of $1 million of reserves. Its reserves consist of its checking account with the Central Bank, which are its own warehouse receipts for cash. Its fractional reserve is 1/5, so that it has pyramided 5:1 on top of its reserves.

Now suppose that depositors at the Martin Bank wish to redeem $500,000 of their demand deposits into cash. The only cash (assuming that they don't insist on gold) they can obtain is Central Bank notes. But to obtain them, the Martin Bank has to go to the Central Bank and draw down its account by $500,000. In that case, the transactions are as follows (Figure 9.2).

Martin Bank

Assets		Equity & Liabilities	
Demand deposits at Central Bank	$500,000	Demand deposits	$500,000

Central Bank

Assets	Equity & Liabilities	
	Demand deposits of Martin Bank	-$500,000
	Central Bank notes	+$500,000

FIGURE 9.2 — DRAWING DOWN RESERVES

In a regime of free banking, the more frequently that bank clients desire to shift from deposits to notes need not cause any change in the total money supply. If the customers of the Martin Bank were simply willing to shift $500,000 of demand liabilities from deposits to notes (or vice versa), only the *form* of the bank's liabilities would change. But in this case, the need to go to the Central Bank to purchase notes means that Martin Bank reserves are drawn down by the same amount as its liabilities, which means that its fraction of reserves/deposits is lowered considerably. For now its reserves are $500,000 and its demand deposits $4.5 million, the fraction having fallen from 1/5 to 1/9. From the point of view of the Central Bank itself, however, nothing has changed except the form of its liabilities. It has $500,000 less owed to the Martin Bank in its demand deposits, and instead it has printed $500,000 of new Central Bank notes, which are now redeemable in gold to members of the public, who can cash them in through their banks or perhaps at the offices of the Central Bank itself.

If nothing has changed for the Central Bank itself, neither has the total money supply changed. For in the country as a whole, there are now $500,000 less of Martin Bank deposits as part of the money supply, compensated by $500,000 more in Central Bank notes. Only the form, not the total amount, of money has changed.

But this is only the *immediate* effect of the cashing in of bank deposits. For, as we have noted, the Martin Bank's fraction of reserves/deposits has been sharply lowered. Generally, under central banking, a bank will maintain a certain fraction of reserves/deposits, either because it is legally forced to do so, as it is in the United States, or because that is the custom based on market experience. (Such a custom will also prevail—at significantly far higher fractions—under free banking.) If the Martin Bank wishes to or must remain at a fraction of 1/5, it will meet this situation by sharply contracting its loans and selling its assets until the 1/5 fraction is restored. But if its reserves are now down to $500,000 from $1,000,000, it will then wish to contract its demand deposits outstanding from $4.5 million to $2.5 million. It will do so by failing to renew its loans, by rediscounting its IOUs to other financial institutions, and by selling its bonds and other assets on the market. In this way, by contracting its holding of IOUs and deposits, it will contract down to $2.5 million. The upshot is shown in Figure 9.3.

But this means that the Martin Bank has contracted its contribution to the total money supply of the country by $2.5 million.

The Central Bank has $500,000 more in outstanding bank notes in the hands of the public, for a net *decrease* in the total money supply of $2 million. In short, under central banking, a demand for cash—and the subsequent issue of new cash—has the

Martin Bank

Assets		Equity & Liabilities
IOUs	$2 million	Demand deposits $2.5 million
Reserves at Central Bank	$500,000	
Total Assets	$2.5 million	

FIGURE 9.3 — ULTIMATE RESULT OF DRAWING DOWN RESERVES

paradoxical effect of *lowering* the money supply, because of the banks' need to maintain their reserve/deposit ratios. In contrast, the deposit of cash by the public will have the opposite inflationary effect, for the banks' reserve/deposit ratio will rise, and the banks will be able to expand their loans and issues of new deposits. Figure 9.4 shows how this works. Let us take the original Martin Bank balance sheet of Figure 9.1. People decide to deposit $500,000 of their previously issued Central Bank notes and get the equivalent in checking accounts instead. The Martin Bank's balance sheet will change as follows (Figure 9.4):

Step 1: Martin Bank

Assets		Equity & Liabilities
IOUs	$4 million	Demand deposits $5.5 million
Central Bank notes	$500,000	
Demand deposits at Central Bank	$1 million	
Total Assets	$5.5 million	

FIGURE 9.4 — DEPOSITING CASH: PHASE I

But then, the Martin Bank will take this bonanza of cash and deposit it at the Central Bank, adding to its cherished account at the Central Bank, as shown in Figure 9.5:

Step 2: Martin Bank

Assets		Equity & Liabilities
IOUs	$4 million	Demand deposits $5.5 million
Demand deposits at Central Bank	$1.5 million	
Total Assets	$5.5 million	

FIGURE 9.5 — DEPOSITING CASH: PHASE II

But now, in Step 3, the banks will undoubtedly try to maintain their preferred 1/5 ratio. After all, excess reserves beyond the legal or customary fraction is burning a hole in the bank's pocket; banks make money by creating new money and lending it out. After Step 2, the Martin Bank's fractional reserve ratio is $1.5/$5.5, or a little over 27 percent, as compared to the preferred 20 percent. It will therefore expand its loans and issue new deposits until it is back down to its preferred 1/5 ratio. In short, it will pyramid 5:1 on top of its new total reserves of $1.5 million. The result will be Step 3 (Figure 9.6).

Step 3: Martin Bank

Assets		Equity & Liabilities
IOUs	$6 million	Demand deposits $7.5 million
Demand deposits at Central Bank	$1.5 million	
Total Assets	$7.5 million	

FIGURE 9.6 — DEPOSITING CASH: PHASE III

The Martin Bank has expanded its contribution to the money supply by $2.5 million over its original $5 million. As for the Central Bank, its own notes outstanding have declined by $500,000. This amount was received in cash from the Martin Bank, and the Martin Bank account at the Central Bank is credited by an increased $500,000 in return. The Central Bank notes themselves were simply retired and burned, since these obligations were returned to their issuer. The Central Bank balance sheet has changed as follows (Figure 9.7):

Central Bank

Assets	Equity & Liabilities	
	Demand deposits	
	of Martin Bank	+$500,000
	Central Bank notes	– $500,000

FIGURE 9.7 — DEPOSITING CASH: THE CENTRAL BANK

Thus, as a result of $500,000 of cash being deposited in the banks by the public, the Martin Bank has created $2.5 million in new bank deposits, the Central Bank has decreased its notes outstanding by $500,000, and the net result is a $2 million *increase* in the money supply. Again, paradoxically, a drop in paper money outstanding has led to a multiple *expansion* in the supply of money (paper money + bank demand deposits) in the country.

We should note, by the way, that the total money supply only includes money held by the public (demand deposits + Central Bank notes). It does *not* include demand deposits of the banks at the Central Bank or vault cash held by the banks, for this money is simply held in reserve against outstanding (and greater) components of the money supply. To include *intra*bank cash or deposits as part of the money supply would be double counting, just as it would have been double counting to include *both* gold in the banks *and* warehouse receipts for gold as part of the money supply. Warehouse receipts are surrogates for reserves, even when they are pyramided on top of them, so that reserves cannot *also* be included in an account of the supply of money.

Under central banking, then, the total supply of money, M, equals cash in the hands of the public plus demand deposits owned by the public. Cash, in turn, consists of gold coin or bullion among the public, plus Central Bank notes. Or, putting this in equation form,

$$M = \text{gold in public} + \text{Central Bank notes in public} + \text{Demand deposits of the commercial banks}$$

When a nation is taken off the gold standard, gold dollars or francs are no longer part of the money supply, and so the money supply equation becomes (as it is in the United States and all other countries now):

$$M = \text{Central Bank notes} + \text{Demand deposits}$$

It is clear that, even under central banking, if the public is or becomes unwilling to hold any money in bank deposits or notes and insists on using only gold, the inflationary potential of the banking system will be severely limited. Even if the public insists on holding bank notes rather than deposits, fractional reserve bank expansion will be highly limited. The more the public is willing to hold checking accounts rather than cash, the greater the inflationary potential of the central banking system.

But what of the other limits on bank inflation that existed under free banking? True, the Central Bank—at least under the gold standard—can still go bankrupt if the public insists on cashing in their deposits *and* Central Bank paper for gold. But, given the prestige of the Central Bank conferred by government, and with government using the Central Bank for its own deposits and conferring the monopoly privilege of note issue, such bankruptcy will be most unlikely. Certainly the parameters of bank inflation have been greatly widened. Furthermore, in most cases government has conferred another crucial privilege on the Central Bank: making its notes legal tender for all debts in money. Then, if A has contracted with B for a debt of $10,000 in money, B *has* to accept payment in Central Bank notes; he cannot insist, for example, on gold. All this is important in propping up the Central Bank and its associated commercial banks.

What of the dread bank run? Cannot a bank still be subjected to drastic loss of confidence by its clients, and hence demands for redemption, either in gold or in Central Bank notes? Yes, it can, under the gold standard, and bank runs often swept through the American banking system until 1933. But under central banking as contrasted to free banking, the Central Bank stands ready at all times to lend its vast prestige and resources—to be, as the Englishman Walter Bagehot called it in the mid-nineteenth century— *a lender of last resort*. In the tradition of central banking, the Central Bank always stands ready to bail out banks in trouble, to provide them with reserves by purchasing their assets or lending them reserves. In that way, the Central Bank can help the banks through most storms.

But what of the severe free market limits on the expansion of any bank? Won't an expanding Bank A quickly lose reserves to Bank B, and face bankruptcy? Yes, as in free banking, one bank's expansion will meet a severe shock by other banks calling upon it for redemption. But now, under central banking, *all banks can expand together*, on top of new reserves that are pumped in, across the board, by the benevolent Central Bank. Thus, if Bank A and Bank B each increase their reserves, and both expand on top of such reserves, then neither will lose reserves on net to the other, because the redemption of each will cancel the other redemption out.

Through its centralization of gold, and especially through its monopoly of note issue, the Central Bank can see to it that all banks in the country can inflate harmoniously and uniformly together. The Central Bank eliminates hard and noninflated money, and substitutes a coordinated bank credit inflation throughout the nation. That is precisely its purpose. In short, the Central Bank functions as a government cartelizing device to coordinate the banks so that they can evade the restrictions of free markets and free banking and inflate uniformly together. The banks do not chafe under central banking control; instead, they lobby for and welcome it. It is their passport to inflation and easy money.

Since banks are more or less released from such limitations of free banking as bank runs and redemption by other banks by the actions of the Central Bank, the only remaining limitation on credit inflation is the legal or customary minimum reserve ratio a bank keeps of total reserves/total deposits. In the United States since the Civil War, these minimal fractions are *legal reserve requirements*. In all except the most unusual times, the banks, freed of all restrictions except reserve requirements, keep "fully loaned up," that is, they pyramid to the maximum permissible amount on top of their total reserves. Suppose, then, that we aggregate all the commercial banks in the country in one set of T-accounts, and also consider the Central Bank T-account. Let us assume that, in some way or other, total bank reserves, in the form of demand deposits at the Central Bank, increase by $1 billion, that the legal minimum reserve ratio is 1/5, and that the banks make it a practice to keep fully loaned up, that is, always pyramiding 5:1 on top of total reserves. What then happens is shown in Figure 9.8.

We have not finished the Central Bank balance sheet because we have not yet explored how the increase in commercial bank reserves has come about. But whichever way, the banks' fraction of total reserves to demand deposits is now higher, and they can and do expand their credit by another $4 billion and therefore their demand deposits by a total of $5 billion. They do so by writing out new or increased demand deposits *out of thin air* (as fake warehouse receipts for cash) and lending them out or buying IOUs with that new "money." This can be seen in Step 2 (Figure 9.9).

Step 1: All Commercial Banks

Assets		Equity & Liabilities
		Demand deposits + $1 billion
Reserves	+ $1 billion	

Central Bank

Assets		Equity & Liabilities
		Demand deposits to banks + $1 billion

FIGURE 9.8 — INCREASING BANK RESERVES

Step 2: All Commercial Banks

Assets		Equity & Liabilities	
IOUs	+ $4 billion	Demand deposits + $5 billion	
Reserves	+ $1 billion		
Total Assets	+ $5 billion	Total Liabilities	+ $5 billion

Central Bank

Assets		Equity & Liabilities
		Demand deposits to banks + $1 billion

FIGURE 9.9 — PYRAMIDING ON TOP OF NEW RESERVES

Thus, an increase of $1 billion in total commercial bank reserves has led, over a short period of time, to a $5 billion increase in demand deposits, and hence in the total money supply of the country.

If banks remain fully loaned up, then the amount that, in the aggregate, they will pyramid on top of reserves can be precisely known: It is the inverse of the minimum reserve requirement. Thus, if the legal reserve requirement is 1/5 (total reserves/total deposits), the banks will be able to pyramid 5:1 on top of new reserves. If the reserve requirement is 1/10, then the banks will be able to pyramid 10:1 on top of total new reserves. The amount banks can pyramid new deposits on top of reserves is called the *money multiplier*, which is the inverse of the minimum reserve requirement. In short,

$$\text{MM (money multiplier)} = \frac{1}{\text{reserve requirement}}$$

If the banks remain fully loaned up then, we can alter our equation for the nation's money supply to the following:

$$M = \text{Cash} + (\text{total bank reserves x MM})$$

Since banks earn their profits by creating new money and lending it out, banks will keep fully loaned up unless highly unusual circumstances prevail. Since the origin of the Federal Reserve System, U.S. banks have remained fully loaned up except during the Great Depression of the 1930s, when banks were understandably fearful of bankruptcies crashing around them, and could find few borrowers who could be trusted to remain solvent and repay the loan. In that era, the banks allowed *excess reserves* to pile up, that is, reserves upon which they did not pyramid loans and deposits by the legally permissible money multiplier.

The determinants of the money supply under central banking, then, are *reserve requirements* and *total reserves*. The Central Bank can determine the amount of the money supply at any time by manipulating and controlling either the reserve requirements and/or the total of commercial bank reserves.

In the United States, Congressional statute and Federal Reserve Board dictation combine to fix legal reserve requirements. Let us see what happens when a reserve requirement is changed. Suppose that the Fed cuts the reserve requirement in half, from 20 percent to 10 percent—a seemingly extreme example which has, however, been realistic at various times in American history. Let us see the results. Figure 9.10 assumes a hypothetical balance sheet for commercial banks, with the banks fully loaned up to the 5:1 money multiplier.

All Commercial Banks

A				E & L
IOUs	$40 billion	Demand deposits	$50 billion
Reserves	$10 billion		
Total Assets	$50 billion	Total Liabilities	$50 billion

Central Bank

A			E & L
		Demand deposits to banks	$10 billion

FIGURE 9.10 — BANKS, RESERVE REQUIREMENT AT 20 PERCENT

The banks are fully loaned up, with total reserves of $10 billion in legal reserve requirement at 20 percent, and demand deposits therefore at $50 billion.

Now, in Figure 9.11, we see what happens when the Fed lowers the reserve requirement to 10 percent. Because of the halving of reserve requirements, the banks have now expanded another $50 billion of loans and investments (IOUs), thereby increasing

demand deposits by another $50 billion. Total demand deposits
in the country are now $100 billion, and the total money supply
has now increased by $50 billion.

All Commercial Banks

A			E & L	
IOUs	$90 billion	Demand deposits	$100 billion
Reserves	$10 billion		
Total Assets	$100 billion	Total Liabilities	$100 billion

Central Bank

A		E & L	
		Demand deposits to banks	$10 billion

FIGURE 9.11 — LOWERING THE RESERVE REQUIREMENT

One way for the Central Bank to inflate bank money and the
money supply, then, is to lower the fractional reserve requirement. When the Federal Reserve System was established in 1913,
the Fed lowered reserve requirements from 21 percent to 10 percent by 1917, thereby enabling a concurrent doubling of the
money supply at the advent of World War I.

In 1936 and 1937, after four years of money and price inflation during an unprecedentedly severe depression under the New
Deal, the Fed, frightened at a piling up of excess reserves that
could later explode in inflation, quickly doubled bank reserve
requirements, from approximately 10 percent to 20 percent.

Frightened that this doubling helped to precipitate the severe
recession of 1938, the Fed has since been very cautious about
changing reserve requirements, usually doing so by only 1/4 to
1/2 of 1 percent at a time. Generally, true to the inflationary

nature of all central banking, the Fed has lowered requirements. Raising reserve requirements, then, is contractionary and deflationary; lowering them is inflationary. But since the Fed's actions in this area are cautious and gradual, the Fed's most important day-to-day instrument of control of the money supply has been to fix and determine total bank reserves.

X.

CENTRAL BANKING: DETERMINING TOTAL RESERVES

The crucial question then is what determines the level of total bank reserves at any given time. There are several important determinants, which can be grouped into two classes: those controlled by actions of the public, or the market; and those controlled by the Central Bank.

1. THE DEMAND FOR CASH

The major action by the public determining total bank reserves is its demand for cash.[1] We saw (in chapter IX and in Figures 9.1–9.7) how the public's increased demand for cash will put contractionary pressure on a bank, while decreased desire for cash will add to its inflation of the money supply. Let us now repeat this for the aggregate of commercial banks. Let us assume that the public's demand for cash in exchange for its demand

---

[1] In this chapter, we will assume that cash is the notes of the Central Bank.

deposits increases. Figure 10.1 shows a hypothetical banking system, and Figure 10.2 shows the immediate effect on it of an increase in the public's demand for cash, that is, their redeeming some of its deposits for cash.

All Commercial Banks

Assets		Equity & Liabilities	
IOUs	$40 billion	Demand deposits	$50 billion
Reserves	$10 billion		
Total Assets	$50 billion	Total Liabilities	$50 billion

Central Bank

Assets		Equity & Liabilities	
		Demand deposits	
		to banks	$10 billion
		Central Bank notes	$15 billion

FIGURE 10.1 — A HYPOTHETICAL BANKING SYSTEM:
ALL COMMERCIAL BANKS

The hypothetical banking system is depicted as one with a 20 percent reserve ratio, fully loaned up. "Reserves" in the commercial banks' asset column are of course exactly equal to "Demand deposits to banks" in the Central Bank's liabilities column, since they are one and the same thing. The asset side of the Central Bank balance sheet is not being considered here; in our example, we simply assume that Central Bank notes outstanding in the hands of the public is $15 billion. Total money supply in the country, then, is Demand deposits plus Central Bank notes, or

$$\$50 \text{ billion} + \$15 \text{ billion} = \$65 \text{ billion}$$

Now let us assume that the public wishes to draw down its demand deposits by $2 billion in order to obtain cash. In order to obtain cash, which we will assume is Central Bank notes, the banks must go to the Fed and draw down $2 billion worth of *their* checking accounts, or demand deposits, at the Fed. The initial impact of this action can be seen in Figure 10.2.

Step 1: All Commercial Banks

Assets		Equity & Liabilities	
		Demand deposits	– $2 billion
Reserves	– $2 billion		

Central Bank

Assets		Equity & Liabilities	
		Demand deposits	– $2 billion
		Central Bank notes	+ $2 billion

FIGURE 10.2 — INCREASE IN THE DEMAND FOR CASH: PHASE I

In short, depositors demand $2 billion in cash; the banks go to the Central Bank to buy the $2 billion; and the Central Bank, in exchange, prints $2 billion of new notes and gives them to the banks.

At the end of Step 1, then, the money supply remains the same, since demand deposits have gone down by $2 billion but Central Bank notes outstanding have increased by the same amount. The composition of the money supply has been changed but not yet the total. The money supply is still $65 billion, except that there is now $2 billion less of demand deposits and $2 billion more of Central Bank notes in the hands of the public.

But this is only the first step, because the crucial fact is that bank reserves have *also* gone down by $2 billion, by the same amount that Central Bank notes in the hands of the public have increased.

But since reserves have gone down, and the banks keep fully loaned up, this means that banks must contract their loans and demand deposits until the new total of deposits is again brought down to maintain the legal reserve ratio. As a result, bank loans and investments must contract by another $8 billion, so that the fall in reserves can be matched by a fivefold fall in total deposits. In short, the $2 billion drop in reserves must be matched by a total of $10 billion drop in demand deposits. At the end of the completed Step 2, therefore, the balance sheets of the banks and of the Central Bank look as follows (Figure 10.3).

Step 2: All Commercial Banks

Assets		Equity & Liabilities	
IOUs	$32 billion	Demand deposits	$40 billion
Reserves	$8 billion		
Total assets	$40 billion	Total liabilities	$40 billion

Central Bank

Assets		Equity & Liabilities	
		Demand deposits to banks	$8 billion
		Central Bank notes	$17 billion

FIGURE 10.3 — INCREASES IN THE DEMAND FOR CASH: CONCLUSION

The eventual result, then, of an increased demand for cash by the public is a drop in demand deposits of $10 billion, resulting from the drop of bank reserves of $2 billion. The total money supply has gone down by $8 billion. For demand deposits have fallen by $10 billion, and cash in the hands of the public has risen by $2 billion, making a net drop of $8 billion in the supply of money.

Thus, an increased demand for cash causes an *equal* drop in bank reserves, which in turn has a money multiplier effect in decreasing total demand deposits, and hence a slightly less intense effect in cutting the total amount of money.

If the public's demand for cash drops, on the other hand, and it puts more of its cash in the banks, then the exact reverse happens. Suppose we begin with the situation in Figure 10.1, but now the public decides to take $2 billion out of the $15 billion of Central Bank notes in its possession and deposits them in exchange for checking accounts. In this case, demand deposits increase by $2 billion, and the banks take the ensuing extra cash and deposit it in the Central Bank, increasing their reserves there by $2 billion. The $2 billion of old Central Bank notes goes back into the coffers of the Central Bank, where they are burned, or otherwise retired or liquidated. This situation is shown in Figure 10.4.

Step 1: All Commercial Banks

Assets		Equity & Liabilities	
Reserves	+ $2 billion	Demand deposits	+ $2 billion

Central Bank

Assets		Equity & Liabilities	
		Demand deposits	+ $2 billion
		Central Bank notes	– $2 billion

FIGURE 10.4 — DECREASE IN THE DEMAND FOR CASH: PHASE I

In short, the immediate result of the public's depositing $2 billion of cash in the banks is that, while the total money supply remains the same, only changing the composition between demand deposits and cash, total bank reserves rise by $2 billion.

Receiving the new reserves, the banks then expand credit, lending new demand deposits which they have created out of thin air. They pyramid deposits on top of the new reserves in accordance with the money multiplier, which in our stipulated case is 5:1. The final result is depicted in the balance sheets in Figure 10.5.

Step 2: All Commercial Banks

Assets		Equity & Liabilities	
IOUs	$48 billion	Demand deposits	$60 billion
Reserves	$12 billion		
Total assets	$60 billion	Total liabilities	$60 billion

Central Bank

Assets		Equity & Liabilities	
		Demand deposits to banks	$12 billion
		Central Bank notes	$13 billion

FIGURE 10.5 — DECREASE IN THE DEMAND FOR CASH: CONCLUSION

Thus, the public's depositing $2 billion of cash in the banks increases reserves by the same amount; the increase in reserves enables the banks to pyramid $8 billion more of deposits by increasing loans and investments (IOUs) by $8 billion. Demand deposits have therefore increased by $10 billion from the reduction in the public's holding of cash. The total money supply has increased by $8 billion since Central Bank notes outstanding have dropped by $2 billion.

In short, the public's holding of cash is a *factor of decrease* of bank reserves. That is, if the public's holding of cash increases, bank reserves immediately *decrease by the same amount*, whereas if the public's holding of cash falls, bank reserves immediately *increase by the same amount*. The movement of bank reserves is equal and inverse to the movement in the public's holding of cash. The more cash the public holds, the greater the anti-inflationary effect, and vice versa.

The public's demand for cash can be affected by many factors. Loss of confidence in the banks will, of course, intensify the demand for cash, to the extent of breaking the banks by bank runs. Despite the prestige and resources of the Central Bank, bank runs have been a powerful weapon against bank credit expansion. Only in 1933, with the establishment of the Federal Deposit Insurance Corporation, was the government of the U.S. able to stop bank runs by putting the unlimited taxing and counterfeiting power of the federal government behind every bank deposit. Since 1933, the FDIC has "insured" every bank deposit (up to a high and ever-increasing maximum), and behind the FDIC—implicitly but powerfully—is the ability of the Federal Reserve to print money in unlimited amounts. The commercial banks, it is true, are now far "safer," but that is a dubious blessing indeed; for the "safety" means that they have lost their major incentive not to inflate.

Over time, one powerful influence toward a falling demand for cash is the growth of clearing systems, and devices such as credit cards. People then need to carry less cash than before.[2] On the other hand, the growth of the underground economy in recent years, in order to avoid income taxes and other forms of government regulation, has required an increase in strictly cash transactions, transactions which do not appear on the books of

---

[2]But note that our previous concept of "cash balances" includes not only cash but also demand deposits and any other form of money, whereas now we are dealing with the public's demand for *cash* per se as against deposits or other forms of money.

any government-regulated bank. In fact, it is now customary for economists to try to gauge the extent of illegal, underground transactions by estimating the increase in the proportion of cash transactions in recent years.

The major movement in the public's demand for cash is seasonal. Traditionally, the public cashes in a substantial amount of demand deposits before Christmas in order to use cash for tips or presents. This has a deflationary seasonal effect on bank reserves. Then, in January, the cash pours back into the banks, and reserves rise once again. Generally, the Fed keeps watch on the public's demand for cash and neutralizes it accordingly, in ways which will be explored below.

2. THE DEMAND FOR GOLD

As in the case of the demand for cash in the form of Central Bank notes, an increase in the public's demand for gold will be a factor of decrease in lowering bank reserves, and a fall in the demand for gold will have the opposite effect. Under the gold standard, with a Central Bank (as in the U.S. from 1913 to 1933), almost all of the gold will be deposited in the Central Bank by the various banks, with the banks getting increased reserves in return. An increase in the public's demand for gold, then, will work very similarly to an increased demand for Central Bank notes. To obtain the gold, the public goes to the banks and draws down demand deposits, asking for gold in return. The banks must go to the Central Bank and buy the gold by drawing down their reserves.

The increase in the public's demand for gold thus decreases bank reserves by the same amount, and will, over several months, exert a multiple deflationary effect over the amount of bank money in existence. Conversely, a decrease in the public's demand for gold will add the same amount to bank reserves and exert a multiple inflationary effect, depending on the money multiplier.

Under the present fiat standard, there are no requirements that the Central Bank redeem in gold, or that gold outflows be checked in order to save the banking system. But to the extent that gold is still used by the public, the same impact on reserves still holds. Thus, suppose that gold flows in, say, from South Africa, either from outright purchase or as a result of an export surplus to that country. If the importers from South Africa deposit their gold in the banks, the result is an increase by the same amount in bank reserves as the banks deposit the gold at the Central Bank, which increases its gold assets by the same amount. The public's demand for gold remains a factor of decrease of bank reserves. (Or, conversely, the public's increased deposit of gold at the banks, that is, lowered demand for gold, raises bank reserves by the same amount.)

So far, we have seen how the public, by its demand for gold or nowadays its demand for cash in the form of Central Bank notes, will help determine bank reserves by an equivalent factor of decrease. We must now turn to the major instruments by which the Central Bank itself helps determine the reserves of the banking system.

3. LOANS TO THE BANKS

One method by which the Central Bank expands or contracts total bank reserves is a simple one: it increases or decreases its outstanding loans of reserves to various banks. In the mid-nineteenth century, the English financial writer Walter Bagehot decreed that the Central Bank must always stand ready to bail out banks in trouble, to serve as the "lender of last resort" in the country. Central Banks generally insist that borrowing from them is a "privilege," not a right conferred upon commercial banks, and the Federal Reserve even maintains this about members of the Federal Reserve System. In practice, however, Central Banks try to serve as an ultimate "safety net" for banks, though they will not lend reserves indiscriminately; rather, they will enforce patterns of behavior upon borrowing banks.

In the United States, there are two forms of Federal Reserve loans to the banks: *discounts* and *advances*. Discounts, the major form of Fed loans to banks in the early days of the Federal Reserve System, are temporary purchases (*rediscounts*) by the Central Bank of IOUs or discounts owed to banks. These days, however, almost all of the loans are outright advances, made on the collateral of U.S. government securities. These loans are incurred by the banks in order to get out of difficulty, usually to supply reserves temporarily that had fallen below the required ratio. The loans are therefore made for short periods of time—a week or two—and banks will generally try to get out of debt to the Fed as soon as possible. For one thing, banks do not like to be in continuing, quasi-permanent debt to the Fed, and the Fed would discourage any such tendency by a commercial bank.

Figure 10.6 describes a case where the Central Bank has loaned $1 million of reserves to the Four Corners Bank, for a two-week period.

Four Corners Bank

Assets		Equity & Liabilities	
		IOU to Central Bank	+ $1 million
Reserves	+ $1 million		

Central Bank

Assets		Equity & Liabilities	
IOU from Four Corners Bank	+ $1 million	Demand deposit to Four Corners Bank	+ $1 million

FIGURE 10.6 — CENTRAL BANK LOANS TO BANKS

Thus, the Central Bank has loaned $1 million to the Four Corners Bank, by opening up an increase in the Four Corners checking account at the Central Bank. The Four Corners' reserves have increased by $1 million, offset by a liability of $1 million due in two weeks to the Central Bank.

When the debt is due, then the opposite occurs. The Four Corners Bank pays its debt to the Central Bank by having its account drawn down by $1 million. Its reserves drop by that amount, and the IOU from the Four Corners Bank is canceled. Total reserves in the banking system, which had increased by $1 million when the loan was made, drop by $1 million two weeks later. Central Bank loans to banks are a factor of increase of bank reserves.

It might be thought that since the loan is very short-term, loans to banks can play no role in the bank's inflationary process. But this would be as simplistic as holding that bank loans to customers can't really increase the money supply for any length of time if their loans are very short-term.[3] This doctrine forgets that if outstanding bank loans, short-term or no, increase permanently, then they serve to increase reserves over the long run and to spur an inflationary increase in the money supply. It is, admittedly, a little more difficult to increase the supply of outstanding loans permanently if they are short-term, but it is scarcely an insurmountable task.

Still, partly because of the factors mentioned above, outstanding loans to banks by the Federal Reserve are now a minor aspect of Central Bank operations in the United States. Another reason for the relatively minor importance of this factor has been the spectacular growth, in the last few decades, of the *federal funds market*. In the federal funds market, banks with temporary excess reserves at the Fed lend them literally overnight to banks in temporary difficulties. By far the greatest part of bank borrowing of reserves is now conducted in the federal funds market rather than at what is known as the *discount window* of the Federal Reserve.

---

[3]This was one of the tenets of the "banking school" of monetary thought, prominent in the nineteenth century and still held in some quarters.

Thus, during the 1920s, banks' borrowed reserves from the Federal Reserve were at approximately 4 to 1 over borrowings from the federal fund market. But by the 1960s, the ratio of Federal Reserve to federal funds borrowing was 1 to 8 or 10. As J. Parker Willis summed up, "It may be said that in the 1920s Federal Funds were considered a supplement to discounting, but that in the 1960s discounting had become a supplement to trading in Federal Funds."[4]

To get an idea of the relative importance of loans to banks, on January 6, 1982, the Federal Reserve Banks owned $1.5 billion of IOUs from banks; in contrast, they owned almost $128 billion of U.S. government securities (the major source of bank reserves). Over the previous 12 months, member banks borrowing from the Fed had increased by $335 million, whereas U.S. government securities owned by the Fed increased by almost $9 billion.

If the Fed wishes to encourage bank borrowings from itself, it will lower the rediscount rate or discount rate of interest it charges the banks for loans.[5] If it wishes to discourage bank borrowings, it will raise the discount rate. Since lower discount rates stimulate bank borrowing and hence increase outstanding reserves, and higher discount rates do the reverse, the former is widely and properly regarded as a proinflationary, and the latter an anti-inflationary, device. Lower discount rates are inflationary and higher rates the reverse.

All this is true, but the financial press pays entirely too much attention to the highly publicized movements of the Fed's (or other Central Banks') discount rates. Indeed, the Fed uses changes in these rates as a psychological weapon rather than as a measure of much substantive importance.

---

[4]J. Parker Willis, *The Federal Funds Market* (Boston: Federal Reserve Bank of Boston, 1970), p. 62.

[5]Interest rates on Fed loans to banks are still called "discount rates" despite the fact that virtually all of them are now outright loans rather than discounts.

Still, despite its relative unimportance, it should be pointed out that Federal Reserve rediscount rate policy has been basically inflationary since 1919. The older view was that the rediscount rate should be at a *penalty* rate, that is, that the rate should be so high that banks would clearly borrow only when in dire trouble and strive to repay very quickly. The older tradition was that the rediscount rate should be well above the prime rate to top customers of the banks. Thus, if the prime rate is 15 percent and the Fed discount rate is 25 percent, any bank borrowing from the Fed is a penalty rate and is done only *in extremis*. But if the prime rate is 15 percent and the Fed discount rate is 10 percent, then the banks have an incentive to borrow heavily from the Fed at 10 percent and use these reserves to pyramid loans to prime (and therefore relatively riskless) customers at 15 percent, reaping an assured differential profit. Yet, despite its unsoundness and inflationary nature, the Fed has kept its discount rate well below prime rates ever since 1919, in inflationary times as well as any other. Fortunately, the other factors mentioned above have kept the inflationary nature of member bank borrowing relatively insignificant.[6]

4. OPEN MARKET OPERATIONS

We come now to by far the most important method by which the Central Bank determines the total amount of bank reserves, and therefore the total supply of money. In the United States, the Fed by this method determines total bank reserves and thereby the total of bank demand deposits pyramiding by the money multiplier on top of those reserves. This vitally important method is *open market operations*.

---

[6]On the penalty rate question, see Benjamin M. Anderson, *Economics and the Public Welfare,* 2nd ed. (Indianapolis: Liberty Press, 1979), pp. 72, 153–54. Also see Seymour E. Harris, *Twenty Years of Federal Reserve Policy* (Cambridge, Mass.: Harvard University Press, 1933), vol. 1, pp. 3–10, 39–48.

Open market, in this context, does not refer to a freely competitive as opposed to a monopolistic market. It simply means that the Central Bank moves outside itself and into the market, where it buys or sells assets. The purchase of any asset is an *open market purchase*; the sale of any asset is an *open market sale.*

To see how this process works, let us assume that the Federal Reserve Bank of New York, for some unknown reason, decides to purchase an old desk of mine. Let us say that I agree to sell my desk to the Fed for $100.

How does the Fed pay for the desk? It writes a check on itself for the $100, and hands me the check in return for the desk, which it carts off to its own offices. Where does it get the money to pay the check? By this time, the answer should be evident: it creates the money out of thin air. *It creates the $100 by writing out a check for that amount.* The $100 is a new liability it creates upon itself out of nothing. This new liability, of course, is solidly grounded on the Fed's unlimited power to engage in legalized counterfeiting, for if someone should demand cash for the $100 liability, the Fed would cheerfully print a new $100 bill and give it to the person redeeming the claim.

The Fed, then, has paid for my desk by writing a check on itself looking somewhat as follows:

FEDERAL RESERVE BANK OF NEW YORK
Pay to the Order of Murray N. Rothbard $100.00

        (Signed)
        Mr. Blank
        Officer
        Federal Reserve Bank of New York

There is only one thing I can do with this check. I cannot deposit or cash it at the Fed, because the Fed takes only deposit accounts of banks, not individuals. The only thing I can do is deposit it at a commercial bank. Suppose I deposit it in my account at Citibank. In that case, I now have an increase of $100

in my demand deposit account at Citibank; the bank, in turn, has
a $100 check on the Fed. The bank greets the check with enthu-
siasm, for it now can rush down to the Fed and deposit the check,
thereby obtaining an increase in its reserves at the Fed of $100.

Figure 10.7 shows what has happened as a result of the Fed's
purchase of my desk. The key monetary part of the transaction
was not the desk, which goes to grace the increased furniture asset
column of the Fed's ledger, but that the Fed has written a check
upon itself. I can use the check only by depositing it in a bank,
and as soon as I do so, my own money supply in the form of
demand deposits goes up by $100. More important, my bank
now deposits the check on the Fed at that institution, and its total
reserves also go up by $100. The money supply has gone up by
$100, but the key point is that reserves have gone up by the same
amount, so that the banking system will, over a few months, pyramid more loans and demand deposits on top of the new reserves,
depending on the required reserve ratio and hence the money
multiplier.

Citibank

Assets		Equity & Liabilities	
		Demand deposits to Rothbard	+ $100
Reserves at Fed	+ $100		
Total assets	+ $100	Total demand deposits	+ $100

Federal Reserve Bank

Assets		Equity & Liabilities	
Desk	+ $100	Demand deposits to banks	+ $100

FIGURE 10.7 — OPEN MARKET PURCHASE

Note that bank reserves have increased by the same amount (in this case, $100) as the Fed's open market purchase of the desk; open market purchases are a *factor of increase* of bank reserves, and in practice by far the most important such factor.

An *open market sale* has precisely the reverse effect. Suppose that the Fed decides to auction off some old furniture and I buy one of its desks for $100. Suppose too, that I pay for the sale with a check to the Fed on my bank, say, Citibank. In this case, as we see in Figure 10.8, my own money stock of demand deposits is decreased by $100, in return for which I receive a desk. More important, Citibank has to pay the Fed $100 as it presents the check; Citibank pays for it by seeing its reserve account at the Fed drawn down by $100.

Citibank

Assets		Equity & Liabilities	
		Demand deposits to Rothbard	– $100
Reserves at Fed	– $100		
Total assets	– $100	Total demand deposits	– $100

Federal Reserve Bank

Assets		Equity & Liabilities	
Desk	– $100	Demand deposits to banks	– $100

FIGURE 10.8 — OPEN MARKET SALE

Total money supply has initially gone down by $100. But the important thing is that total bank reserves have gone down by $100, which will force a contraction of that times the money multiplier of bank loans and deposits, and hence of the total money supply.

Therefore, if open market purchases of assets by the Fed are a *factor of increase* of reserves by the same amount, the other side of the coin is that open market sales of assets are a *factor of decrease*.

From the point of view of the money supply it doesn't make any difference *what* asset the Fed buys; the only thing that matters is the Fed's writing of a check, or someone writing the Fed a check. And, indeed, under the Monetary Control Act of 1980, the Fed now has unlimited power to buy any asset it wishes and up to any amount—whether it be corporate stocks, bonds, or foreign currency. But until now virtually the only asset the Fed has systematically bought and sold has been U.S. government securities. Every week, the System Manager (a vice president of the Federal Reserve Bank of New York) buys or sells U.S. government securities from or to a handful of top private dealers in government securities. The System Manager acts under the orders of the Fed's Federal Open Market Committee, which meets every month to issue directives for the month. The Fed's System Manager mostly buys, but also sells, an enormous amount, and every year the accumulated purchases of U.S. Treasury bills and bonds drive up bank reserves by the same amount, and thereby act to fix total reserves wherever the Fed wishes, and hence to determine the total money supply issued by the banks.

One reason for selecting government bonds as the major asset is that it is by far the biggest and most liquid capital market in the country. There is never any problem of illiquidity, or problem of making a purchase or sale in the government securities market.

How Fed open market purchases have been the driving force of monetary expansion may be quickly seen by noting that the Fed's assets of U.S. government securities, totaling $128 billion in January 1982, was by far the bulk of its total assets. Moreover, this figure contrasts with $62 billion owned in 1970, and $27 billion owned in 1960. This is roughly a 17 percent (uncompounded) annual increase in U.S. government securities owned by the Fed over the past two decades. There is no need to worry about the ever-shifting definition of money, the ever-greater numbers of Ms. All that need be done to stop inflation in its tracks forever is to pass a law ordering the Fed never to buy any more assets, ever again. Repeatedly, governments have distracted attention from their own guilt for inflation, and scapegoated various groups and institutions on the market. Repeatedly, they have tried and failed to combat inflation by freezing wages and prices, equivalent to holding down the mercury column of a thermometer by brute force in order to cure a fever. But all that need be done is one freeze that governments have never agreed to: freezing the Central Bank. Better to abolish central banking altogether, but if that cannot be accomplished, then, as a transitional step, the Central Bank should be frozen, and prevented from making further loans or especially open market purchases. Period.

Let us see how a government bond purchase by the Fed on the open market increases reserves by the same amount. Suppose that the Fed's System Manager buys $1,000,000 of government bonds from private bond dealers. (Note that these are *not* newly issued bonds, but old bonds previously issued by the Treasury, and purchased by individuals, corporations, or financial institutions. There is a flourishing market for old government securities.) In Figure 10.9, we show the System Manager's purchase of $1,000,000 in government bonds from the securities dealer firm of Jones & Co. The Fed pays for the bonds by writing a check for $1,000,000 upon itself. Its assets increase by $1,000,000, balanced by its liabilities of newly-created deposit money consisting of a check upon itself. Jones & Co. has only one option: to deposit the check in a commercial bank. If it deposits the check at Citibank, it now has an increase of its own money supply of $1,000,000. Citibank then takes the check to the Fed, deposits it there, and in turn acquires a new reserve of $1,000,000, upon which the banking system pyramids reserves in accordance with the money multiplier.

Citibank

Assets		Equity & Liabilities	
		Demand deposits to Jones & Co.	+ $1 million
Reserves	+ $1 million		
Total assets	+ $1 million	Total demand deposits	+ $1 million

Federal Reserve Bank

Assets		Equity & Liabilities	
U.S. Government Securities	+ $1 million	Demand deposits to banks	+ $1 million

FIGURE 10.9 — FED PURCHASE OF GOVERNMENT SECURITIES FROM DEALER

Thus, a Fed purchase of a $1,000,000 bond from a private bond dealer has resulted in an increase of total bank reserves of $1,000,000, upon which the banks can pyramid loans and demand deposits.

If the Fed should buy bonds from commercial banks directly, the increase in total reserves will be the same. Thus, suppose, as in Figure 10.10, the Fed buys a $1,000,000 government bond from Citibank. In that case, the results for both are as shown in Figure 10.10.

Here when the Fed purchases a bond directly from a bank, there is no initial increase in demand deposits, or in total bank assets or liabilities. But the key point is that Citibank's reserves have, once again, increased by the $1,000,000 of the Fed's open market purchase, and the banking system can readily pyramid a multiple amount of loans and deposits on top of the new reserves.

Citibank

Assets		Equity & Liabilities
U.S. Government		
bonds	– $1 million	
Reserves	+ $1 million	

Federal Reserve Bank

Assets		Equity & Liabilities	
U.S. Government		Demand deposits to	
bonds	+ $1 million	banks	+ $1 million

FIGURE 10.10 — FED PURCHASE OF GOVERNMENT SECURITIES FROM BANK

Thus, the factors of increase of total bank reserves determined by Federal Reserve (that is, Central Bank) policy, are: open market purchases and loans to banks, of which the former are far more important. The public, by increasing its demands for cash (and for gold under the gold standard) can reduce bank reserves by the same amount.

XI.

Central Banking: The Process of Bank Credit Expansion

1. Expansion from Bank to Bank

U p till now, we have simply asserted that the banks, in the aggregate, will pyramid on top of their reserves in accordance with the money multiplier. But we have not shown in detail *how* the individual banks pyramid on top of reserves. If there were only one commercial bank in the country, with a few million branches, there would be no problem. If the Fed buys $1 million of securities, and bank reserves increase by that amount, this monopoly bank will simply lend out $4 million more, thereby driving its total demand deposits up by an increased $5 million. It will obtain the increased $4 million by simply creating it out of thin air, that is, by opening up deposit accounts and allowing checks to be written on those accounts. There will be no problem of interbank redemption, for every person and firm in the country will have its account with the same monopoly bank. Thus, if the monopoly bank lends $2 million to General Motors, GM will spend the money on some person or firm who *also* has an account at the same bank. Therefore, the $1 million in new reserves can readily and swiftly sustain an increase of 5:1 in loans and deposits.

But suppose, as in the United States, we have a competitive banking system, with literally thousands of commercial banks. How can any one bank expand? How does the existence of the Fed enable the banks to get around the ironclad restrictions on inflationary credit expansion imposed under a regime of free banking?

To see the answer, we have to examine the detailed bank-to-bank process of credit expansion under central banking. To make it simple, suppose we assume that the Fed buys a bond for $1,000 from Jones & Co., and Jones & Co. deposits the bond in Bank A, Citibank. The first step that occurs we have already seen (Figure 10.9) but will be shown again in Figure 11.1. Demand deposits, and therefore the money supply, increase by $1,000, held by Jones & Co., and Citibank's reserves also go up by $1,000.

Bank A
Citibank

Assets		Equity & Liabilities	
		Demand deposits	
		to Jones & Co.	+ $1,000
Reserves	+ $1,000		

Federal Reserve

Assets		Equity & Liabilities	
U.S. Government		Demand deposits	
Securities	+ $1,000	to Citibank	+ $1,000

FIGURE 11.1 — THE CENTRAL BANK BUYS SECURITIES

At this point, Citibank cannot simply increase demand deposits by another $4,000 and lend them out. For while it could do so and remain with a required minimum reserve/deposit ratio of 20 percent, it could not keep that vital status for long. Let us make the reasonable assumption that the $4,000 is loaned to R.H. Macy & Co., and that Macy's will spend its new deposits on someone who is a client of another, competing bank. And if Citibank should be lucky enough to have Macy's spend the $4,000 on another of its clients, then *that* client, or another one soon thereafter, will spend the money on a nonclient. Suppose that Macy's spends $4,000 on furniture from the Smith Furniture Co. But the Smith Furniture Co. is the client of another bank, ChemBank, and it deposits Macy's Citibank check into its Chem-Bank account. ChemBank then calls on Citibank to redeem its $4,000. But Citibank hasn't *got* the $4,000, and this call for redemption will make Citibank technically bankrupt. Its reserves are only $1,000, and it therefore will not be able to pay the $4,000 demanded by the competing bank.

Figure 11.2 reveals the straits of Citibank, imposed by the existence of competing banks:

Bank A Citibank		Bank B Chembank	
Assets	Equity & Liabilities	Assets	Equity & Liabilities
from Macy's + $4,000	Demand deposits to Jones & Co. + $1,000		Demand deposits to Smith + $4,000
Reserves +$1,000	Demand deposits to Chembank + $4,000	Due from Citibank + $4,000	

FIGURE 11.2 — REDEMPTION OF ONE BANK FROM ANOTHER

In short, when Citibank's demand deposits were owed to Macy's, its own client, everything was fine. But now, not from loss of confidence or from a sudden demand for cash, but in the course of regular, everyday trade, Macy's demand deposits have been transferred to ChemBank, and ChemBank is asking for reserves at the Fed for redemption. But Citibank doesn't have any reserves to spare and is therefore insolvent.

One bank, therefore, cannot blithely heap 5:1 on top of new reserves. But if it cannot expand 500 percent on top of its reserves, what *can* it do? It can and does expand much more moderately and cautiously. In fact, to keep within its reserve requirements now and in the foreseeable future, it expands not by 500 percent but by 1 minus the minimum reserve requirement. In this case, it expands by 80 percent rather than by 500 percent. We will see in the figures below how each bank's expanding by 80 percent in a central banking system causes all banks, in the aggregate, in a short period of time, to expand by the money multiplier of 5:1. Each bank's expansion of 80 percent leads to a system or aggregate expansion of 500 percent.

Let us therefore go back to Figure 11.1, and see what Citibank does in fact do. Instead of lending $4,000 to Macy's, it lends out 80 percent of its new reserves, or $800. In Figure 11.3, we see what happens after this *first* step in bank credit expansion across the banking system.

First, the total money supply, which had increased by $1,000 after the Fed's bond purchase, has now increased by $1,800. There has already been an 80 percent further expansion in the money supply, in the form of demand deposits.

But Macy's, of course, has not borrowed money to sit on it. It uses the $800 to purchase something, say furniture, from the Smith Furniture Co. The Smith Furniture Co., we assume, has its account with ChemBank, and deposits its $800 check drawn on Citibank with ChemBank. ChemBank now calls upon Citibank for redemption, that is, for shifting $800 of its reserves at the Fed to ChemBank. But Citibank now has ample reserves, for it can afford to pay $800 out of its $1,000 new reserves, and it will still

Bank A
Citibank

Assets		Equity & Liabilities	
IOUs from Macy's	+ $800	Demand deposits	
		to Jones & Co.	+ $1,000
		to Macy's	+ $800
Reserves	+ $1,000		
Total assets	+ $1,800	Total demand deposits	+ $1,800

FIGURE 11.3 — CREDIT EXPANSION WITH COMPETING BANKS:
THE FIRST BANK

have $200 left to offset the $1,000 demand deposit owed to Jones & Co. (It doesn't *have* to offset the Macy's deposit any longer because that has already been transferred to ChemBank.) Figure 11.4 shows what happens as the result of the loan of $800 to Macy's, and the spending by Macy's of $800 on the Smith Furniture Co. which deposits the check in ChemBank.

Note what has happened. Bank A, Citibank, having expanded the money supply by 80 percent on top of $1,000, is now out of the picture. Ultimately, its increase of the money supply is back to the original $1,000, but now another bank, Bank B, is exactly in the same position as Citibank had been before, except that its new reserves are $800 instead of $1,000. Right now, Bank A has increased the money supply by the original reserve increase of $1,000, but Bank B, ChemBank, has also increased the money supply by an extra $800. Note that the increased $1,000 in total reserves at the Fed has shifted, so that there is now a $200 increase to Bank A and an $800 increase to Bank B.

And so ChemBank is in the exact same position as Citibank had been, except to a lesser extent. Citibank had enjoyed a new reserve of $1,000; ChemBank now enjoys a new reserve of $800.

	Bank A *Citibank*		Bank B *Chembank*
Assets	Equity & Liabilities	Assets	Equity & Liabilities
IOUs from Macy's + $800	Demand deposits to Jones & Co. + $1,000		Demand deposits to Smith + $800
Reserves + $200		Reserves + $800	

Federal Reserve

Assets	Equity & Liabilities
U.S. Government Securities + $1,000	Demand deposits to banks Citibank + $200 Chembank + $800

FIGURE 11.4 — CREDIT EXPANSION WITH COMPETING BANKS:
THE FIRST AND SECOND BANKS

Where the reserve came from is unimportant. ChemBank proceeds to do exactly the same thing as Citibank had done before: expand on top of its new reserves by another 80 percent. That is, ChemBank makes a loan of $640 to someone else, by writing out an increase in the latter's deposit account. Suppose that ChemBank lends $640 to Joe's Diner. ChemBank's balance sheet is now as shown in Figure 11.5.

The analogy with Figure 11.3 is clear. ChemBank has expanded on top of its new reserves by 80 percent, lending that out to Joe's Diner.

But Joe's Diner, too, does not borrow in order to stay idle. It takes the $640 and, say, purchases a new counter from the Robbins Appliance Co. The Robbins Appliance Co. keeps its accounts

Bank B
Chembank

Assets		Equity & Liabilities	
IOU from Joe's Diner + $640		Demand deposits	
		to Smith	+ $800
Reserves	+ $800	to Joe's Diner	+ $640
Total assets	+ $1,440	Total demand deposits	+ $1,440

FIGURE 11.5 — THE SECOND BANK EXPANDS

at Bank C, the Bank of Great Neck. The $640 of deposits from Joe's Diner gets transferred to Robbins, and is in turn deposited in the Bank of Great Neck. Figure 11.6 shows what now happens to Banks B and C:

Bank B *Chembank*		Bank C *Bank of Great Neck*	
Assets	Equity & Liabilities	Assets	Equity & Liabilities
IOU from Joe's Diner + $640	Demand deposits to Smith + $800		Demand deposits to Robbins + $640
Reserves +$160		Reserves + $640	

FIGURE 11.6 — THE SECOND AND THIRD BANKS

Clearly, what happens is a repeat of what happened to Banks A and B, as seen in Figure 11.4. When the Bank of Great Neck cashed in $640 in reserves from ChemBank, it left ChemBank with $160 worth of reserves, just enough to satisfy the 20 percent reserve requirement from Smith's demand deposits. In the same way, Citibank was left with $200, just enough to meet the reserve requirement for the increased demand deposit of $1,000 to Jones & Co. Bank B is now out of the picture, having contributed $800 to the expansion of the money supply, just as Bank A is out of the picture, having received the initial impact of $1,000 of new reserves on the banking system. Bank C is now, after the operations of this process, in the same position as Banks A and B had been before, except it now has fewer new reserves, in this case $640.

We can now sum up the results of the process so far, looking, in Figure 11.7, at the balance sheets for Banks A, B, and C, as well as the Federal Reserve Bank.

Thus we see that any increase in reserves (whether from increased deposits of cash, loans by the Fed, or open market purchase) must take place in one particular bank. That bank, in a competitive banking system, cannot itself increase its loans and deposits by the money multiplier. But it can and does expand by 1 minus the reserve requirement, in our example 80 percent. As it does so, the process of bank credit expansion has a ripple effect outward from the initial bank. Each outward ripple is less intense. For each succeeding bank increases the money supply by a *lower* amount (in our example, Bank A increases demand deposits by $1,000, Bank B by $800, and Bank C by $640), each bank increases its loan by a lower amount (Bank A by $800, Bank B by $640), and the increased reserves get distributed to other banks, but in lesser degree (Bank A by $200, Bank B by $160).

The next step will be for Bank C to expand by 80 percent of its new reserves, which will be $512. And so on from bank to bank, in ever decreasing ripple effects. As the ripples widen, each bank in the process will increase its demand deposits by 80 percent of the preceding bank's.

Bank A

Assets		Equity & Liabilities	
IOU from Macy's	+ $800	Demand deposits to Jones & Co.	+ $1,000
Reserves	+ $200		

Bank B

Assets		Equity & Liabilities	
IOU from Joe's Diner	+ $640	Demand deposits to Smith	+ $800
Reserves	+ $160		

Bank C

Assets		Equity & Liabilities	
		Demand deposits to Robbins	+ $640
Reserves	+ $640		

Federal Reserve

Assets		Equity & Liabilities	
U.S. Government securities	$1,000	Demand deposits to	
		Bank A	+ $200
		Bank B	+ $160
		Bank C	+ $640

FIGURE 11.7 — CREDIT EXPANSION UNDER COMPETING BANKS:
SURVEY OF THE PROCESS

$1,000 + $800 + $640 + $512 + $410 + $328 + $262 + . . .

At the end of 14 banks in this chain, the grand total is $4,780, and it is evident that we are rapidly and asymptotically approaching an increased money supply of $5,000.

In this way, competing banks under the aegis of a central bank can increase the money supply by the money multiplier in the aggregate even though each individual bank expands by only 1 minus the money multiplier. The mystery of the inflation process in the modern world has finally been unraveled.

2. THE CENTRAL BANK AND THE TREASURY

We have seen that modern inflation consists in a chronic and continuing issue of new money by the Central Bank, which in turn fuels and provides the reserves for a fractional reserve banking system to pyramid a multiple of checkbook money on top of those reserves. But where in all this are government deficits? Are deficits inflationary, and if so, to what extent? What is the relationship between the government as Central Bank and the government in its fiscal or budgetary capacity?

First, the process of bank money creation we have been exploring has no necessary connection to the fiscal operations of the central government. If the Fed buys $1 million of assets, this will create $5 million of new money (if the reserve ratio is 20 percent) or $10 million of new money (if the ratio is 10 percent). The Fed's purchases have a multiple leverage effect on the money supply; furthermore, in the United States, Fed operations are off-budget items and so do not even enter the fiscal data of government expenditures. If it is pointed out that almost all the Fed's purchases of assets are U.S. government bonds, then it should be rebutted that these are *old* bonds, the embodiment of past federal deficits, and do not require any current deficits for the process to continue. The Treasury could enjoy a balanced budget (total annual revenues equal to total annual spending) or even a surplus (revenues greater than spending), and still the Fed could merrily create new reserves and hence a multiple of new bank money. Monetary inflation does not require a budget deficit.

On the other hand, it is perfectly possible, theoretically, for the federal government to have a deficit (total spending greater than total revenues) which does not lead to any increase in the money supply and is therefore not inflationary. This bromide was repeated continually by the Reagan economists in late 1981 in their vain effort to make the country forget about the enormous deficits looming ahead. Thus, suppose that Treasury expenditures are $500 billion and revenues are $400 billion; the deficit is therefore $100 billion. If the deficit is financed strictly by selling new bonds to the public (individuals, corporations, insurance companies, etc.), then there is no increase in the money supply and hence no inflation. People's savings are simply shifted from the bank accounts of bond buyers to the bank accounts of the Treasury, which will quickly spend them and thereby return those deposits to the private sector. There is movement within the same money supply, but no increase in that supply itself.

But this does not mean that a large deficit financed by voluntary savings has no deleterious economic effects. Inflation is not the only economic problem. Indeed, the deficit will siphon off or "crowd out" vast sums of capital from productive private investment to unproductive and parasitic government spending. This will cripple productivity and economic growth, and raise interest rates considerably. Furthermore, the parasitic tax burden will increase in the future, due to the forced repayment of the $100 billion deficit plus high interest charges.

There is another form of financing deficits which is now obsolete in the modern Western world but which was formerly the standard method of finance. That was for the central government to simply print money (Treasury cash) and spend it. This, of course, was highly inflationary, as—in our assumed $100 billion deficit—the money supply would increase by $100 billion. This was the way the U.S. government, for example, financed much of the Revolutionary and Civil War deficits.

The third method is, like the first one, compatible with modern banking procedures, but combines the worst features of the other two modes. This occurs when the Treasury sells new bonds to the commercial banks. In this method of *monetizing the debt* (creating new money to pay for new debt), the Treasury sells, say, $100 billion of new bonds to the banks, who create $100 billion of new demand deposits to pay for the new bonds. As in the second method above, the money supply has increased by $100 billion—the extent of the deficit—to finance the shortfall. But, as in the *first* method, the taxpayers will now be forced over the years to pay an additional $100 billion to the banks *plus* a hefty amount of interest. Thus, this third, modern method of financing the deficit combines the worst features of the other two: it is inflationary, *and* it imposes future heavy burdens on the taxpayers.

Note the web of special privilege that is being accorded to the nation's banks. First, they are allowed to create money out of thin air which they then graciously lend to the federal government by buying its bonds. But then, second, the taxpayers are forced in ensuing years to pay the banks back with interest for buying government bonds with their newly created money.

Figure 11.8 notes what happens when the nation's banks buy $100 billion of newly-created government bonds.

Commercial Banks

Assets	Equity & Liabilities
U.S. Government securities + $100 billion	Demand deposits to the Treasury + $100 billion

FIGURE 11.8 — BANKS BUY BONDS

The Treasury takes the new demand deposits and spends them on private producers, who in turn will have the new deposits, and in this way they circulate in the economy.

But if banks are always fully loaded up, how did they get enough reserves to enable them to create the $100 billion in new deposits? That is where the Federal Reserve comes in; the Fed must create new bank reserves to enable the banks to purchase new government debt.

If the reserve requirement is 20 percent, and the Fed wishes to create enough new reserves to enable the banks to buy $100 billion of new government bonds, then it buys $25 billion of *old* bonds on the open market to fuel the desired inflationary transaction.[1] First,

---

[1]Not *$20* billion, as one might think, because the Fed will have to buy enough to cover not only the $100 billion, but also the amount of its own purchase which will add to the demand deposits of banks through the accounts of government bond dealers. The formula for figuring out how much the Fed should buy (X) to achieve a desired level of bank purchases of the deficit (D) is:

$$X = \frac{D}{MM - 1}$$

The Fed should buy X, in this case $25 billion, in order to finance a desired deficit of $100 billion. In this case, X equals $100 billion divided by MM (the money multiplier) or 5 minus 1. Or X equals $100 billion/4, or $25 billion. This formula is arrived at as follows: We begin by the Fed wishing to buy whatever amount of old bonds, when multiplied by the money multiplier, will yield the deficit plus X itself. In other words, it wants an X which will serve as the base of the pyramid for the federal deficit plus the amount of demand deposits acquired by government bond dealers. This can be embodied in the following formula:

$$MM \cdot X = D + X$$

But then: $$MM \cdot X - X = D$$

and, $$X \cdot MM - 1 = D$$

Therefore, $$X = \frac{D}{MM - 1}$$

the Fed buys $25 billion of old bonds on the open market; this creates increased demand deposits in the banks of $25 billion, matched by $25 billion in new reserves. Then, the Treasury issues $100 billion of new bonds, which the banks now buy because of their new reserves. Their total increase of new demand deposits is $125 billion, precisely the money multiple pyramiding on top of $25 billion of new reserves. The changes in the balance sheets of the commercial banks and of the Fed are depicted in Figure 11.9.

Commercial Banks

A		E & L	
(new) U.S. Government securities	+ $100 billion	Demand deposits to government bond dealers	+ $25 billion
		to the Treasury	+ $100 billion
Reserves	+ $25 billion		
Total assets	+ $125 billion	Total demand deposits	+ $125 billion

Federal Reserve

A		E & L	
(old) U.S. Government securities	+ $25 billion	Demand deposits to banks	+ $25 billion

FIGURE 11.9 — FED AIDING BANKS TO FINANCE DEFICITS

Thus, under the assumed conditions of a 20 percent reserve requirement, the Fed would need to buy $25 billion of old bonds to finance a Treasury deficit of $100 billion. The total increase in the money supply of the entire operation would be $125 billion.

If the Fed were to finance new Treasury bond issues directly, as it was only allowed by law to do for a while during World War

II, this step would be wildly inflationary. For the Treasury would now have an increased $100 billion not just of newly-created bank money, but of "high-powered" bank money—demand deposits at the Fed. Then, as the Treasury spent the money, its claims on the Fed would filter down to the private economy, and total bank reserves would increase by $100 billion. The banking system would then pyramid loans and deposits on top of that by 5:1 until the money supply increased by no less than $500 billion. Hence we have the highly inflationary nature of direct Fed purchases of new bonds from the Treasury.

Figure 11.10 depicts the two steps of this process. In the first step, Step 1, the Fed buys $100 billion of new government bonds, and the Treasury gets increased demand deposits at the Fed.

Step 1: Federal Reserve

Assets	Equity & Liabilities
(new) U.S. Government securities + $100 billion	Demand deposits to the Treasury + $100 billion

FIGURE 11.10 — FED PURCHASE OF NEW GOVERNMENT SECURITIES

Then, as the Treasury spends the new money, its checks on the Fed will filter down toward various private sellers. The latter will deposit these checks and acquire demand deposits at their banks; and the banks will rush down and deposit the checks with the Fed, thereby earning an increase in their reserve accounts. Figure 11.11 shows what happens in Step 2 at the end of this process.

Thus, the upshot of the Fed's direct purchase of the Treasury deficit is for total bank reserves to rise by the same amount, and for the Treasury account to get transferred into the reserves of the banks. On top of these reserves, the banking system will pyramid deposits 5:1 to a total increased money supply of $500 billion.

Step 2: Commercial Banks

Assets	Equity & Liabilities
Reserves at the Fed + $100 billion	Demand deposits to the public + $100 billion

Federal Reserve

Assets	Equity & Liabilities
(new) U.S. Government securities + $100 billion	Demand deposits to banks + $100 billion

FIGURE 11.11 — EFFECT OF FED PURCHASE ON BANKS

Thus, we see that the chronic and accelerating inflation of our time has been caused by a fundamental change in the monetary system. From a money, centuries ago, based solidly on gold as the currency, and where banks were required to redeem their notes and deposits immediately in specie, we now have a world of fiat paper moneys cut off from gold and issued by government-privileged Central Banks. The Central Banks enjoy a monopoly on the printing of paper money, and through this money they control and encourage an inflationary fractional reserve banking system which pyramids deposits on top of a total of reserves determined by the Central Banks. Government fiat paper has replaced commodity money, and central banking has taken the place of free banking. Hence our chronic, permanent inflation problem, a problem which, if unchecked, is bound to accelerate eventually into the fearful destruction of the currency known as *runaway inflation*.

XII.

THE ORIGINS OF CENTRAL BANKING

1. THE BANK OF ENGLAND

How did this momentous and fateful institution of central banking appear and take hold in the modern world? Fittingly, the institution began in late seventeenth century England, as a crooked deal between a near-bankrupt government and a corrupt clique of financial promoters.

Banking in England, in the 1690s, consisted of scriveners—loan bankers who loaned out borrowed money, and goldsmiths, who had accepted gold on deposit and were beginning to make loans. The harrowing and expensive Civil Wars had finally concluded, in 1688, with the deposition of James II and the installation of William and Mary on the throne of Great Britain. The Tory party, which had been in favor, now lost its dominance, and was replaced by the Whig party of noble landlords and merchant companies enjoying monopoly privileges from the government. Whig foreign policy was mercantilist and imperialist, with colonies sought and grabbed for the greater glory of the Crown, trading advantages, investments in raw material, and markets for shipping and exports. England's great rival was the mighty French Empire, and England set out in a successful half-century-long effort to attack and eventually conquer that rival empire.

A policy of war and militarism is expensive, and the British government found, in the 1690s, that it was short of money and its credit poor. It seemed impossible after a half-century of civil wars and a poor record of repayment for the government to tap sufficient savings by inducing people to buy its bonds. The British government would have loved to levy higher taxes, but England had just emerged from a half-century of civil wars, much of which had been waged over the king's attempt to extend his taxing power. The taxing route was therefore politically unfeasible.

A committee of the House of Commons was therefore formed in early 1693 to figure out how to raise money for the war effort. There came to the committee the ambitious Scottish promoter, William Paterson, who, on behalf of his financial group, proposed a remarkable new scheme to Parliament. In return for a set of important special privileges from the State, Paterson and his clique would form the Bank of England, which would issue new notes, much of which would be used to finance the English deficit. In short, since there were not enough private savers willing to finance the deficit, Paterson and his group were graciously willing to buy government bonds, provided they could do so with newly-created out-of-thin-air bank notes carrying a raft of special privileges with them. This was a splendid deal for Paterson and company, and the government benefited from the flimflam of a seemingly legitimate bank's financing their debts. (Remember that the device of open government paper money had only just been invented in Massachusetts in 1690.) As soon as the Bank of England was chartered by Parliament in 1694, King William himself and various members of Parliament rushed to become shareholders of the new money factory they had just created.

From the beginning, the Bank of England invested itself, aided and abetted by the government, with an impressive aura of mystery—to enhance its prestige and the public's confidence in its operations. As one historian perceptively writes:

> From 27 July 1694, when the books were opened with the words "*Laus Deo* in London," the Bank was surrounded with an aura of prestige and mystery which has never entirely evaporated—a sense that it was not as other businesses, yet as businesslike as any. It was like some great ship, with its watch of directors always on duty during its business hours, and its studied display of operational efficiency. The un-English title of "director," the Italianate contraction "*Compa*" on its notes, were deliberate touches of the exotic and modern, showing those who handled the new currency or dealt with the Bank that, though this was something new in England, it had borrowed its tradition from the glorious banks of Genoa and Amsterdam. And although the Bank had grown from, and continued as the preserve of, a particular business syndicate who as a group and as individuals had many other interests, it bred and drew a particular type of man, capable of sustaining its gravity.[1]

William Paterson urged that the English government grant his Bank notes legal tender power, which would have meant that everyone would be compelled to accept them in payment of money debt, much as Bank of England or Federal Reserve notes are legal tender today. The British government refused, believing that this was going too far, but Parliament did give the new Bank the advantage of holding all government deposits, as well as the power to issue new notes to pay for the government debt.

The Bank of England promptly issued the enormous sum of £760,000, most of which was used to buy government debt. This had an immediate and considerable inflationary effect, and in the short span of two years, the Bank of England was insolvent after a bank run, an insolvency gleefully abetted by its competitors, the private goldsmiths, who were happy to return to it the swollen Bank of England notes for redemption in specie.

It was at this point that a fateful decision was made, one which set a grave and mischievous precedent for both British and

---

[1]John Carswell, *The South Sea Bubble* (Stanford, Calif.: Stanford University Press, 1960), pp. 27–28.

American banking. In May 1696, the English government simply allowed the Bank of England to "suspend specie payment"—that is, to refuse to pay its contractual obligations of redeeming its notes in gold—yet to continue in operation, issuing notes and enforcing payments upon its *own* debtors. The Bank of England suspended specie payment, and its notes promptly fell to a 20 percent discount against specie, since no one knew if the Bank would ever resume payment in gold.

The straits of the Bank of England were shown in an account submitted at the end of 1696, when its notes outstanding were £765,000, backed by only £36,000 in cash. In those days, few noteholders were willing to sit still and hold notes when there was such a low fraction of cash.

Specie payments resumed two years later, but the rest of the early history of the Bank of England was a shameful record of periodic suspensions of specie payment, despite an ever-increasing set of special privileges conferred upon it by the British government.

In 1696, for example, the Whig magnates who ran the Bank of England had a scare: the specter of competition. The Tories tried to establish a competing National Land Bank, and almost succeeded in doing so. As one historian writes, "Free trade in banking seemed a possibility. Bank of England stock fell on the market."[2]

Though the Land Bank failed, the Bank of England moved quickly. The following year, it induced Parliament to pass a law prohibiting any new corporate bank from being established in England. Furthermore, counterfeiting of Bank of England notes was now made punishable by death. As Sir John Clapham, in his

---

[2]Marvin Rosen, "The Dictatorship of the Bourgeoisie: England, 1688–1721," *Science and Society* XLV (Spring 1981): 44. This is an illuminating article, though written from a Marxist perspective.

sycophantic history of the Bank of England, put it, "Bank notes were not yet King's money, but they were getting near to it."[3]

In 1708, Parliament followed up this privilege with a further one: It was now unlawful for any corporate body other than the Bank of England to issue demand notes, and added a similar prohibition for any partnership of more than six persons. Not only could such bodies not issue notes redeemable on demand, but they also could not make short-term loans under six months. In this way, the Bank of England was enormously privileged by Parliament by being the only corporation or even moderately sized institution allowed to issue bank notes; its only competitors could now be very small banks with fewer than seven partners.

Despite these provisions, the Bank soon suffered the competition of powerful Tory-connected rivals, launched during a brief Tory ascendancy during the reign of Queen Anne. The South Sea Company, created in 1711 and headed by Prime Minister Robert Harley, was a formidable rival to the Bank, but it collapsed nine years later after a bout of inflationary monetary expansion and stock speculation. In the wake of the South Sea collapse, the Bank of England was itself subject to a bank run and was again allowed to suspend specie payments indefinitely. Still, the ignominious end of the "South Sea Bubble" left the Bank of England striding like a colossus, unchallenged, over the English banking system.[4]

A similar run on the Bank of England was precipitated in 1745, by the rising of Bonnie Prince Charlie in Scotland, and once more the Bank was permitted to suspend payments for a while.

During the late eighteenth century, the Bank of England's policy of monetary expansion formed the base of a pyramid for a flood of small, private partnerships in note issue banks. These

---

[3]John Clapham, *The Bank of England* (Cambridge: Cambridge University Press, 1958), pp. 1, 50.

[4]On the South Sea Bubble, see Carswell, *The South Sea Bubble*. For more on the early history of the Bank of England, in addition to Clapham, see J. Milnes Holden, *The History of Negotiable Instruments in English Law* (London: The Athlone Press, 1955), pp. 87–94, 191–98.

"country banks" increasingly used Bank of England notes as reserves and pyramided their own notes on top of them. By 1793, there were nearly 400 fractional reserve banks of issue in England. Inflationary financing of the lengthy, generations-long wars with France, beginning in the 1790s, led to the suspension of specie payment by one-third of English banks in 1793, followed by the Bank of England's suspension of specie payments in 1797. That suspension was joined in by the other banks, who then had to redeem their obligations in Bank of England notes.

This time, the suspension of specie payments by the Bank lasted 24 years, until 1821, after the end of the wars with France. During that period, the Bank of England's notes, in fact though not in law, served as legal money for England, and after 1812 until the end of the period, was *de jure* legal tender as well. As might be expected, this period proved to be a bonanza for inflationary bank credit and for creation of new, unsound banks. In 1797, there were 280 country banks in England and Wales. By 1813, the total number of banks was over 900. These banks pyramided on top of a swiftly rising total of Bank of England notes. Total bank notes outstanding in 1797 were £11 million. By 1816, the total had more than doubled, to £24 million.[5]

The fiat money period proved a bonanza for the Bank of England as well. The Bank's profits zoomed, and when specie payments finally resumed, Bank stocks fell by a substantial 16 percent.[6]

In 1826, banking was liberalized in England, since all corporations and partnerships were now permitted to issue demand notes; however, the effect of the liberalization was minuscule, since the new freedom was restricted to outside a 65-mile radius from London. Furthermore, in contrast to the Bank of England, the new bank corporations were subjected to unlimited liability. Thus, the monopoly of the Bank was kept inside London and its environs, limiting competition to *country* banking.

---

[5]Estimated total of country bank notes, in 1810, was £22 million.

[6]See Vera C. Smith, *The Rationale of Central Banking* (London: E.S. King & Son, 1936), p. 13.

In 1833, banking was liberalized further, but only slightly: *deposit* but *not* note issue corporate banking was allowed within London. More significantly, however, the Bank of England now received the permanent privilege of its notes functioning as *legal tender*. Furthermore, country banks, which previously were required to redeem their notes in specie, now had the option of redeeming them in Bank of England notes. These actions strengthened the Bank's position immeasurably and from that point on, it functioned as a full central bank, since country banks now took to keeping virtually all of their reserves at the Bank of England, demanding cash, or gold, from the Bank as necessary.

2. FREE BANKING IN SCOTLAND

After the founding of the Bank of England, English banking, during the eighteenth and first half of the nineteenth centuries, was riven by inflation, periodic crises and panics, and numerous—and in one case, lengthy—suspensions of specie payment. In contrast, neighboring Scottish banking, not subject to Bank of England control and, indeed, living in a regime of free banking, enjoyed a far more peaceful and crisis-free existence. Yet the Scottish experience has been curiously neglected by economists and historians. As the leading student of the Scottish free banking system concludes:

> Scotland, an industrialized nation with highly developed monetary, credit, and banking institutions, enjoyed remarkable macroeconomic stability through the eighteenth and early nineteenth centuries. During this time, Scotland had no monetary policy, no central bank, and virtually no political regulation of the banking industry. Entry was completely free and the right of note-issue universal. If the conjunction of these facts seems curious by today's light, it is because central banking has come to be taken for granted in this century, while the theory of competitive banking and note-issue has been neglected.[7]

---

[7]Lawrence H. White, "Free Banking in Scotland Prior to 1845" (unpublished essay, 1979), p. 1.

Scotland enjoyed a developing, freely competitive banking system from 1727 to 1845. During that period, Scottish bank notes were never legal tender, yet they circulated freely throughout the country. Individual banks were kept from overissue by a flourishing note exchange clearinghouse system. Since each bank was forced to toe the mark by being called upon for redemption, each bank would ordinarily accept each other's notes.[8]

Whereas English country banks were kept weak and unreliable by their limitation to partnerships of six or fewer, free Scottish banks were allowed to be corporate and grew large and nationwide, and therefore enjoyed much more public confidence. An important evidence of the relative soundness of Scottish banks is that Scottish notes circulated widely in the northern counties of England, while English bank notes never traveled northward across the border. Thus, in 1826, the citizens of the northern English counties of Cumberland and Westmoreland petitioned Parliament against a proposed outlawing of their use of Scottish bank notes. The petition noted that Scotland's freedom from the six-partner restriction "gave a degree of strength to the issuers of notes, and of confidence to the receivers of them, which several banks established in our counties have not been able to command. The natural consequence has been, that Scotch notes have formed the greater part of our circulating medium." The petitioners added that, with one exception, they had never suffered any losses from accepting Scottish notes for the past 50 years, "while in the same period the failures of banks in the north of England have been unfortunately numerous, and have occasioned the most ruinous losses to many who were little able to sustain them."[9]

---

[8]On the success of the Scottish note-exchange system, see William Graham, *The One Pound Note in the History of Banking in Great Britain*, 2nd ed. (Edinburgh: James Thin, 1911), p. 59; White, "Free Banking," pp. 8–19.

[9]Graham, *The One Pound Note*, pp. 366–67; White, "Free Banking," p. 41. The Cumberland and Westmoreland experience well supports Professor Klein's argument that, under free banking, "high confidence monies will

In contrast to the English banking system, the Scottish, in its 120 years of freedom from regulation, never evolved into a central banking structure marked by a pyramiding of commercial banks on top of a single repository of cash and bank reserves. On the contrary, each bank maintained its own specie reserves, and was responsible for its own solvency. The English "one-reserve system," in contrast, was not the product of natural market evolution. On the contrary, it was the result, as Bagehot put it, "of an accumulation of legal privileges on a single bank." Bagehot concluded that "the natural system—that which would have sprung up if Government had left banking alone—is that of many banks of equal or not altogether unequal size." Bagehot, writing in the mid-nineteenth century, cited Scotland as an example of freedom of banking where there was "no single bank with any sort of predominance."[10]

Moreover, Scottish banking, in contrast to English, was notably freer of bank failures, and performed much better and more stably during bank crises and economic contractions. Thus, while English banks failed widely during the panic of 1837, a contemporary writer noted the difference in the Scottish picture:

---

drive out low confidence monies." Klein has stressed the importance of public confidence under free banking; people will only be disposed to accept the money of a fully trustworthy issuer, "so that issuers," as White sums up Klein's argument, "must compete to convince the public of their superior reliability." In a system of private bank notes redeemable in specie, "the primary aspect of reliability is the assurance that convertibility will be maintained by the continued existence of the note-issuing bank." Benjamin Klein, "The Competitive Supply of Money," *Journal of Money, Credit and Banking* 6 (1974): 433; White, "Free Banking," p. 40.

[10]Walter Bagehot, *Lombard Street* (Homewood, Ill.: Irwin, 1962), pp. 32–33; White, "Free Banking," pp. 42–43. Furthermore, Scottish free banking was never plagued by any problem of counterfeiting. Counterfeiting is generally a function of the length of time any given note remains in circulation, and the average Scottish bank note lasted a very brief time until a competing bank would return it to the issuing bank through the clearinghouse for redemption. Emmanual Coppieters, *English Bank Note Circulation 1694–1954* (The Hague: Martinus Nijhoff, 1955), pp. 64–65; White, "Free Banking," pp. 43–44.

"While England, during the past year, has suffered in almost every branch of her national industry, Scotland has passed comparatively uninjured through the late monetary crisis."[11]

3. The Peelite Crackdown, 1844–1845

In 1844, Sir Robert Peel, a classical liberal who served as Prime Minister of Great Britain, put through a fundamental reform of the English banking system (followed the next year by imposing the same reform upon Scotland). Peel's Act is a fascinating example of the ironies and pitfalls of even the most well-meaning politico-economic reform. For Sir Robert Peel was profoundly influenced by the neo-Ricardian British economists known as the Currency School, who put forth a caustic and trenchant analysis of fractional reserve banking and central banking similar to that of the present book. The Currency School was the first group of economists to show how expansion of bank credit and bank notes generated inflations and business cycle booms, paving the way for the inevitable contraction and attendant collapse of business and banks. Furthermore, the Currency School showed clearly how the Central Bank, in England's case the Bank of England, had generated and perpetrated these inflations and contractions, and how it had borne the primary responsibility for unsound money and for booms and busts.

What, then, did the Currency School propose, and Sir Robert Peel adopt? In a praiseworthy attempt to end fractional reserve banking and institute 100 percent money, the Peelites unfortunately decided to put absolute monetary power in the hands of the very central bank whose pernicious influence they had done so much to expose. In attempting to eliminate fractional reserve banking, the Peelites ironically and tragically put the fox in charge of the proverbial chicken coop.

---

[11]Robert Bell, *Letter to James W. Gilbart . . .* (Edinburgh: Bell & Bradfute, 1838), p. 8; White, "Free Banking," p. 38.

Specifically, Peel's Act of 1844 provided (a) that all further issues of bank notes by the Bank of England must be backed 100 percent by new acquisitions of gold or silver[12]; (b) that no new bank of issue (issuing bank notes) could be established; (c) that the average note issue of each existing country bank could be no greater than the existing amount of issue; and (d) that banks would lose their note issue rights if they were merged into or bought by another bank, these rights being largely transferred to the Bank of England. Provisions (b), (c), and (d) effectively eliminated the country banks as issuers of bank notes, for they could not issue any more (even if backed by gold or silver) than had existed in 1844. Thereby the effective monopoly of bank note issue was placed into the not very clean hands of the Bank of England. The quasi-monopoly of note issue by the Bank had now been transformed into a total legally enforceable monopoly. (In 1844, the Bank of England note circulation totaled £21 million; total country bank note circulation was £8.6 million, issued by 277 small country banks.)

By these provisions, the Peelites attempted to establish one bank in England—the Bank of England—and then to keep it limited to essentially a 100 percent receiver of deposits. In that way, fractional reserve banking, inflationary booms, and the business cycle were supposed to be eliminated. Unfortunately, Peel and the Currency School overlooked two crucial points. First, they did not realize that a monopoly bank privileged by the State could not, in practice, be held to a restrictive 100 percent rule. Monopoly power, once created and sustained by the State, will be used and therefore abused. Second, the Peelites overlooked an important contribution to monetary theory by such American Currency School economists as Daniel Raymond and William M. Gouge:

---

[12]In fact, the maximum limit of Bank of England notes not backed by gold was set at £14 million; circulation of bank notes in 1844 was £21 million, making the restriction on the Bank even more rigorous.

that demand deposits are fully as much part of the money supply
as bank notes. The British Currency School stubbornly insisted
that demand deposits were purely nonmonetary credit, and
therefore looked with complacency on its issue. Fractional
reserve banking, according to these theorists, was only pernicious
for bank *notes*; issue of demand deposits was not inflationary and
was not part of the supply of money.

The result of this tragic error on bank deposits meant that
fractional reserve banking did not end in England after 1844, but
simply changed to focusing on demand deposits instead of notes.
In fact, the pernicious modern system now came into full flower.
Both the Bank of England and the country banks, deprived of the
right to issue notes at will, began to issue deposits to a fare-thee-
well. And since only the Bank of England could now issue notes,
the country banks relied on the Central Bank to issue notes,
which remained as legal tender, while they themselves pyramided
demand deposits on top of them.

As a result, inflationary booms of bank credit continued
immediately after 1844, leading to the final collapse of the Currency School. For as crises arose when domestic and foreign citizens called upon the banks for redemption of their notes, the
Bank of England was able to get Parliament to "suspend" Peel's
Act, allowing the Bank to issue enough fractional reserve legal
tender notes to get the entire banking system out of trouble. Peel's
Act requiring 100 percent issue of new Bank of England notes was
suspended periodically: in 1847, 1857, 1866, and finally, in
1914, when the old gold standard system went into the discard.
How seriously the government and the Bank of England kept to
the spirit of noninflationary banking may be seen by the fact that
when the last vestiges of Peel's Act were scrapped in 1928, the
authorized maximum of the Bank of England was permanently
raised from the traditional, but now unfortunately obsolete, £14
million to the now realistic £260 million, while any further issues
could simply be authorized by the British government without an
act of Parliament. Vera C. Smith justly writes that:

> The 1847, 1857 and 1866 crises showed the Government always ready, on the only occasions when it was necessary, to exempt the Bank from the provisions of the Bank Act (Peel's Act), and the opinion was necessarily expressed in some quarters that the clause of the Act, limiting the fiduciary issue of the Bank, was a mere paper provision having no practical application, since the Bank of England could always rely on the Government to legalise a breach of it every time it got into a difficult position. The relations between the Bank and the Government were, in fact, a tradition too long established for either the Bank, or the public, or the Government, to envisage anything other than full Government support to the Bank in time of stress. It had always been a privileged and protected institution.[13]

If the political flaw of trusting a monopoly Bank of England combined with the economic flaw of overlooking deposits to make the English banking system worse than before, the effect on Scotland was far worse. For the Currency School theorists were totally ignorant of the beneficial workings of the Scottish free banking system, and in their haste to impose a uniform monetary scheme on the entire United Kingdom, they proceeded to destroy Scottish free banking as well.

Peel's Act to Regulate the Issue of Bank Notes was imposed on Scotland in July 1845. No new banks of issue were allowed in Scotland any longer; and the note issue of each existing bank could only increase if backed 100 percent by specie in the bank's vault. In effect, then, the Scottish banks were prevented from further note issue (though not absolutely so as in the case of England), and they, too, shifted to deposits and were brought under the Bank of England's note issue suzerainty.

One interesting point is the lack of any protests by the Scottish banks at this abrogation of their prerogatives. The reason is

---

[13]Smith, *Rationale of Central Banking*, pp. 18–19.

that Peel's 1845 Act suppressed all new entrants into Scottish note banking, thereby cartelizing the Scottish banking system, and winning the applause of the existing banks who would no longer have to battle new competitors for market shares.[14]

---

[14]As White says,

> The bankers of Scotland did not protest loudly against the Act of 1845, as it bestowed upon them a shared legal monopoly of the note-issue. . . . Peel in essence bought the support of all the existing Scottish banks by suppressing new entrants. In freezing the authorized issues at 1844 levels, the Act of 1845 also hampered rivalry for market shares among existing banks. ("Free Banking," p. 34)

XIII.

CENTRAL BANKING IN THE
UNITED STATES I: THE ORIGINS

1. THE BANK OF NORTH AMERICA AND THE FIRST BANK
OF THE UNITED STATES

The first commercial bank in the United States was also designed to be the first central bank.[1] The charter of the Bank of North America was driven through the Continental Congress by Robert Morris in the spring of 1781. Morris, a wealthy Philadelphia merchant and Congressman, had assumed virtually total economic and financial power during the Revolutionary War. As a war contractor, Morris siphoned off millions from the public treasury into contracts to his own mercantile and shipping firm and to those of his associates. Morris was also leader of the powerful Nationalist forces in the embattled new

---

[1]There were very few privately-owned banks in colonial America, and they were short-lived.

country whose aim was to reimpose in the new United States a system of mercantilism and big government similar to that in Great Britain, against which the colonists had rebelled. The object was to have a strong central government, particularly a strong president or king as chief executive, built up by high taxes and heavy public debt. The strong central government was to impose high tariffs to subsidize domestic manufacturers, develop a big navy to open up and subsidize foreign markets for American exports, and launch a massive system of internal public works. In short, the United States was to have a British system without Great Britain.

Part of the Morris scheme was to organize and head a central bank, to provide cheap credit and expanded money for himself and his allies. The new privately owned Bank of North America was deliberately modeled after the Bank of England. Its money liabilities were to be grounded upon specie, with a controlled monetary inflation pyramiding credit upon a reserve of specie.

The Bank of North America received a federal charter very quickly in a Congress dominated by its founder and major owner. Like the Bank of England, the Bank of North America was granted the monopoly privilege of its notes being receivable in all duties and taxes to state and federal governments, and at par with specie. Furthermore, no other banks were allowed to operate in the country. In return for this monopoly license to issue paper money, the Bank graciously agreed to lend most of its newly created money to the federal government. In return for this agreement, of course, the hapless taxpayers would have to pay the Bank principal and interest.[2]

---

[2]When he failed to raise the legally required specie capital to launch the Bank of North America, Robert Morris, in an act tantamount to embezzlement, simply appropriated specie loaned to the U.S. by France and invested it on behalf of the government in his own bank. In this way, Morris appropriated the bulk of specie capital for his bank out of government funds. A multiple of these funds was then borrowed back from Morris's bank by Morris as government financier for the pecuniary benefit of Morris as

Despite the monopoly privileges conferred upon the Bank of North America and its nominal redeemability in specie, the market's lack of confidence in the inflated notes led to their depreciation outside the Bank's home base in Philadelphia. The Bank even tried to bolster the value of its notes by hiring people to urge redeemers of its notes not to insist on specie—a move scarcely calculated to improve long-run confidence in the Bank.

After a year of operation, Morris's political power slipped, and he moved quickly to shift the Bank of North America from a central bank to a purely commercial bank chartered by the state of Pennsylvania. By the end of 1783, all the federal government's stock in the Bank, amounting to 5/8 of its capital, had been sold into private hands, and all U.S. government debt to the Bank repaid. The first experiment with a central bank in the United States had ended.

But the U.S. was not to be allowed to be without a central bank for very long. In 1787–88, the Nationalist forces pushed through a new Constitution replacing the decentralist Articles of Confederation. The Nationalists were on their way to re-establishing the mercantilist and statist British model, even though they were grudgingly forced to accept the libertarian Bill of Rights as the price for the Anti-Federalists—who commanded the support of the majority of Americans—not insisting on a second constitutional convention to return to something very like the decentralized Articles.

The successful Federalists (the term the Nationalists called themselves) proceeded to put through their cherished program: high tariffs, domestic taxes, public works, and a high public debt. A crucial part of their program was put through in 1791 by their leader, Secretary of the Treasury, Alexander Hamilton, a disciple of Robert Morris. Hamilton put through Congress the First Bank

---

banker; and finally, Morris channeled most of the money into war contracts for his friends and business associates. See Murray N. Rothbard, *Conceived in Liberty*, Vol. IV, *The Revolutionary War, 1775–1784* (New Rochelle, N.Y.: Arlington House, 1979), p. 392.

of the United States, a privately owned central bank, with the federal government owning 1/5 of the shares. Hamilton argued that an alleged "scarcity" of specie had to be overcome by infusions of paper money, to be issued by the new Bank and invested in the public debt and in subsidies of cheap credit to manufacturers. The Bank notes were to be legally redeemable in specie on demand, and they were to be kept at par with specie by the federal government's accepting its notes in taxes, thus giving it a quasi-legal tender status. The federal government would also confer upon the Bank the privileges of being the depository for its funds. Furthermore, for the 20-year period of its charter, the First Bank of the United States was to be the only bank with the privilege of having a national charter.

The First Bank of the United States was modeled after the old Bank of North America, and in a significant gesture of continuity the latter's longtime president and former partner of Robert Morris, Thomas Willing of Philadelphia, was made president of the new Bank.

The First Bank of the United States promptly fulfilled its inflationary potential by issuing millions of dollars in paper money and demand deposits, pyramiding on top of $2 million of specie. The BUS invested heavily in $8.2 million of loans to the U.S. government by 1796. As a result, wholesale prices rose from an index of 85 in 1791 to a peak of 146 in 1796, an increase of 72 percent. In addition, speculation mounted in government securities and real estate. Pyramiding on top of BUS expansion, and aggravating the paper money expansion and the inflation, was a flood of newly created commercial banks. Only three commercial banks had existed at the inception of the Constitution, and only four by the time of the establishment of the BUS. But eight new banks were founded shortly thereafter, in 1791 and 1792, and 10 more by 1796. Thus, the BUS and its monetary expansion spurred the creation of 18 new banks in five years, on top of the original four.

Despite the official hostility of the Jeffersonians to commercial as well as central banks, the Democratic-Republicans, under the control of quasi-Federalist moderates rather than militant Old

Republicans, made no move to repeal the charter of the BUS before its expiration in 1811. Moreover, they happily multiplied the number of state chartered banks and bank credit during the two decades of the BUS existence. Thus in 1800, there were 28 state banks; by 1811, the number had grown to 117, a fourfold increase.[3]

When the time came for rechartering the BUS in 1811, the re-charter bill was defeated by one vote each in the House and Senate. Recharter was fought for by the quasi-Federalist Madison administration, aided by nearly all the Federalists in Congress, but was narrowly defeated by the bulk of the Democratic-Republicans, led by the hard money Old Republican forces. In view of the widely held misconception among historians that central banks serve, and are looked upon, as restraints on state bank inflation, it is instructive to note that the major forces in favor of recharter

---

[3]On the quasi-Federalists as opposed to the Old Republicans, on banking and on other issues, see Richard E. Ellis, *The Jeffersonian Crisis: Courts and Politics in the Young Republic* (New York: Oxford University Press, 1971) p. 277 and passim. Ellis perceptively writes:

> For all their hostility to banks during the 1790's, the Jeffersonians, once in power, established more state banks than the Federalists had ever thought of creating. Much of this was deliberate on the part of the moderates and bitterly opposed by the radicals. . . . The real meaning of Jeffersonian Democracy, it would seem, is to be found in the political triumph of the moderate Republicans and their eventual amalgamation with the moderate wing of the Federalist party. This represented a victory of moderation over the extremism of the ultra-nationalist, neo-mercantile wing of the Federalist party on the one hand, and the particularistic, Anti-Federalist-Old Republican wing of the Democratic party on the other.

Very true, although the use of the term "moderate" by Ellis, of course, loads the semantic dice. Ellis notes that one quasi-Federalist hailed the triumph of the center over "Federalism, artfully employed to disguise monarchy" on the one hand, and Democracy, "unworthily employed as a cover for anarchy" on the other. Ibid., pp. 277–78.

were merchants, Chambers of Commerce, and most of the state banks. Merchants found that the BUS had expanded credit at cheap interest rates, and eased the eternal complaints about a "scarcity of money." Even more suggestive is the support of the state banks, which hailed the BUS as "advantageous" and worried about a contraction of credit should the Bank be forced to liquidate. The Bank of New York, which had been founded by Alexander Hamilton, even lauded the BUS because it had been able "in case of any sudden pressure upon the merchants to step forward to their aid in a degree which the state institutions were unable to do."[4]

But free banking was not to have much of a chance. The very next year, the United States launched an unsuccessful war against Great Britain. Most of the industry and most of the capital was in New England, a pro-British region highly unsympathetic to the War of 1812. New England capital and the conservative New England banks were not about to invest heavily in debt to finance the war. Therefore, the U.S. government encouraged an enormous expansion in the number of banks and in bank notes and deposits to purchase the growing war debt. These new and recklessly inflationary banks in the Middle Atlantic, Southern, and Western states, printed enormous quantities of new notes to purchase government bonds. The federal government then used these notes to purchase arms and manufactured goods in New England.

Thus, from 1811 to 1815, the number of banks in the country increased from 117 to 246. The estimated total of specie in all banks fell from $14.9 million in 1811 to $13.5 million in 1815,

---

[4]John Thom Holdsworth, *The First Bank of the United States* (Washington, D.C.: National Monetary Commission, 1910), p. 83. Holdsworth, the premier historian of the First BUS, saw this overwhelmingly supported by the state banks, but still inconsistently clung to the myth that the BUS functioned as a restraint on their expansion: "The state banks, though their note issues and discounts had been kept in check by the superior resources and power of the Bank of the United States, favored the extension of the charter, and memorialized Congress to that effect." Ibid., p. 90. Odd that they would be acting so contrary to their self-interest!

whereas the aggregate of bank notes and deposits rose from $42.2 million in 1811 to $79 million four years later, an increase of 87.2 percent, pyramiding on top of a 9.4 percent decline in specie.

What happened next provides a fateful clue to the problem of why free banking did not work as well before the Civil War as in our theoretical model. It didn't work well (although its record was not nearly as bad as that of central banking) because it wasn't really tried. Remember that a crucial aspect of the free banking model is that the moment a bank cannot pay its notes or deposits in specie, it must declare bankruptcy and close up shop. But the federal and state governments did not allow this crucial process of insolvency—fundamental to the capitalist system—to work itself out.

Specifically, in the War of 1812, as the federal government spent the new inflated notes in New England, the conservative New England banks called on the banks of the other regions for redemption in specie. By August 1814, it became clear that the banks of the nation apart from New England could not pay, that they were insolvent. Rather than allow the banks of the nation to fail, the governments, state and federal, decided in August 1814 to allow the banks to continue in business while refusing to redeem their obligations in specie. In other words, the banks were allowed to refuse to pay their solemn contractual obligations, while they could continue to issue notes and deposits and force *their debtors* to fulfill their contractual obligations. This was unfair and unjust, as well as a special privilege of mammoth proportions to the banking system; not only that, it provided carte blanche, an open sesame, for bank credit inflation.

Free banking did not work well in the U.S. because it was never fully tried. The banks were allowed to continue to "suspend specie payments" while remaining in business for 2½ years, even though the war was over by early 1815. This general suspension was not only highly inflationary at the time; it set a precedent for all financial crises from then on. Whether the U.S. had a central bank or not, the banks were assured that if they inflated together and then got in trouble, government would bail them out and permit them to suspend specie payments for years. Such general suspensions of specie payments occurred in 1819, 1837, 1839, and 1857, the last three during an era generally considered to be that of "free banking."

2. THE SECOND BANK OF THE UNITED STATES

The United States emerged from the War of 1812 in a chaotic monetary state, its monetary system at a fateful crossroads. The banks, checked only by the varying rates of depreciation of their notes, multiplied and expanded wildly, freed from the obligation of redeeming their notes and deposits in specie. Clearly, the nation could not continue indefinitely with discordant sets of individual banks issuing fiat money. It was apparent that there were only two ways out of this pressing problem. One was the hard money path, advocated by the Old Republicans, and, for their own purposes, the Federalists. The federal and state governments would then have sternly compelled the recklessly inflating banks to redeem promptly in specie and, when most of the banks outside of New England failed to do so, force them to liquidate. In that way, the mass of depreciated and inflated notes would have been liquidated quickly, and specie would have poured back out of hoards and into the country to supply a circulating medium. America's inflationary experience would have been ended, perhaps forever.

Instead, the centrist Democrat-Republican establishment in 1816 turned to the second way: the old Federalist path of a new inflationary central bank, the Second Bank of the United States. Modeled closely after the First Bank, the Second Bank, a private corporation with 1/5 of its stock owned by the federal government, was to create a uniform national paper currency, purchase a large part of the public debt, and receive deposits of Treasury funds. The BUS notes and deposits were to be redeemable in specie, and they were given quasi-legal tender status by the federal government's receiving them in payment of taxes.

That the purpose of establishing the BUS was to support rather than restrain the state banks in their inflationary course is shown by the shameful deal that the BUS made with the state banks as soon as it opened its doors in January 1817. While it was enacting the BUS charter in April 1816, Congress passed a resolution of Daniel Webster, at that time a Federalist champion of hard money, requiring that after February 20, 1817, the U.S. would accept in payments for taxes only specie, Treasury notes, BUS notes, or state bank notes redeemable in specie on demand. In short, no irredeemable state bank notes would be accepted after that date. Instead of using this opportunity to compel the banks to redeem, however, the BUS, meeting with representatives from the leading urban banks outside Boston, agreed to issue $6 million worth of credit in New York, Philadelphia, Baltimore, and Virginia before insisting on specie payments on debts due from the state banks. In return for that massive inflation, the state banks graciously consented to resume specie payments. Moreover, the BUS and the state banks agreed to mutually support each other in any emergency, which, of course, meant in practice that the far stronger BUS was committed to the propping up of the weaker state banks.

Several of the Congressional opponents delivered trenchant critiques of the establishment of the BUS. Senator William H. Wells, Federalist from Delaware, noted in some surprise that:

> This bill came out of the hands of the Administration ostensibly for the purpose of correcting the diseased state of our paper currency, by restraining and curtailing the over issue of banking paper; and yet it came prepared to inflict upon us the same evil; being itself nothing more than simply a paper-making machine. . . . The disease, it is said, under which the people labor, is the banking fever of the States; and this is to be cured by giving them the banking fever of the United States.[5]

---

[5]*Annals of Congress*, 14 Cong., 1 sess., April 1, 1816, p. 267.

In the House of Representatives, Artemas Ward, Jr., Federalist from Massachusetts, pointed out that the remedy for the evil of inflated and depreciated paper was simple: "refusing to receive the notes of those banks, which do not pay specie, in dues to the Government." This would naturally be done, Ward pointed out, but for an alliance, which he considered "disgraceful to the country and unjust to individuals," between the Secretary of the Treasury and the banks, without which the evil never would have existed. The leader in the battle against the Bank, Daniel Webster, Federalist of New Hampshire, pointed out that "there was no remedy for the state of depreciation of the paper currency, but the resumption of specie payments," which the government should force the banks to undertake.

But the most eloquent attack on the new BUS was that of the fiery Old Republican from Virginia, John Randolph of Roanoke. After pointing out that only specie can soundly function as money, Randolph prophetically warned that a central bank

> would be an engine of irresistible power in the hands of any administration; that it would be in politics and finance what the celebrated proposition of Archimedes was in physics—a place, the fulcrum from which, at the will of the Executive, the whole nation could be huffed to destruction, or managed in any way, at his will and discretion.

The Bank, Randolph charged, would serve "as a crutch," and, as far as he understood it, it was a broken one: "it would tend, instead of remedying the evil, to aggravate it."

"We do not move forthrightly against the insolvent banks," Randolph warned, because of fear and greed:

> Every man you meet in this House or out of it, with some rare exceptions, which only served to prove the rule, was either a stockholder, president, cashier, clerk or doorkeeper, runner, engraver, paper-maker, or mechanic in some other way to a bank . . .
>
>   However great the evil of their conduct might be . . . who was to bell the cat—who was to take the bull by the horns? . . . There were very few, he said, who dared to speak truth

> to this mammoth; the banks were so linked together with
> the business of the world, that there were very few men
> exempt from their influence. The true secret is, said he, the
> banks are creditors as well as debtors

and so their debtors fear to tackle the banks.

Randolph went on to pinpoint the fraudulent nature of fractional reserve banking:

> . . . [i]t was as much swindling to issue notes with intent not
> to pay, as it was burglary to break open a house. If they were
> unable to pay, the banks were bankrupts . . .[6]

The BUS was driven through Congress by the Madison
administration and particularly by Secretary of the Treasury
Alexander J. Dallas, whose appointment had been pushed for that
purpose. Dallas, a wealthy Philadelphia lawyer, was a close friend,
counsel, and financial associate of Philadelphia merchant and
banker, Stephen Girard, reputedly one of the two wealthiest men
in the country. Girard had been the largest single stockholder of
the First BUS, and during the War of 1812, he became a very
heavy investor in the war debt of the federal government. As a
prospective large stockholder of the BUS and as a way of creating
a buyer for his public debt, Girard began to urge a new Central
Bank. Dallas's appointment as Secretary of Treasury in 1814 was
successfully engineered by Girard and his close friend, wealthy
New York merchant and fur trader, John Jacob Astor, also a heavy
investor in the war debt.[7]

As a result of the deal between the BUS and the state banks,
the resumption of specie payments by the latter after 1817 was
more nominal than real, thereby setting the stage for continued

---

[6]*Annals of Congress*, 14 Cong., 1 sess., pp. 1066, 1091, 1110ff.

[7]On the Girard-Dallas connection, see Bray Hammond, *Banks and Politics in America* (Princeton, N.J.: Princeton University Press, 1957), pp.
231–46, 252; and Philip H. Burch, Jr., *Elites in American History*, vol. I,
The Federalist Years to the Civil War (New York: Holmes & Meier, 1981),
pp. 88, 97, 116–17, 119–21.

inflation, and for renewed widespread suspensions of specie payment during the 1819–21 panic and depression. A mark of this
failure of redemption was that varying discounts on bank notes
against specie continued from 1817 on.

The problem was aggravated by the fact that the BUS lacked
the courage to insist on payment of notes from the state banks. As
a result, the BUS piled up large balances against the state banks,
reaching over $2.4 million during 1817 and 1818. As the major
historian of the BUS writes: "So many influential people were
interested in the [state banks] as stockholders that it was not
advisable to give offense by demanding payment in specie, and
borrowers were anxious to keep the banks in the humor to
lend."[8]

From its inception, the Second BUS launched a massive inflation of money and credit. Lax about insisting on the required payments of its capital in specie, the Bank failed to raise the $7 mil-
lion legally required to be subscribed in specie. During 1817 and
1818, its specie never rose above $2.5 million and at the peak of
its initial expansion, BUS specie was $21.8 million. Thus, in a
scant year and a half of operation, the BUS added a net of $19.2
million to the money supply.

Outright fraud abounded at the BUS, especially at the
Philadelphia and Baltimore branches, which made 3/5 of all BUS
loans.[9] Furthermore, the BUS attempt to provide a uniform
national currency foundered on the fact that the western and
southern branches could inflate credit and bank notes, and that

[8]Ralph C.H. Catterall, *The Second Bank of the United States* (Chicago:
University of Chicago Press, 1902), p. 36.

[9]The main culprits in the massive BUS fraud were James A. Buchanan,
president of the Baltimore branch, his partner Samuel Smith of the leading
Baltimore mercantile firm of Smith & Buchanan, and the Baltimore BUS
cashier, James W. McCulloch, who was simply an impoverished clerk at the
mercantile house. Smith, an ex-Federalist, was a Senator from Maryland and
a powerful member of the national quasi-Federalist Democratic-Republican
establishment. See ibid., pp. 28–50, 503.

the inflated notes would then come into the more conservative branches in New York and Boston, which would be obligated to redeem the inflated notes at par. In this way, the conservative branches were stripped of specie while the western branches continued to inflate unchecked.

The expansionary operations of the BUS impelled an inflationary expansion of state banks on top of the enlargement of the central bank. The number of incorporated state banks rose from 232 in 1816 to 338 in 1818, with Kentucky alone chartering 40 new banks in the 1817–18 legislative session. The estimated total money supply in the nation rose from $67.3 million in 1816 to $94.7 million in 1818, a rise of 40.7 percent in two years. Most of this increase was supplied by the BUS.[10] This enormous expansion of money and credit impelled a full-scale inflationary boom throughout the country.

Starting in July 1818, the government and the BUS began to see what dire straits they were in; the enormous inflation of money and credit, aggravated by the massive fraud, had put the BUS in danger of going under and illegally failing to maintain specie payments. Over the next year, the BUS began a series of enormous contractions, forced curtailment of loans, contractions of credit in the south and west, refusal to provide uniform national currency by redeeming its shaky branch notes at par, and at last, seriously enforcing the requirement that its debtor banks redeem in specie. These heroic actions, along with the ouster of President William Jones, managed to save the BUS, but the contraction of money and credit swiftly brought to the United States its first widespread economic and financial depression. The first nationwide "boom-bust" cycle had arrived in the United States, ignited by rapid and massive inflation and quickly succeeded by contraction of money and credit. Banks failed, and private banks

---

[10]Figures are adapted from tables, converted pro rata to 100 percent of the banks, in J. Van Fenstermaker, "The Statistics of American Commercial Banking, 1782–1818," *Journal of Economic History* (September 1965): 401, 405–06.

curtailed their credits and liabilities and suspended specie payments in most parts of the country.

Contraction of money and credit by the BUS was almost incredible, notes and deposits falling from $21.8 million in June 1818 to $11.5 only a year later. The money supply contributed by the BUS was thereby contracted by no less than 47.2 percent in one year. The number of incorporated banks at first remained the same, and then fell rapidly from 1819 to 1822, dropping from 341 in mid-1819 to 267 three years later. Total notes and deposits of state banks fell from an estimated $72 million in mid-1818 to $62.7 million a year later, a drop of 14 percent in one year. If we add in the fact that the U.S. Treasury contracted total treasury notes from $8.81 million to zero during this period, we get a total money supply of $103.5 million in 1818, and $74.2 million in 1819, a contraction in one year of 28.3 percent.

The result of the contraction was a rash of defaults, bankruptcies of business and manufacturers, and a liquidation of unsound investments during the boom. Prices in general plummeted: the index of export staples fell from 158 in November 1818 to 77 in June 1819, an annualized drop of 87.9 percent in seven months.

In the famous charge of the Jacksonian hard money economist and historian William M. Gouge, by its precipitate and dramatic contraction "the Bank was saved, and the people were ruined."[11]

The Bank of the United States was supposed to bring the blessings of a uniform paper currency to the United States. Yet from the time of the chaotic 1814–17 experience, the notes of the state banks had circulated at varying rates of depreciation, depending on how long the public believed they could keep redeeming their obligations in specie.

During the panic of 1819, obstacles and intimidation were often the lot of those who attempted to press the banks to fulfill their contractual obligations to pay in specie. Thus, Maryland and

---

[11]William M. Gouge, *A Short History of Paper Money and Banking in the United States* (New York: Augustus M. Kelley, 1968), p. 110.

Pennsylvania engaged in almost bizarre inconsistency. Maryland, on February 15, 1819, enacted a law "to compel . . . banks to pay specie for their notes, or forfeit their charters." Yet, two days after this seemingly tough action, it passed another law relieving banks of any obligation to redeem notes held by professional money brokers, the major force ensuring such redemption. The latter act was supposed "to relieve the people of this state . . . from the evil arising from the demands made on the banks of this state for gold and silver by brokers." Pennsylvania followed suit a month later. In this way, these states could claim to be enforcing contract and property rights while trying to prevent the most effective means of such enforcement.

Banks south of Virginia largely went off specie payment during the Panic of 1819, and in Georgia at least general suspension continued almost continuously down to the 1830s. One customer complained during 1819 that in order to collect in specie from the largely state-owned Bank of Darien in Georgia, he was forced to swear before a justice of the peace, five bank directors, and the bank cashier, that each and every note he presented to the bank was his own and that he was not a "money broker" or an agent for anyone else. Furthermore, he was forced to pay a fee of $1.36 on each note in order to obtain the specie to which he was entitled.[12]

In North Carolina, furthermore, banks were not penalized by the legislature for suspending specie payments to brokers, though they were for suspending payments to other depositors. Thus encouraged, the three leading banks of North Carolina met in June 1819 and agreed not to pay specie to brokers or their agents. Their notes, however, immediately fell to a 15 percent discount outside the state. In the course of this partial default, of course,

---

[12]Ibid., pp. 141–42. Secretary of the Treasury William H. Crawford, a powerful political leader from Georgia, tried in vain to save the Bank of Darien by depositing Treasury funds in the bank. Murray N. Rothbard, *The Panic of 1819: Reactions and Policies* (New York: Columbia University Press, 1962), p. 62.

the banks continued to require their own debtors to pay them at par in specie.

Many states permitted banks to suspend specie payments during the Panic of 1819, and four Western states—Tennessee, Kentucky, Missouri, and Illinois—established state-owned banks to try to combat the depression by issuing large amounts of inconvertible paper money. In all states trying to prop up bank paper, a quasi-legal tender status was conferred on it by agreeing to receive the notes in taxes or debts due to the state. All the inconvertible paper schemes led to massive depreciation and disappearance of specie, succeeded by rapid liquidation of the new state-owned banks.

XIV.

CENTRAL BANKING IN THE UNITED STATES II: THE 1820s TO THE CIVIL WAR

1. THE JACKSONIAN MOVEMENT AND THE BANK WAR

Out of the debacle of the Panic of 1819 emerged the beginnings of the Jacksonian movement dedicated to *laissez-faire*, hard money, and the separation of money and banking from the State. During the 1820s, the new Democratic Party was established by Martin Van Buren and Andrew Jackson to take back America for the Old Republican program. The first step on the agenda was to abolish the Bank of the United States, which was up for renewal in 1836. The imperious Nicholas Biddle, head of the BUS who was continuing the chain of control over the Bank by the Philadelphia financial elite,[1] decided to

---

[1]See Philip H. Burch, *Elites in American History: The Civil War to the New Deal* (Teaneck, N.J.: Holmes and Meier, 1981).

force the issue early, filing for renewal in 1831. Jackson, in a dramatic message, vetoed renewal of the Bank charter, and Congress failed to pass it over his veto.

Triumphantly reelected on the Bank issue in 1832, President Jackson disestablished the BUS as a central bank by removing Treasury deposits from the BUS in 1833, placing them in a number of state banks (soon called "pet banks") throughout the country. At first, the total number of pet banks was seven, but the Jacksonians, eager to avoid a tight-knit oligarchy of privileged banks, increased the number to 91 by the end of 1836. In that year, as its federal charter ran out, Biddle managed to get a Pennsylvania charter for the Bank, and the new United States Bank of Pennsylvania managed to function as a regular state bank for a few years thereafter.

Historians long maintained that Andrew Jackson, by his reckless act of eliminating the BUS and shifting government funds to pet banks, freed the state banks from the restraints imposed upon them by a central bank. In that way, the banks allegedly were allowed to pyramid money on top of specie, precipitating an unruly inflation later succeeded by two bank panics and a disastrous inflation.

Recent historians, however, have demonstrated that the correct picture was precisely the reverse.[2] First, under the regime of Nicholas Biddle, BUS notes and deposits had risen, from January 1823 to January 1832, from $12 million to $42.1 million, an annual increase of 27.9 percent. This sharp inflation of the base of the banking pyramid led to a large increase in the total money supply, from $81 million to $155 million, or an annual increase of 10.2 percent. Clearly, the driving force of this monetary expansion

<hr>

[2]For an excellent survey and critique of historical interpretations of Jackson and the Bank War, see Jeffrey Rogers Hummel, "The Jacksonians, Banking and Economic Theory: A Reinterpretation," *The Journal of Libertarian Studies* 2 (Summer 1978): 151–65.

of the 1820s was the BUS, which acted as an inflationary spur rather than as a restraint on the state banks.

The fact that wholesale prices remained about the same over this period does not mean that the monetary inflation had no ill effects. As "Austrian" business cycle theory points out, any bank credit inflation creates a boom-and-bust cycle; there is no need for prices actually to rise. Prices did not rise because an increased product of goods and services offset the monetary expansion. Similar conditions precipitated the great crash of 1929. Prices need not rise for an inflationary boom, followed by a bust, to be created. All that is needed is for prices to be kept up by the artificial boom, and be *higher than they would have been* without the monetary expansion. Without the credit expansion, prices would have fallen during the 1820s, as they would have a century later, thereby spreading the benefits of a great boom in investments and production to everyone in the country.

Recent historians have also demonstrated that most of the state banks warmly supported recharter of the Bank of the United States. With the exception of the banks in New York, Connecticut, Massachusetts, and Georgia, the state banks overwhelmingly backed the BUS.[3] But if the BUS was a restraining influence on their expansion, why did they endorse it?

In short, the BUS had a poor inflationary record in the 1820s, and the state banks, recognizing its role as a spur to their own credit expansion, largely fought on its behalf in the recharter struggle of the early 1830s.

Furthermore, the inflationary boom of the 1830s began, not with Jackson's removal of the deposits in 1833, but three years earlier, as an expansion fueled by the central bank. Thus, the total money supply rose from $109 million in 1830 to $155 million at the end of 1831, a spectacular expansion of 35 percent in one

---

[3]See Jean Alexander Wilburn, *Biddle's Bank: The Crucial Years* (New York: Columbia University Press, 1970), pp. 118–19.

year. This monetary inflation was sparked by the central bank, which increased its notes and deposits from January 1830 to January 1832 by 45.2 percent.[4]

There is no question, however, that the money supply and the price level rose spectacularly from 1833 to 1837. Total money supply rose from $150 million at the beginning of 1833 to $276 million four years later, an astonishing rise of 84 percent, or 21 percent per annum. Wholesale prices, in turn, rose from 84 in the spring of 1834 to 131 in early 1837, a rise of 52 percent in a little less than three years—or an annual rise of 19.8 percent.

The monetary expansion, however, was not caused by state banks going hog wild. The spark that ignited the inflation was an unusual and spectacular inflow of Mexican silver coins into the United States—brought about by the minting of debased Mexican copper coins which the Mexican government tried to keep at par value with silver. The system of fractional reserve banking, however, fundamentally was to blame for magnifying the influx of specie and pyramiding notes and deposits upon the specie base. In 1837, the boom came to an end, followed by the inevitable bust, as Mexico was forced to discontinue its copper coin issue by the outflow of silver, and the Bank of England, worried about inflation at home, tightened its own money supply and raised interest rates.[5] The English credit contraction in late 1836 caused a bust in the American cotton export trade in London, followed by contractionist pressure on American trade and banks.

In response to this contractionist pressure—demands for specie—the banks throughout the United States (including the old

---

[4]See Peter Temin, *The Jacksonian Economy* (New York: W.W. Norton, 1969).

[5]Mexico was shown to be the source of the specie inflow by Temin, *Jacksonian Economy*, p. 80, while the cause of the inflow in the minting of debased Mexican copper coins is pinpointed in Hugh Rockoff, "Money, Prices, and Banks in the Jacksonian Era," in R. Fogel and S. Engerman, eds., *The Reinterpretation of American Economic History* (New York: Harper & Row, 1971), p. 454.

BUS) promptly suspended specie payments in May 1837. The governments allowed them to do so, and continued to receive the notes in taxes. The notes began to depreciate at varying rates, and interregional trade within the United States was crippled.

The banks, however, could not hope to be allowed to continue on a fiat basis indefinitely, so they reluctantly began contracting their credit in order to go back eventually on specie. Finally, the New York banks were compelled by law to resume paying in specie, and other banks followed in 1838. During the year 1837, the money supply fell from $276 million to $232 million, a large drop of 15.6 percent in one year. Specie continued to flow into the country, but increased public distrust in the banks and demands to redeem in specie put enough pressure on the banks to force the contraction. In response, wholesale prices fell precipitately, by over 30 percent in seven months, declining from 131 in February 1837 to 98 in September of that year.

This healthy deflation brought about speedy recovery by 1838. Unfortunately, public confidence in the banks returned as they resumed specie payment, so that the money supply rose slightly and prices rose by 25 percent. State governments ignited the new boom of 1838 by recklessly spending large Treasury surpluses which President Jackson had distributed pro rata to the states two years earlier. Even more money was borrowed to spend on public works and other forms of boondoggle. The states counted on Britain and other countries purchasing these new bonds, because of the cotton boom of 1838. But the boom collapsed the following year, and the states had to abandon the unsound projects of the boom. Cotton prices fell and severe deflationist pressure was put upon the banks and upon trade. Moreover, the BUS had invested heavily in cotton speculation, and was forced once again to suspend specie payments in the fall of 1839. This touched off a new wave of general bank suspensions in the South and West, although this time the banks of New York and New England continued to redeem in specie. Finally, the BUS, having played its role of precipitating boom and bust for the last time, was forced to close its doors forever in 1841.

The crisis of 1839 ushered in four years of massive monetary and price deflation. Many unsound banks were finally eliminated, the number of banks declining during these years by 23 percent. The money supply fell from $240 million at the beginning of 1839 to $158 million in 1843, a seemingly cataclysmic drop of 34 percent, or 8.5 percent per annum. Wholesale prices fell even further, from 125 in February 1839 to 67 in March 1843, a tremendous drop of 42 percent, or 10.5 percent per year. The collapse of money and prices after 1839 also brought the swollen state government debts into jeopardy.

State government debt had totaled a modest $26.5 million in 1830. By 1835 it had reached $66.5 million, and by 1839 it had escalated to $170 million. It was now clear that many states were in danger of default on the debt. At this point, the Whigs, taking a leaf from their Federalist forebears, called for the federal government to issue $200 million worth of bonds in order to assume all the state debt.

The American people, however, strongly opposed federal aid, including even the citizens of the states in difficulty. The British noted in wonder that the average American seemed far more concerned about the status of his personal debts than about the debts of his state. To the worried question, Suppose foreign capitalists did not lend any further to the states? the *Floridian* replied, "Well who cares if they don't. We are now as a community heels over head in debt and can scarcely pay the interest."[6]

---

[6]*The Floridian*, March 14, 1840. Quoted in Reginald C. McGrane, *Foreign Bondholders and American State Debts* (New York: Macmillan, 1935), pp. 39–40. Americans also pointed out that the banks, including the BUS, who were presuming to take the lead in denouncing repudiation of state debt, had already suspended specie payments and were largely responsible for the contraction.

> Let the bondholders look to the United States Bank and to the other banks for their payment declared the people. Why should the poor be taxed to support the opulent classes in foreign lands who, it was believed, held the bulk of these securities. (p. 48)

The implication was clear: The disappearance of foreign credit to the states would be a good thing; it would have the healthy effect of cutting off their further wasteful spending, as well as avoiding the imposition of a crippling tax burden to pay for the interest and principal. There was in this astute response an awareness by the public that they and their governments were separate and sometimes even hostile entities rather than all part of one and the same organism.

The advent of the Jacksonian Polk administration in 1845 put an end to the agitation for Federal assumption of the debt, and by 1847, four western and southern states had repudiated all or part of their debts, while six other states had defaulted from three to six years before resuming payment.[7]

Evidently, the 1839–43 contraction and deflation was a healthy event for the economy, since it liquidated unsound investments, debts, and banks, including the pernicious Bank of the United States. But didn't the massive deflation have catastrophic effects—on production, trade, and employment—as we have generally been led to believe? Oddly enough, no. It is true that real investment fell by 23 percent during the four years of deflation, but, in contrast, real consumption *increased* by 21 percent and real GNP by 16 percent during this period. It seems that only the initial months of the contraction worked a hardship. And most of the deflation period was an era of economic growth.[8]

---

[7]The four states which repudiated all or part of their debts were Mississippi, Arkansas, Florida, and Michigan; the others were Maryland, Pennsylvania, Louisiana, Illinois, and Indiana.

[8]In a fascinating comparative analysis, Professor Temin contrasts this record with the disastrous contraction a century later, from 1929–33. During the latter four years, the money supply and prices fell by slightly less than in the earlier period, and the number of banks in existence by more. But the impact on the real economy was strikingly different. For in the later deflation, real consumption and GNP fell substantially, while real investment fell catastrophically. Temin properly suggests that the very different impact of the two deflations stemmed from the downward flexibility of wages and prices in the nineteenth century, so that massive monetary

The Jacksonians had no intention of leaving a permanent system of pet banks, and so Jackson's chosen successor Martin Van Buren fought to establish the Independent Treasury System, in which the federal government conferred no special privilege or inflationary prop on any bank; instead of a central bank or pet banks, the government was to keep its funds solely in specie, in its own Treasury vaults or "subtreasury" branches. Van Buren managed to establish the Independent Treasury in 1840, but the Whig administration repealed it the following year. Finally, however, Democratic President Polk installed the Independent Treasury System in 1846, lasting until the Civil War. At long last, the Jacksonians had achieved their dream of severing the federal government totally from the banking system, and placing its finances on a purely hard money, specie basis. From now on, the battle over money would shift to the arena of the states.

2. Decentralized Banking from the 1830s to the Civil War

After the financial crises of 1837 and 1839, the Democratic Party became even more Jacksonian, more ardently dedicated to hard money, than ever before. The Democrats strived during the 1840s and 1850s, for the outlawing of all fractional reserve bank paper. Battles were fought during the late 1840s, at constitutional conventions of many western states, in which the Jacksonians would succeed in outlawing such banking, only to find the Whigs repealing the prohibition a few years later. Trying to find some way to overcome the general revulsion against banks, the Whigs adopted the concept of *free banking*, which had been enacted in New York and Michigan in the late 1830s. Spreading outward from New York, the free banking concept triumphed in 15 states

---

contraction lowered prices but did not cripple real production, growth, or living standards. In contrast, the government of the 1930s placed massive roadblocks on the downward fall of prices and particularly wages, bringing about a far greater impact on production and unemployment. Temin, *Jacksonian Economy*, pp. 155ff.

by the early 1850s. On the eve of the Civil War, 18 out of the 33 states in the U.S. had adopted free banking laws.[9]

It must be emphasized that free banking before the Civil War was scarcely the same as the economic concept of free banking we have set forth earlier. Genuine free banking, as we have noted, exists where entry into the banking business is totally free, where banks are neither subsidized nor controlled, and where at the first sign of failure to redeem in specie, the bank is forced to declare insolvency and close its doors.

Free banking before the Civil War, however, was very different. Vera C. Smith has gone so far as to call the banking system before the Civil War, "decentralization without freedom," and Hugh Rockoff labeled free banking as the "antithesis of laissez-faire banking laws."[10] We have already seen that general suspensions of specie payments were periodically allowed whenever the banks overexpanded and got into trouble; the last such episode before the Civil War being in the Panic of 1857. It is true that under free banking incorporation was more liberal, since any bank meeting the legal regulations could be incorporated automatically without having to lobby for a special legislative charter. But the banks were subject to a myriad of regulations, including edicts by state banking commissioners, along with high minimum capital requirements which greatly restricted entry into the banking business. The most pernicious aspect of free banking was that the expansion of bank notes and deposits was tied directly to the amount of state government bonds which the bank had invested in and posted as security with the state. In effect, then, state government bonds became the reserve base upon which the banks

---

[9]Hugh Rockoff, *The Free Banking Era: A Re-Examination* (New York: Arno Press, 1975), pp. 3–4.

[10]Vera C. Smith, *The Rationale of Central Banking* (London: P.S. King & Son, 1936), p. 36, also ibid., pp. 148–49, Hugh Rockoff, "Varieties of Banking and Regional Economic Development in the United States, 1840–1860," *Journal of Economic History* 35 (March 1975): 162, quoted in Hummel, "Jacksonians," p. 157.

were allowed to pyramid a multiple expansion of bank notes and deposits. This meant that the more public debt the banks purchased, the more they could create and lend out new money. Thus, banks were induced to monetize the public debt, state governments were encouraged to go into debt, and government and bank inflation were intimately linked.

In addition to allowing periodic suspension of specie payments, federal and state governments conferred upon the banks the highly valuable privilege of having their notes accepted in taxes. And the general prohibition of interstate (and sometimes intrastate) branch banking greatly inhibited the speed by which one bank could demand payment from another in specie. The clearing of notes and deposits, and hence the free market limit on bank credit expansion, was thereby weakened.

The desire of state governments to finance public works was an important factor in their subsidizing and propelling the expansion of bank credit. Even Bray Hammond, scarcely a hard money advocate, admits that "the wildcats lent no money to farmers and served no farmer interest. They arose to meet the credit demands not of farmers (who were too economically astute to accept wildcat money) but of states engaged in public improvements."[11]

Despite the flaws and problems in the decentralized nature of the pre-Civil War banking system, the banks were free to experiment on their own to improve the banking system. The most successful such device, which imposed a rapid and efficient clearing

---

[11]Bray Hammond, *Banks and Politics in America: From the Revolution to the Civil War* (Princeton, N.J.: Princeton University Press, 1957), p. 627. On the neglected story of the Jacksonians versus their opponents on the state level after 1839, see William G. Shade, *Banks or No Banks: The Money Issue in Western Politics, 1832–1865* (Detroit: Wayne State University Press, 1972); Herbert Ershkowitz and William Shade, "Consensus or Conflict? Political Behavior in the State Legislatures During the Jacksonian Era," *Journal of American History* 58 (December 1971): 591–621; and James Roger Sharp, *The Jacksonians versus the Banks: Politics in the States After the Panic of 1837* (New York: Columbia University Press, 1970).

system on the banks of New England, was the privately developed Suffolk System.

In 1824, the Suffolk Bank of Boston, concerned for years about an influx of depreciated notes from various country banks in New England, decided to purchase country bank notes and systematically call on the country banks for redemption. By 1825, country banks began to give in to the pressure to deposit specie with the Suffolk, so as to make redemption of their notes by that bank far easier. By 1838, furthermore, almost every bank in New England was keeping such deposits, and was redeeming its liabilities in specie through the medium of the Suffolk Bank.

From the beginning to the end of the Suffolk System (1825–58), each country bank was obliged to maintain a permanent specie deposit of at least $2,000 ranging upward for larger sizes of bank. In addition to the permanent minimum deposit, each bank had to keep enough specie at the Suffolk Bank to redeem all the notes that Suffolk received. No interest was paid by the Suffolk Bank on these deposits, but Suffolk performed the invaluable service of accepting at par all the notes received from other New England banks, crediting the depositor banks' accounts the following day.

As the result of Suffolk acting as a private clearing bank, every New England bank could automatically accept the notes of any other bank at par with specie. In contrast to the general state bank approval of the Bank of the United States (and later of the Federal Reserve System), the banks greatly resented the existence of the Suffolk Bank's tight enforcement of specie payments. They had to play by the Suffolk rules, however, else their notes would depreciate rapidly and circulate only in a very narrow area. Suffolk, meanwhile, made handsome profits by lending out the permanent, noninterest paying deposits, and by making overdrafts to the member banks.

Suffolk System members fared very well during general bank crises during this period. In the Panic of 1837, not one Connecticut bank failed, or even suspended specie payments; all were members of the Suffolk System. And in 1857, when specie payment was

suspended in Maine, all but three banks (virtually all members of
the Suffolk System) continued to pay in specie.[12]

The Suffolk System ended in 1858 when a competing clearing
bank, the Bank of Mutual Redemption, was organized, and the
Suffolk System petulantly refused to honor the notes of any banks
keeping deposits with the new bank. The country banks then
shifted to the far laxer Bank of Mutual Redemption, and the Suffolk Bank stopped its clearing function in October 1858, becoming just another bank. Whatever the error of management in that
year, however, the Suffolk System would have been swept away in
any case by the universal suspension of specie payments at the
start of the Civil War, by the National Banking System installed
during the war, and by the prohibitive federal tax on state bank
notes put through during that fateful period.[13]

---

[12]John Jay Knox, historian and former U.S. Comptroller of the Currency, concluded from his study of the Suffolk System that private clearing
house service is superior to that of a government central bank:

> the fact is established that private enterprise could be
> entrusted with the work of redeeming the circulating notes
> of the banks, and that it could thus be done as safely and
> much more economically than the same service can be per-
> formed by the Government.

John Jay Knox, *A History of Banking in the United States* (New York: Brad-
ford Rhodes & Co., 1900), pp. 368–69.

[13]On the Suffolk System, see George Trivoli, *The Suffolk Bank: A Study
of a Free-Enterprise Clearing System* (London: The Adam Smith Institute,
1979).

XV.

CENTRAL BANKING IN THE UNITED STATES III: THE NATIONAL BANKING SYSTEM

1. THE CIVIL WAR AND THE NATIONAL BANKING SYSTEM

The Civil War wrought an even more momentous change in the nation's banking system than had the War of 1812. The early years of the war were financed by printing paper money—*greenbacks*—and the massive printing of money by the Treasury led to a universal suspension of specie payments by the Treasury itself and by the nation's banks, at the end of December 1861. For the next two decades, the United States was once again on a depreciating inconvertible fiat standard.

The money supply of the country totaled $745 million in 1860; by 1863, the money supply had zoomed to $1.44 billion, an increase of 92.5 percent in three years, or 30.8 percent per annum. The result of this large monetary inflation was a severe inflation of prices. Wholesale prices rose from 100 in 1860, to

211 at the end of the war, a rise of 110.9 percent, or 22.2 percent per year.

After the middle of 1863, the federal government stopped issuing the highly depreciated greenbacks, and began to issue large amounts of public debt. The accumulated deficit during the war totaled $2.61 billion, of which the printing of greenbacks financed only $430 million, almost all in the first half of the war.

The Civil War public debt brought into prominence in American finance one Jay Cooke, who became known as "The Tycoon." The Ohio-born Cooke had joined the moderately sized Philadelphia investment banking firm of Clark & Dodge as a clerk at the age of 18. In a few years, Cooke worked himself up to the status of junior partner, and in 1857 he left the firm to go into canal and railroad promotion and other business ventures. Cooke probably would have remained in relative obscurity, except for the lucky fact that he and his brother Henry, editor of the leading Republican newspaper in Ohio, the *Ohio State Journal*, were good friends of U.S. Senator Salmon P. Chase. Chase, a veteran leader of the antislavery movement, had lost the Republican presidential nomination in 1860 to Abraham Lincoln. The Cookes then determined to feather their nest by lobbying to make Salmon Chase Secretary of the Treasury. After extensive lobbying by the Cookes, the Chase appointment was secured, after which Jay Cooke quickly set up his own investment banking house of Jay Cooke & Co.

Everything was in place; it now remained to seize the opportunity. As the Cookes' father wrote of Henry: "I took up my pen principally to say that H.D.'s (Henry) plan in getting Chase into the Cabinet and (John) Sherman into the Senate is accomplished, and that now is the time for making money, by honest contracts out of the government."[1]

---

[1]In Henrietta Larson, *Jay Cooke, Private Banker* (Cambridge, Mass.: Harvard University Press, 1936), p. 103.

Now indeed was their time for making money, and Cooke lost no time in seizing the advantage. After wining and dining his old friend, Cooke was able to induce Chase to take an unprecedented step in the fall of 1862: granting the House of Cooke a monopoly on the underwriting of the public debt. Cooke promptly hurled himself into the task of persuading the mass of the public to buy U.S. government bonds. In doing so, Cooke perhaps invented the art of public relations and of mass propaganda; certainly he did so in the realm of selling bonds. As Edward Kirkland, author of *Industry Comes of Age: Business Labor & Public Policy 1860–1897*, writes:

> With characteristic optimism, he [Cooke] flung himself into a bond crusade. He recruited a small army of 2,500 sub-agents among bankers, insurance men, and community leaders and kept them inspired and informed by mail and telegraph. He taught the American people to buy bonds, using lavish advertising in newspapers, broadsides, and posters. God, destiny, duty, courage, patriotism—all summoned "Farmers, Mechanics, and Capitalists" to invest in loans.[2]

Loans which of course they had to purchase from Jay Cooke.

And purchase the loans they did, for Cooke's bond sales soon reached the enormous figure of $1 to $2 million a day. Approximately $2 billion in bonds were bought and underwritten by Jay Cooke during the war. Cooke lost his monopoly in 1864, under pressure of rival bankers; but a year later he was reappointed to that highly lucrative post, keeping it until the House of Cooke crashed in the Panic of 1873.

It is not surprising that Jay Cooke acquired enormous political influence in the Republican administrations of the Civil War and after. Hugh McCulloch, Secretary of the Treasury from 1865 to 1869, was a close friend of Cooke's, and when McCulloch left

---

[2]Edward C. Kirkland, *Industry Comes of Age: Business, Labor & Public Policy, 1860–1897* (New York: Holt, Rinehart & Winston, 1961), pp. 20–21.

The Mystery of Banking

office he became head of Cooke's London office. The Cooke brothers were also good friends of General Grant, and so they wielded great influence during the Grant administration.

No sooner had Cooke secured the monopoly of government bond underwriting than he teamed up with his associates Secretary of the Treasury Chase and Ohio's Senator John Sherman to drive through a measure destined to have far more fateful effects than greenbacks on the American monetary system: the National Banking Acts. National banking destroyed the previous decentralized and fairly successful state banking system, and substituted a new, centralized and far more inflationary banking system under the aegis of Washington and a handful of Wall Street banks. Whereas the greenbacks were finally eliminated by the resumption of specie payments in 1879, the effects of the national banking system are still with us. Not only was this system in place until 1913, but it paved the way for the Federal Reserve System by instituting a quasi-central banking type of monetary system. The "inner contradictions" of the national banking system impelled the U.S. either to go on to a frankly central bank or to scrap centralized banking altogether and go back to decentralized state banking. Given the inner dynamic of state intervention, coupled with the common adoption of a statist ideology after the turn of the twentieth century, the course the nation would take was unfortunately inevitable.

Chase and Sherman drove the new system through under cover of the war necessity: setting up national banks to purchase large amounts of U.S. government bonds. Patterned after the free banking system, the nation's banks were tied in a symbiotic relationship with the federal government and the public debt. The Jacksonian independent treasury was *de facto* swept away, and the Treasury would now keep its deposits in a new series of "pets": the national banks, chartered directly by the federal government. In this way, the Republican Party was able to use the wartime emergency, marked by the virtual disappearance of Democrats from Congress, to fulfill the long-standing Whig-Republican dream of a permanently centralized banking system, able to inflate the supply of money and credit in a uniform manner. Sherman conceded that a vital object of the national banking system was to eradicate the doctrine of state's rights, and to nationalize American politics.

The Cooke-Chase connection with the new national banking system was simple but crucial. As Secretary of the Treasury, Salmon Chase wanted an assured market for the government bonds that were being issued heavily during the Civil War. And as the monopoly underwriter of U.S. government bonds for every year but one from 1862 to 1873, Jay Cooke was even more directly interested in an assured and expanding market for his bonds. What better method of obtaining such a market than creating an entirely new banking system, in which expansion was directly tied to the banks' purchase of government bonds—and all from Jay Cooke?

The Cooke brothers played a major role in driving the National Banking Act of 1863 through a reluctant Congress. The Democrats, devoted to hard money, opposed the legislation almost to a man. Only a narrow majority of Republicans could be induced to agree to the bill. After John Sherman's decisive speech in the Senate in favor of the measure, Henry Cooke—now head of the Washington office of the House of Cooke—wrote jubilantly to his brother:

> It will be a great triumph, Jay, and one to which we have contributed more than any other living men. The bank bill had been repudiated by the House, and was without a sponsor in the Senate, and was thus virtually dead and buried when I induced Sherman to take hold of it, and we went to work with the newspapers.[3]

Going to work with the newspapers meant something more than gentle persuasion for the Cooke brothers. For as monopoly underwriter of government bonds, Cooke was paying the

---

[3]Quoted in Robert P. Sharkey, *Money, Class and Party: An Economic Study of Civil War and Reconstruction* (Baltimore: Johns Hopkins Press, 1959), p. 245.

newspapers large sums for advertising, and so the Cookes realized that they could induce the newspapers to grant them an enormous amount of free space "in which to set forth the merits of the new national banking system." Such space meant not only publicity and articles, but more important, the fervent editorial support of most of the nation's press. And so the press, virtually bought for the occasion, kept up a drumroll of propaganda for the new national banking system. As Cooke himself related: "For six weeks or more nearly all the newspapers in the country were filled with our editorials condemning the state bank system and explaining the great benefits to be derived from the national banking system now proposed." And every day the indefatigable Cookes put on the desks of every Congressman the relevant editorials from newspapers in their respective districts.[4]

As established in the bank acts of 1863 and 1864, national banks could be chartered by the Comptroller of the Currency in Washington, D.C. The banks were free in the sense that anyone meeting the legal requirements could obtain a charter, but the requirements were severe. For one thing, the minimum capital requirements were so high—from $50,000 for rural banks to $200,000 in the bigger cities—that small national banks could not be established, particularly in the large cities.

The national banking system created three sets of national banks: *central reserve city*, which was then only New York; *reserve city*, for other cities with over 500,000 population; and *country*, which included all other national banks.

Central reserve city banks were required to keep 25 percent of their notes and deposits in reserve of vault cash of *lawful money*, which included gold, silver, and greenbacks. This provision incorporated the reserve requirement concept which had been a feature of the free banking system. Reserve city banks, on the other hand, were allowed to keep one-half of their required

---

[4]See Bray Hammond, *Sovereignty and an Empty Purse: Banks and Politics in the Civil War* (Princeton, N.J.: Princeton University Press, 1970), pp. 289–90.

reserves in vault cash, while the other half could be kept as demand deposits in central reserve city banks. Finally, country banks only had to keep a minimum reserve ratio of 15 percent to their notes and deposits; and only 40 percent of these reserves had to be in the form of vault cash. The other 60 percent of the country banks reserves could be in the form of demand deposits either at the reserve city or central reserve city banks.

In short, the individualized structure of the pre-Civil War state banking system was replaced by an inverted pyramid of country banks expanding on top of reserve city banks, which in turn expanded on top of New York City banks. Before the Civil War, every bank had to keep its own specie reserves, and any pyramiding of notes and deposits on top of specie was severely limited by calls for redemption in specie by other, competing banks as well as by the general public. But now, all the national banks in the country would pyramid in two layers on top of the relatively small base of reserves in the New York banks. Furthermore, these reserves could consist of inflated greenbacks as well as specie.

The national banks were not compelled to keep part of their reserves as deposits in larger banks, but they tended to do so. They could then expand uniformly on top of the larger banks, and they enjoyed the advantages of having a line of credit with a larger "correspondent" bank as well as earning interest in demand deposits at their bank.[5]

Furthermore, in a way pioneered by the free banking system, every national bank's expansion of notes was tied intimately to its ownership of U.S. government bonds. Every bank could issue notes only if it deposited an equivalent in U.S. securities as collateral with the U.S. Treasury. Hence national banks could only expand their notes to the extent that they purchased U.S. government bonds. This provision tied the national banking system closely to the federal government's expansion of public debt. The

---

[5]Banks generally paid interest on demand deposits until the Federal Government outlawed the practice in 1934.

federal government had an assured, built-in market for its debt, and the more the banks purchased that debt, the more the banking system could inflate.

The pyramiding process was spurred by several other provisions of the National Banking Act. Every national bank was compelled to redeem the obligations of every other national bank at par. This provision erased a severe free market limit on the circulation of inflated notes and deposits: depreciation increasing as one got farther away from the headquarters of the bank. And while the federal government could scarcely make the notes of a private bank legal tender, it conferred quasi-legal tender status on the national banks by agreeing to receive their notes and deposits at par for dues and taxes. And yet, despite these enormous advantages granted by the federal government, national bank notes fell below par with greenbacks in the crises of 1867, and a number of national banks failed that year.[6]

While national banks were required to redeem the notes and deposits of each other at par, the requirement was made more difficult to meet by the government's continuing to make branch banking illegal. Branch banking would have provided a swift method for banks calling on each other for redemption in cash. But, perhaps as a way of blocking such redemption, interstate, and even more, intrastate, banking continued to be illegal. A bank was only required to redeem its own notes at its home office, making redemption still more difficult. Furthermore, the redemption of notes was crippled by the federal government's imposing a maximum limit of $3 million a month by which national bank notes could be contracted.[7] In addition, limits which had been imposed on the issue of national bank notes were removed in 1875, after several years of the banks' straining at the maximum legal limit.

Furthermore, in June 1874, the structure of the national banking system was changed. Congress, in an inflationist move

---

[6]See Smith, *Rationale of Central Banking*, p. 48.

[7]See ibid., p. 132.

after the Panic of 1873, eliminated all reserve requirements on notes, keeping them only on deposits. This action released over $20 million of lawful money from bank reserves and allowed a further pyramiding of demand liabilities. The result was a separation of notes from deposits, with notes tied rigidly to bank holdings of government debt, while demand deposits pyramided on top of reserve ratios in specie and greenbacks.

Reserve requirements are now considered a sound and precise way to limit bank credit expansion, but the precision can cut two ways. Just as government safety codes can *decrease* safety by setting a lower limit for safety measures and inducing private firms to reduce safety downward to that common level, so reserve requirements can serve as lowest common denominators for bank reserve ratios. Free competition, on the other hand, will generally result in banks voluntarily keeping higher reserve ratios. Banks now keep fully loaned up, expanding to the limit imposed by the legal reserve ratio. Reserve requirements are more an inflationary than a restrictive monetary device.

The national banking system was intended to replace the state banks completely, but many state banks refused to join as members, despite the special privileges accorded to the national banks. The reserve and capital requirements for state banks were more onerous, and national banks were prohibited from making loans on real estate. With the state banks refusing to come to heel voluntarily, Congress, in March 1865, completed the Civil War revolution of the banking system by placing a prohibitive 10 percent tax upon all state bank notes. The tax virtually outlawed all note issues by the state banks. From 1865 national banks had a legal monopoly to issue bank notes.

At first, the state banks contracted and withered under the shock, and it looked as if the United States would indeed have only national banks. The number of state banks fell from 1,466 in 1863 to 297 in 1866, and total notes and deposits in state banks fell from $733 million in 1863 to only $101 million in 1866. After several years, however, the state banks began expanding again, albeit in a role subordinated to the national banks. In order to survive, the state banks had to keep deposit accounts at national banks, from whom they could "buy" national bank notes in order to redeem their deposits. In short, the state banks now became the fourth layer of the national pyramid of money and credit, on top of the country and the other national banks. The reserves of the state banks were kept, in addition to vault cash, as demand deposits at national banks, from whom they could redeem in cash. The multilayered structure of bank inflation under the national banking system was now compounded.

Once the national banking system was in place, Jay Cooke plunged in with a will. He not only sold the national banks their required bonds, but he himself set up new national banks which would have to buy his government securities. His agents formed national banks in the smaller towns of the South and West. Furthermore, he set up his own national banks, the First National Bank of Philadelphia and the First National Bank of Washington, D.C.

But the national banking system was in great need of a powerful bank in New York City to serve as the base of the inflationary pyramid for the country and reserve city banks. Shortly after the start of the system, three national banks had been organized in New York, but none of them was large or prestigious enough to serve as the fulcrum of the new banking structure. Jay Cooke, however, was happy to step into the breach, and he quickly established the Fourth National Bank of New York, capitalized at an enormous $5 million. After the war, Cooke favored resumption of specie payments, but only if greenbacks could be replaced one-to-one by new national bank notes. In his unbounded enthusiasm for national bank notes and their dependence on the federal debt, Cooke, in 1865, published a pamphlet proclaiming that in less than 20 years national bank note circulation would total $1 billion.[8] The title of Cooke's pamphlet is revealing: *How our*

---

[8]Actually, Cooke erred, and national bank notes never reached that total. Instead, it was demand deposits that expanded, and reached the billion dollar mark by 1879.

National Debt May Be a National Blessing. The Debt is Public Wealth, Political Union, Protection of Industry, Secure Basis for National Currency.[9]

2. THE NATIONAL BANKING ERA AND THE ORIGINS OF THE FEDERAL RESERVE SYSTEM

After the Civil War, the number of banks and the total of national bank notes and deposits all expanded and, after 1870, state banks began to expand as deposit creating institutions pyramiding on top of the national banks. The number of national banks increased from 1,294 in 1865 to 1,968 in 1873, while the number of state banks rose from 349 to 1,330 in the same period.

As a summary of the national banking era, we can agree with John Klein that

> The financial panics of 1873, 1884, 1893, and 1907 were in large part an outgrowth of . . . reserve pyramiding and excessive deposit creation by reserve city and central reserve city banks. These panics were triggered by the currency drains that took place in periods of relative prosperity when banks were loaned up.[10]

The major effect of the Panic of 1873 was to cause bankruptcies among overinflated banks and in railroads that had ridden the tide of vast government subsidy and bank speculation. In particular, we may note the poetic justice meted out to the extraordinarily powerful Jay Cooke.

By the late 1860s, Cooke had acquired control of the new transcontinental Northern Pacific Railroad. Northern Pacific had received the biggest federal subsidy during the great railroad boom of the 1860s: a land grant of no less than 47 million acres.

Cooke sold Northern Pacific bonds as he had learned to sell government securities: hiring pamphleteers, for example, to write

---

[9]See Sharkey, *Money, Class and Party*, p. 247.

[10]John J. Klein, *Money and the Economy*, 2nd ed. (New York: Harcourt, Brace and World, 1970), pp. 145–46.

propaganda about the alleged Mediterranean climate of the American Northwest. Many leading government officials and politicians were on the Cooke/Northern Pacific payroll, including Rutherford B. Hayes, Vice President Schuyler Colfax, and the private secretary of President Grant, General Horace Porter.

In 1869, Jay Cooke expressed his monetary philosophy in keeping with the grandiose swath he was cutting in American economic and financial life. "Why," he asked,

> should this Grand and Glorious country be stunted and dwarfed—its activities chilled and its very life blood curdled by these miserable "hard coin" theories—the musty theories of a bygone age. These men who are urging on premature resumption know nothing of the great and growing west which would grow twice as fast if it was not cramped for the means . . .

But four years later, the overbuilt Northern Pacific crumbled, and Cooke's government bond operation collapsed. And so the mighty House of Cooke—"stunted and dwarfed" by the market economy—crashed and went bankrupt, igniting the Panic of 1873.[11]

In each of the banking panics after the Civil War, 1873, 1884, 1893, and 1907, there was a general suspension of specie payments. The Panic of 1907 proved to be the most financially acute of them all. The bankers, almost to a man, had long agitated for going further than the national banking system, to go forward frankly and openly, surmounting the inner contradictions of the quasi-centralized system, to a system of central banking.

The bankers found that the helpful cartelization of the national banking system was not sufficient. A central bank, they believed, was needed to provide a *lender of last resort*, a federal governmental Santa Claus who would always stand ready to bail out banks in trouble. Furthermore, a central bank was needed to provide *elasticity* of the money supply. A common complaint by

---

[11]Irwin Unger, *The Greenback Era: A Social and Political History of American Finance, 1865–1879* (Princeton, N.J.: Princeton University Press, 1964), pp. 46–47, 221.

bankers and by economists in the latter part of the national banking era was that the money supply was *inelastic*. In plain English, this meant that there was no governmental mechanism to assure a greater expansion of the money supply—especially during panics and depressions, when banks particularly wished to be bailed out and to avoid contraction. The national banking system was particularly inelastic, since its issue of notes was dependent on the banks' deposit of government bonds at the Treasury. Furthermore, by the end of the nineteenth century, government bonds generally sold on the market at 40 percent over par. This meant that $1,400 worth of gold reserves would have to be sold by the banks to purchase every $1,000 worth of bonds—preventing the banks from expanding their note issues during a recession.[12]

In addition to the chronic desire by the banks to be subsidized and cartelized more effectively, the large Wall Street banks, by the end of the nineteenth century, saw financial control of the nation slipping away. For the state banks and other non-national banks had begun to grow faster and outstrip the nationals. Thus, while most banks were national in the 1870s and 1880s, by 1896 non-national banks constituted 61 percent of the total number, and by 1913, 71 percent. By 1896, moreover, the non-national banks held 54 percent of the total banking resources of the country, and this proportion had grown to 57 percent by 1913. The inclusion of Chicago and St. Louis as central reserve cities after 1887 further diluted Wall Street's power. With Wall Street losing control and no longer able to cope, it was time to turn to the United States government to do the centralizing and cartelizing with Wall Street exerting effective control of the monetary system through the power of Washington.[13]

---

[12]On agitation by bankers and others for the substitution of a central bank for the national banking system, see among others, Robert Craig West, *Banking Reform and the Federal Reserve, 1863–1923* (Ithaca, N.Y.: Cornell University Press, 1977).

[13]See Gabriel Kolko, *The Triumph of Conservatism: A Reinterpretation of American History, 1900–1916* (Glencoe, Ill.: The Free Press, 1963), p. 140.

In addition to the bankers, economists, and businessmen, politicians and political parties were all ripe for a shift to a central banking system. Economists participated in the general intellectual shift in the late nineteenth century from *laissez-faire*, hard money, and minimal government to the new concepts of statism and big government imbibed from Bismarck's Germany. The new collectivist spirit became known as *progressivism*, an ideology also embraced by businessmen and politicians. Having failed to achieve monopoly positions on the free market, big businessmen, after 1900, turned to the states and especially to the federal government to do the subsidizing and cartelizing on their behalf. Not only that: The Democratic Party in 1896 lost its century-long status as the champion of *laissez-faire* and hard money. For statists and inflationists under William Jennings Bryan captured the Democratic Party at its 1896 presidential convention. With the disappearance of the Democratic Party as the libertarian party in American life, both parties soon fell under the statist, progressive spell. A new era was under way, with virtually no one left to oppose the juggernaut.[14]

The growing consensus among the bankers was to transform the American banking system by establishing a central bank. That bank would have an absolute monopoly of note issue and reserve requirements and would then insure a multilayered pyramiding

---

[14]In addition to Kolko, *Triumph of Conservatism*, see James Weinstein, *The Corporate Ideal in The Liberal State, 1900–1918* (Boston: Beacon Press, 1968). On the new collectivist intellectuals, see James Gilbert, *Designing the Industrial State: The Intellectual Pursuit of Collectivism in America, 1880–1940* (Chicago: Quadrangle Books, 1972); and Frank Tariello, Jr., *The Reconstruction of American Political Ideology, 1865–1917* (Charlottesville: University Press of Virginia, 1981). On the transformation of the American party system with the Bryan takeover in 1896, see Paul Kleppner, *The Cross of Culture: A Social Analysis of Midwestern Politics, 1850–1900* (New York: The Free Press, 1970), and idem., "From Ethnoreligious Conflict to Social Harmony: Coalitional and Party Transformations in the 1890s," in S. Lipset, ed., *Emerging Coalitions in American Politics* (San Francisco: Institute for Contemporary Studies, 1978), pp. 41–59.

on top of its notes. The Central Bank could bail out banks in trouble and inflate the currency in a smooth, controlled, and uniform manner throughout the nation.

Banking reform along these lines was considered as early as the beginning of the 1890s, and particularly favorable was the American Bankers Association and especially the larger banks. In 1900, President McKinley's Secretary of the Treasury, Lyman J. Gage, suggested the creation of a central bank. Gage was formerly president of the American Bankers Association, and also former president of the First National Bank of Chicago, an organization close to the then-Rockefeller-controlled National City Bank of New York. In 1908, a special committee of the New York Chamber of Commerce, which included Frank A. Vanderlip, president of the National City Bank, called for a new central bank "similar to the Bank of Germany." Similar recommendations were made the same year by a commission of big bankers set up by the American Bankers Association, and headed by A. Barton Hepburn, chairman of the board of the then-Morgan-controlled Chase National Bank.[15]

The Panic of 1907 galvanized the bankers into accelerating proposals for a new banking system. With intellectuals and politicians now sympathetic to a newly centralized statism, there was virtually no opposition to adopting the European system of central banking. The various shifts in plans and proposals reflected a jockeying for power among political and financial groups, eventually resolved in the Federal Reserve Act of 1913, which the Wilson administration pushed through Congress by a large majority.

Amid all the maneuvering for power, perhaps the most interesting event was a secret summit meeting at Jekyll Island, Georgia in December 1910, at which top representatives of the pro-central banking forces met to hammer out an agreement on the essential features of the new plan. The conferees consisted of Senator Nelson W. Aldrich (R., R.I.), a Rockefeller kinsman who had

---

[15]See Kolko, *Triumph of Conservatism*, pp. 146–53.

headed the pro-central banking studies of the Congressionally created National Monetary Commission; Frank A. Vanderlip of Rockefeller's National City Bank; Paul M. Warburg, of the investment banking firm of Kuhn, Loeb & Co., who had emigrated from Germany to bring to the U.S. the blessings of central banking; Henry P. Davison, a partner of J.P. Morgan & Co.; and Charles Norton, of the Morgan-controlled First National Bank of New York. With such powerful interests as the Morgans, the Rockefellers, and Kuhn, Loeb in basic agreement on a new central bank, who could prevail against it?

One particularly ironic note is that two economists who played an especially important role in establishing the Federal Reserve System were highly conservative men who spent the rest of their lives attacking the Fed's inflationary policies (though not, unfortunately, to the extent of repudiating their own roles in creating the Fed). These were University of Chicago professor J. Laurence Laughlin and his former student, then a professor at Washington & Lee University, H. Parker Willis. Laughlin and Willis played a large part, not only in the technical drafting of the bill and the Fed structure, but also as political propagandists for the new central bank.

XVI.

CENTRAL BANKING IN THE UNITED STATES IV: THE FEDERAL RESERVE SYSTEM

1. THE INFLATIONARY STRUCTURE OF THE FED

The new Federal Reserve System was deliberately designed as an engine of inflation, the inflation to be controlled and kept uniform by the central bank. In the first place, the banking system was transformed so that only the Federal Reserve Banks could print paper notes. The member banks, no longer able to print cash, could only *buy* it from the Fed by drawing down deposit accounts at the Fed. The different reserve requirements for central reserve city, reserve city, and country banks were preserved, but the Fed was now the single base of the entire banking pyramid. Gold was expected to be centralized at the Fed, and now the Fed could pyramid its deposits 2.86:1 on top of gold, and its notes 2.5:1 on top of gold. (That is, its reserve requirements were: 35 percent of total demand deposits/gold, and 40

percent of its notes/gold.)[1] Thus, since gold reserves were centralized from the national banks to the Fed, it could pyramid further
on top of them. All national banks were forced to become members of the Federal Reserve System, while state banks had a voluntary choice; but nonmembers could be controlled because, in
order to get cash for their customers, they had to keep deposit
accounts with member banks who had access to the Fed.

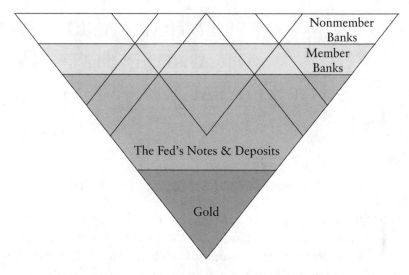

FIG. 16.1 — THE FEDERAL RESERVE PYRAMID

Figure 16.1 depicts the new inverted pyramid created by the
Federal Reserve System in 1913. Nonmember banks pyramid on
top of member banks, which in turn pyramid on top of the Fed,
which pyramids its notes and deposits on top of its centralized
gold hoard. The new central bank, being an arm of the federal

---

[1]Since the establishment of the Federal Reserve System, the reserve
requirement limits on the Fed itself have been progressively weakened, until
now there is no statutory limit whatsoever on the Fed's desire to inflate.

government, carries the great prestige of that status, and also has a legal monopoly on the issue of notes.

How this reserve centralization was designed to be inflationary was pointed out by Phillips, McManus, and Nelson:

> Suppose the total cash reserves of all commercial banks prior to the introduction of central banking amounted to one billion dollars; on the basis of these reserves, and with an assumed minimum reserve-deposit ratio of 10 per cent, the banking system could expand credit to the extent of 10 billion dollars. Now, suppose that the Federal Reserve System is established, and all reserves are transferred to the vaults of the new Reserve Banks, where they become deposits to the credit of (and at the same time are counted as the reserves for) the member banks. Against this billion dollars of deposits the Reserve Banks must maintain a minimum cash reserve of 35 per cent, or 350 million dollars. The remainder of the billion dollars of cash, 650 million dollars, becomes excess reserve for the Reserve Banks. On the basis of such excess reserves the Reserve Banks are able to increase their deposits, and hence the new reserves of the member banks, by the maximum amount of about $1.9 billion . . . .
>
> In other words, the Federal Reserve Banks now have 2.9 billion dollars in deposits to the credit of the member institutions (against which they have the one billion dollars as a reserve, or a reserve ratio of 35 per cent), or conversely, the member banks now have 2.9 billion dollars in legal reserves, on the basis of which it is possible for them to expand credit to a total amount of 29 billion dollars. By virtue of the possession of this new, added, reserve of 1.9 billion dollars . . . the member banks can now add 19 billion dollars new credit to the antecedently existing 10 billion dollars.[2]

---

[2]C.A. Phillips, T.F. McManus, and R.W. Nelson, *Banking and the Business Cycle* (New York: Macmillan, 1937), pp. 26–27. In fact, the inflationary potential of the new centralization was not as great as this, since the previous national banking system was not fully decentralized, but had already been quasi-centralized to pyramid on top of a handful of Wall Street banks.

But this was scarcely the only aspect of inflation built into the structure of the Federal Reserve System. At the beginning of the Fed in 1913, the most important single item of paper money in circulation was the gold certificate, held by the Fed and backed 100 percent by gold assets in the Treasury. But in a few years, the Fed adopted the policy of withdrawing gold certificates from circulation and substituting Federal Reserve Notes. But since the FRN only had to be backed 40 percent by gold certificates, this meant that 60 percent of the released gold was available as a base on which to pyramid a multiple of bank money.

In addition, as part of the creation of the Federal Reserve System, the previous reserve requirements were cut approximately *in half,* thereby allowing for a doubling of demand deposits. The average reserve requirement of all banks before the establishment of the Fed was 21.1 percent. Under the provisions of the original Federal Reserve Act in 1913, this requirement was cut to 11.6 percent, and it was cut further to 9.8 percent in June 1917.[3] It is no accident that the Fed, as a result, was able to engineer a doubling of the money supply from its inception at the end of 1913 until the end of 1919. Total bank demand deposits rose from $9.7 billion in June 1914 to $19.1 billion in January 1920, while the total currency and demand deposits increased from $11.5 billion to $23.3 billion in the same period. Furthermore, the impetus from the Fed is shown by the fact that nonmember bank deposits expanded by only one-third over these six years, whereas member bank deposits increased by 250 percent.

Another inflationary step taken at the origin of the Federal Reserve System was, for the first time, to drastically reduce the reserve requirements on time or *savings* deposits as compared to *demand* deposits. During the era of the national banking system, the reserve requirement, averaging 21.1 percent, applied equally to time or demand deposits. The original Federal Reserve Act greatly reduced the reserve requirements on time deposits of

---

[3]Phillips, et al., *Banking and the Business Cycle*, p. 23n.

commercial banks to 5 percent, and in 1917 it was further lowered to 3 percent.

It is true that if a deposit is a genuine time or savings deposit,
then it is in no sense part of the money supply, and therefore
needs no reserve requirement (assuming that monetary liabilities
should have such requirements). But any *creation* of time deposits
through the making of a loan is deeply suspect as not a time
deposit at all, but rather a crypto-demand deposit. With the drastic reduction of reserve requirements on time deposits upon the
inception of the Fed, the commercial banks had an enormous
incentive to shift borrowers into time deposits, and thereby inflate
further. And, indeed, that is precisely what happened after 1913
and during the 1920s. Deposits that were legally time deposits and
only due in 30 days were really *de facto* demand deposits.

The Federal Reserve staff itself admitted that, during the
1920s,

> there developed a tendency to induce depositors to transfer
> their funds from checking accounts to savings accounts.
> Banks frequently not only allowed such a transfer but
> encouraged it in order to take advantage of lower reserves
> and to obtain a large basis for credit expansion. . . . In many
> cases, particularly in large centers, the aspect of savings was
> impaired by allowing depositors to draw a limited number
> of checks against time deposits.[4]

Time deposits expanded more rapidly than demand deposits
from the outset of the Federal Reserve System. From June 1914
to January 1920, when demand deposits were growing from $9.7
billion to $19.1 billion, or 96.9 percent, time deposits at commer-
cial banks rose from $4.6 billion to $10.4 billion, or 126.1 percent. Then, in the great boom of the 1920s, starting after the recession of 1920–21, total demand deposits rose from $16.7 billion in
July 1921 to $22.8 billion eight years later, in July 1929, an

---

[4]Quoted in M. Friedman and A. Schwartz, *A Monetary History of the
United States 1867–1960* (Princeton N.J.: National Bureau of Economic
Research, 1963), pp. 276–77. Also ibid., p. 277n. See also Phillips, et al.,
Banking and the Business Cycle, pp. 29, 95–101.

increase of 36.5 percent. On the other hand, time deposits in commercial banks expanded from $11.2 billion to $19.7 billion in the same period, a far greater rise of 75.9 percent. The great boom of the 1920s was largely fueled by credit expansion going into time deposits.

Furthermore, Phillips, McManus, and Nelson point out that by far the greatest expansion of time deposits came in Central Reserve Cities (New York and Chicago), where the Fed's open market operations were all conducted. Central Reserve City time deposits rose by 232 percent from December 1921 to December 1929; whereas Reserve City time deposits rose by 132 percent and Country Banks time deposits by 77 percent in the same period. Moreover, most of the rise in time deposits occurred in the three years 1922, 1925, and 1927—precisely the three big years of open market purchases by the Federal Reserve, and hence of creation of new bank reserves by the Fed. Significantly, these facts show that time deposits in the 1920s were not genuine savings, but merely a convenient means by which the commercial banks expanded on top of new reserves generated by open market operations of the Fed.

Phillips, McManus, and Nelson describe the process as follows:

> Chronologically and causally, the order of developments was as follows: Federal Reserve open-market purchases resulted in expansion of member bank reserve balances; this served to instigate increased purchases of investments by the member banks; and the credit generated thereby took the form largely of time deposits. The Reserve Banks pumped credit into the money market, inducing increased reserve to purchase investments . . . which created more deposits in the banking system, and the increased deposits, being unneeded by business men and corporations as demand deposits for current transactions, were shifted to time deposits which could draw interest.[5]

---

[5]Phillips, et al., *Banking and the Business Cycle*, p. 99. On time deposits in the 1920s, see also Murray N. Rothbard, *America's Great Depression*, 3rd

That time or savings deposits were, for all practical purposes, equivalent to demand deposits was noted by Governor George L. Harrison, head of the Federal Reserve Bank of New York, who testified in 1931 that any bank suffering a run must pay both its demand and savings deposits on demand. Any attempt to enforce the official 30-day notice for redemption would probably cause the state or the federal Comptroller of the Currency to close the bank immediately. In fact, the heavy bank runs of 1931–33 took place in time as well as demand deposits. The head of the National City Bank of New York at the time agreed that "no commercial bank could afford to invoke the right to delay payment on these time deposits."[6]

2. THE INFLATIONARY POLICIES OF THE FED

A deeply inflationary structure understandably sets the stage for inflationary policies. Policies are enacted and carried forward by particular people, and so we must examine the controlling groups, and the motivations and procedures for carrying out monetary expansion after the launching of the Federal Reserve. We know in general that the bankers, especially the large ones, were using the federal government as a cartelizing and inflationary device. But what of the specifics? *Which* bankers?

With the passage of the Federal Reserve Act, President Wilson in 1914 appointed one Benjamin Strong to what was then the most powerful post in the Federal Reserve System. Strong was made Governor of the Federal Reserve Bank of New York, and he quickly made this position dominant in the System, autocratically

---

ed. (Sheed and Ward, 1974), pp. 92–94; Benjamin M. Anderson, *Economics and the Public Welfare: A Financial and Economic History of the United States, 1914–46*, 2nd ed. (Indianapolis: Liberty Press, 1979), pp. 140–42.

[6]Quoted in Rothbard, *America's Great Depression*, p. 316n. See also Lin Lin, "Are Time Deposits Money?" *American Economic Review* (March 1937): 76–86. Lin points out that demand and time deposits were interchangeable at par and in cash, and were so regarded by the public.

deciding on Fed policy without consulting or even against the wishes of the Federal Reserve Board in Washington. Strong continued to be the dominant leader of the Fed from 1914 until his death in 1928.

Strong pursued an inflationary policy throughout his reign, first during World War I, and then in spurts of expansion of bank reserves in the early 1920s, 1924, and 1927. While it is true that wholesale prices did not rise, they were prevented from falling from increases of capital investment, productivity, and the supply of goods during the 1920s. The expansion of money and credit generated by the Fed during the 1920s kept prices artificially high, and created an unhealthy boom and investments in capital goods and construction, and in such capital title markets as stocks and real estate. It was only the end of the monetary expansion after Strong's death that brought an end to the boom and ushered in a recession—a recession that was made into chronic depression by massive interference by Presidents Hoover and Roosevelt.

But who was Strong and why did he pursue these inflationary and eventually disastrous policies? In the first place, it must be understood that, like other bureaucrats and political leaders, he did not emerge full-blown out of the thin air in 1914. At the time of his appointment, Strong was head of the Morgan-created Bankers' Trust Company in New York—a bank set up by the Morgans to concentrate on the new field of the trusts. Tempted at first to refuse this high office, Strong was persuaded to take the job by his two closest friends: Henry P. Davison, partner at J.P. Morgan & Co., and Dwight Morrow, another Morgan partner. Yet a third Morgan partner, and another close friend, Thomas W. Lamont, also helped persuade Strong to take up this task. Strong was also an old friend of Elihu Root, statesman and Wall Street corporate lawyer, who had long been in the Morgan ambit, serving as personal attorney for J.P. Morgan himself.

It is not too much to say, therefore, that Strong was a Morgan man, and that his inflationary actions in office accorded with the Morgan outlook. Without the inflationary activity of the Federal Reserve, for example, the United States could not have entered and fought in World War I. The House of Morgan was hip-deep in the Allied cause from 1914 on. Morgan was the fiscal agent for the Bank of England, and enjoyed the monopoly underwriting of all British and French bonds in the United States during World War I. Not only that: J.P. Morgan & Co. was the financier for much of the munitions factories that exported weapons and war materiel to the Allied nations.

Morgan's railroads were in increasingly grave financial trouble, and 1914 saw the collapse of Morgan's $400 million New Haven Railroad. Concentrating on railroads and a bit laggard in moving into industrial finance, Morgan had seen its dominance in investment banking slip since the turn of the century. Now, World War I had come as a godsend to Morgan's fortunes, and Morgan prosperity was intimately wrapped up in the Allied cause.

It is no wonder that Morgan partners took the lead in whipping up pro-British and French propaganda in the United States; and to clamor for the U.S. to enter the war on the Allied side. Henry E. Davison set up the Aerial Coast Patrol in 1915, and Willard Straight and Robert Bacon, both Morgan partners, took the lead in organizing the Businessman's Training Camp at Plattsburgh, New York, to urge universal conscription. Elihu Root and Morgan himself were particularly active in pressing for entering the war on the Allied side. Furthermore, President Wilson was surrounded by Morgan people. His son-in-law, Secretary of the Treasury, William G. McAdoo, had been rescued from financial bankruptcy by Morgan. Colonel Edward M. House, Wilson's mysterious and powerful foreign policy adviser, was connected with Morgan railroads in Texas. McAdoo wrote to Wilson that war exports to the Allies would bring "great prosperity" to the United States, so that loans to the Allies to finance such exports had become necessary.[7]

---

[7]On the role of the Morgans in pushing the Wilson administration into war, see Charles Callan Tansill, *America Goes to War* (Boston: Little, Brown and Co., 1938), chaps. II–IV.

Strong pursued his inflationary policies during the 1920s, largely to help Great Britain escape the consequences of its own disastrous inflationary program. During World War I, all the European countries had inflated greatly to pay for the war, and so were forced to go off the gold standard. Even the United States, in the war for only half the duration of the other warring powers, in effect suspended the gold standard during the war.

After the war, Great Britain, the major world power and in control of the League of Nations's financial and economic policies, made the fateful decision to go back to the gold standard at a highly overvalued par for the pound. Britain wished to regain the prestige it had earned under the gold standard but without paying the price of maintaining a noninflationary sound money policy. It stubbornly insisted on going back to gold at the old prewar par of approximately $4.86, a rate far too high for the postwar pound depreciated by inflation. At one point after the war, the pound had sunk to $3.40 on the foreign exchange market. But, determined to return to gold at $4.86, Great Britain persuaded the other European countries at the Genoa Conference of 1922 to go back, not to a genuine gold standard, but to a phony *gold exchange* standard. Instead of each nation issuing currency directly redeemable in gold, it was to keep its reserves in the form of sterling balances in London, which in turn would undertake to redeem sterling in gold. In that way, other countries would pyramid their currencies on top of pounds, and pounds themselves were being inflated throughout the 1920s. Britain could then print pounds without worrying about the accumulated sterling balances being redeemed in gold.

The overvalued pound meant that Britain was chronically depressed during the 1920s, since its crucial export markets suffered permanently from artificially high prices in terms of the pound. Britain might have overcome this problem by massive monetary deflation, thereby lowering its prices and making its exports more competitive. But Britain wanted to inflate not deflate, and so it tried to shore up its structure by concocting a gold exchange standard, and by going back to a gold *bullion* rather than gold coin standard, so that only large traders could actually redeem paper money or deposits in gold. In addition, Britain induced other European countries to go back to gold themselves at overvalued pars, thereby discouraging their own exports and stimulating imports from Britain.

After a few years, however, sterling balances piled up so high in the accounts of other countries that the entire jerry-built international monetary structure of the 1920s had to come tumbling down. Britain had some success with the European countries, which it could pressure or even coerce into going along with the Genoa system. But what of the United States? That country was too powerful to coerce, and the danger to Britain's inflationary policy of the 1920s was that it would lose gold to the U.S. and thereby be forced to contract and explode the bubble it had created.

It seemed that the only hope was to persuade the United States to inflate as well so that Britain would no longer lose much gold to the U.S. That task of persuasion was performed brilliantly by the head of the Bank of England, Montagu Norman, the architect of the Genoa system. Norman developed a close friendship with Strong and would sail periodically to the United States *incognito* and engage in secret conferences with Strong, where unbeknown to anyone else, Strong would agree to another jolt of inflation in the United States in order to "help England." None of these consultations was reported to the Federal Reserve Board in Washington. In addition, Strong and Norman kept in close touch by a weekly exchange of foreign cables. Strong admitted to his assistant in 1928 that "very few people indeed realized that we were now paying the penalty for the decision which was reached early in 1924 to help the rest of the world back to a sound financial and monetary basis"—that is, to help Britain maintain a phony and inflationary form of gold standard.[8]

---

[8]O. Ernest Moore to Sir Arthur Salter, May 25, 1928. Quoted in Rothbard, *America's Great Depression*, p. 143. In the fall of 1926, a leading banker admitted that bad consequences would follow the Strong cheap money policy, but asserted "that cannot be helped. It is the price we must

Why did Strong do it? Why did he allow Montagu Norman to lead him around by the nose and to follow an unsound policy in order to shore up Britain's unsound monetary structure? Some historians have speculated that Norman exerted a Svengali-like personal influence over the New Yorker. It is more plausible, however, to look at the common Morgan connection between the two central bankers. J.P. Morgan & Co., as we have seen, was the fiscal agent for the Bank of England and for the British government. Norman himself had longtime personal and family ties with New York international bankers. He had worked for several years as a young man in the New York office of Brown Brothers & Co., and he was a former partner in the associated London investment banking firm of Brown, Shipley & Co. Norman's grandfather, in fact, had been a partner in Brown, Shipley, and in Brown Brothers. In this case, as in many others, it is likely that the ties that bound the two men were mainly financial.

---

pay for helping Europe." H. Parker Willis, "The Failure of the Federal Reserve," *North American Review* (1929): 553.

XVII.

CONCLUSION: THE PRESENT BANKING SITUATION AND WHAT TO DO ABOUT IT

1. THE ROAD TO THE PRESENT

With the Federal Reserve System established and in place after 1913, the remainder of the road to the present may be quickly sketched. After Fed inflation led to the boom of the 1920s and the bust of 1929, well-founded public distrust of all the banks, including the Fed, led to widespread demands for redemption of bank deposits in cash, and even of Federal Reserve notes in gold. The Fed tried frantically to inflate after the 1929 crash, including massive open market purchases and heavy loans to banks. These attempts succeeded in driving interest rates down, but they foundered on the rock of massive distrust of the banks. Furthermore, bank fears of runs as well as bankruptcies by their borrowers led them to pile up excess reserves in a manner not seen before or since the 1930s.

Finally, the Roosevelt administration in 1933 took America off the gold standard domestically, so that within the United States the dollar was now fiat paper printed by the Federal Reserve. The dollar was debased, its definition in terms of gold being changed from 1/20 to 1/35 gold ounce. The dollar remained on the gold standard internationally, with dollars redeemable to foreign governments and central banks at the newly debased weight. American citizens were forbidden to own gold, and private citizens' stocks of gold were confiscated by the U.S. government under cover of the depression emergency. That gold continues to lie buried at Fort Knox and in other depositories provided by the U.S. Treasury.

Another fateful Roosevelt act of 1933 was to provide federal guarantee of bank deposits through the Federal Deposit Insurance Corporation. From that point on, bank runs, and bank fears thereof, have virtually disappeared. Only a dubious hope of Fed restraint now remains to check bank credit inflation.

The Fed's continuing inflation of the money supply in the 1930s only succeeded in inflating prices without getting the United States out of the Great Depression. The reason for the chronic depression was that, for the first time in American history, President Herbert Hoover, followed closely and on a larger scale by Franklin Roosevelt, intervened massively in the depression process. Before 1929, every administration had allowed the recession process to do its constructive and corrective work as quickly as possible, so that recovery generally arrived in a year or less. But now, Hoover and Roosevelt intervened heavily: to force businesses to keep up wage rates; to lend enormous amounts of federal money to try to keep unsound businesses afloat; to provide unemployment relief; to expand public works; to inflate money and credit; to support farm prices; and to engage in federal deficits. This massive government intervention prolonged the recession indefinitely, changing what would have been a short, swift recession into a chronic debilitating depression.

Franklin Roosevelt not only brought us a chronic and massive depression; he also managed to usher in the inflationary boom of

1933–37 *within* a depression. This first inflationary depression in history was the forerunner of the inflationary recessions (or "stagflations") endemic to the post-World War II period. Worried about excess reserves piling up in the banks, the Fed suddenly doubled reserve requirements in 1937, precipitating the recession-within-a-depression of 1937–38.

Meanwhile, since only the United States remained on even a partial gold standard, while other countries moved to purely fiat standards, gold began to flow heavily into the United States, an inflow accelerated by the looming war conditions in Europe. The collapse of the shaky and inflationary British-created gold exchange standard during the depression led to a dangerous world of competing and conflicting national currencies and protectionist blocs. Each nation attempted to subsidize exports and restrict imports through competing tariffs, quotas, and currency devaluations.

The pervasive national and regional economic warfare during the 1930s played a major though neglected role in precipitating World War II. After the war was over, Secretary of State Cordell Hull made the revealing comment that

> war did not break out between the United States and any country with which we had been able to negotiate a trade agreement. It is also a fact that, with very few exceptions, the countries with which we signed trade agreements joined together in resisting the Axis. The political lineup follows the economic lineup.[1]

A primary war aim for the United States in World War II was to reconstruct the international monetary system from the conflicting currency blocs of the 1930s into a new form of international gold exchange standard. This new form of gold exchange

---

[1]Cordell Hull, *Memoirs* (New York: Macmillan, 1948), vol. 1, p. 81. See in particular, Murray N. Rothbard, "The New Deal and the International Monetary System," in L. Liggio and J. Martin, eds., *Watershed of Empire: Essays on New Deal Foreign Policy* (Colorado Springs, Colo.: Ralph Myles, 1976), pp. 19–64.

standard, established at an international conference at Bretton
Woods in 1944 by means of great American pressure, closely
resembled the ill-fated British system of the 1920s. The difference
is that world fiat currencies now pyramided on top of dollar
reserves kept in New York instead of sterling reserves kept in London; once again, only the base country, in this case the U.S., continued to redeem its currency in gold.

It took a great deal of American pressure, wielding the club of
Lend–Lease, to persuade the reluctant British to abandon their
cherished currency bloc of the 1930s. By 1942, Hull could expect
confidently that "leadership toward a new system of international
relationship in trade and other economic affairs will devolve very
largely upon the United States because of our great economic
strength. We would assume this leadership, and the responsibility
that goes with it, primarily for reasons of pure national self-interest."[2]

For a while, the economic and financial leaders of the United
States thought that the Bretton Woods system would provide a
veritable bonanza. The Fed could inflate with impunity, for it was
confident that, in contrast with the classical gold standard, dollars
piling up abroad would stay in foreign hands, to be used as
reserves for inflationary pyramiding of currencies by foreign central banks. In that way, the United States dollar could enjoy the
prestige of being backed by gold while not really being
redeemable. Furthermore, U.S. inflation could be lessened by
being "exported" to foreign countries. Keynesian economists in
the United States arrogantly declared that we need not worry
about dollar balances piling up abroad, since there was no chance
of foreigners cashing them in for gold; they were stuck with the
resulting inflation, and the U.S. authorities could treat the international fate of the dollar with "benign neglect."

During the 1950s and 1960s, however, West European countries reversed their previous inflationary policies and came
increasingly under the influence of free market and hard money

[2]Rothbard, "New Deal," p. 52.

authorities. The United States soon became the most inflationist of the major powers. Hard money countries, such as West Germany, France, and Switzerland, increasingly balked at accepting the importation of dollar inflation, and began to accelerate their demands for redemption in gold. Gold increasingly flowed out of the United States and into the coffers of foreign central banks.

As the dollar became more and more inflated, especially relative to the newly sounder currencies of Western Europe, the free gold markets began to doubt the ability of the United States to maintain the cornerstone of the Bretton Woods system: redeemability of the dollar into gold (to foreign central banks) at $35 an ounce. To keep the gold price down to $35, the Treasury began to find it necessary in the 1960s to sell more and more gold for dollars in the free gold markets of London and Zurich. In this way, private citizens of European and other countries (U.S. citizens were not allowed to own any gold) were able to obtain a kind of redeemability for their dollars at $35 an ounce of gold. As continuing inflationary policies of the United States accelerated the hemorrhaging of gold on the London and Zurich markets, the United States began the unraveling of the Bretton Woods system by installing the two-tier gold system of 1968. The idea was that the United States was no longer committed to support the dollar in the free gold markets or to maintain the price at $35 an ounce. A bifurcated gold market was to be constructed: The free market would be left strictly alone by the central banks of the world, and the central banks pledged themselves never to have anything to do with the free gold markets and to continue to settle their mutual foreign balances at $35 an ounce.

The two-tier system only succeeded in buying a little time for the Bretton Woods system. American inflation and gold outflow proceeded apace, despite the pleas of the U.S. that foreign central banks abstain from redeeming their dollars in gold. Pressure to redeem by European central banks led President Nixon, on August 15, 1971, to end Bretton Woods completely and to go off the gold standard internationally and adopt a pure fiat standard. The short-lived and futile Smithsonian Agreement of December

1971 tried to retain fixed exchange rates but without any gold standard—an effort doomed to inevitable failure, which came in March 1973.[3]

Thus, President Nixon in effect declared national bankruptcy and completed the failure to honor commitments to redeem in gold initiated by Franklin Roosevelt in 1933. In the meanwhile, Congress had progressively removed every statutory restriction on the Fed's expansion of reserves and printing of money. Since 1971, therefore, the U.S. government and the Fed have had unlimited and unchecked power to inflate; is it any wonder that these years have seen the greatest sustained inflationary surge in U.S. history?

2. THE PRESENT MONEY SUPPLY

In considering the present monetary situation, the observer is struck with a phenomenon we mentioned at the beginning of this work: the bewildering series of Ms: Which of them *is* the money supply? The various Ms have been changing with disconcerting rapidity, as economists and monetary authorities express their confusion over *what* the Fed is supposed to be controlling. In particularly shaky shape are the Friedmanite monetarists, whose entire program consists of ordering the Fed to increase the money supply at a steady, fixed rate. But *which* M is the Fed supposed to watch?[4] The puzzle for the Friedmanites is aggravated by their

---

[3]For a brief summary of the progressive breakdown of world currencies from the classical gold standard to the end of the Smithsonian agreement, see Murray N. Rothbard, *What Has Government Done to Our Money?* 2nd ed. (Santa Ana, Calif.: Rampart College, January 1974), pp. 50–62. On the two-tier gold market, see Jacques Rueff, *The Monetary Sin of the West* (New York: Macmillan, 1972).

[4]That is only one of the two major problems confronting the Friedmanites: the other is *what* fixed rate should the Fed follow? Monetarist answers have ranged from 3 to 5 percent (with even higher rates allowed for a gradual transition period) and down to zero (for those Friedmanites who have noted that in recent years the demand for money has fallen by about 3 percent per year).

having no theory of how to define the supply of money, which they define in a question-begging way by whichever of the Ms correlates most closely with Gross National Product (correlations which can and do change).[5]

Everyone concedes that what we can call the old M-1 (currency or Federal Reserve Notes + demand deposits) was part of the money supply. The controversial question was and still is: Should anything *else* be included? One grievous problem in the Fed's trying to regulate the banks is that they keep coming up with new monetary instruments, many of which might or might not be treated as part of the money supply. When savings banks began to offer checking services as part of their savings accounts, it became clear even to Friedmanites and other stubborn advocates of only checking accounts as part of the money supply, that these accounts—NOW and ATS—must be included as part of any intelligible definition of the money supply. Old M-1 then became M-1A, and NOW and ATS figures were included in a new M-1B. Finally, in 1982, the Fed sensibly threw in the towel by calling a new M-1 figure the previous M-1B and scrapping the M-1A estimates.[6]

The inclusion of new forms of checking accounts at savings and savings and loan banks in the new M-1, however, by no means eliminates the problem of treating these thrift institutions. For regular savings accounts at these institutions, and indeed at commercial banks, while not checkable, can be easily withdrawn in the form of a cashier's or certified check from these banks. What genuine difference, then, is there between an officially checkable account and one that can be drawn down by a simple

---

[5]For an excellent critique of the question-begging nature of Friedmanite definitions of money, see Leland B. Yeager, "The Medium of Exchange," in R. Clower, ed., *Monetary Theory* (London: Penguin Books, 1970), pp. 37–60.

[6]Recently, however, Fed apologists are beginning to excuse the disconcertingly large increases in M-1 as "only" in NOW and ATS accounts.

cashier's check? The typical answer that a savings account must be withdrawn by presenting a passbook in person hardly seems to offer any genuine obstacle to withdrawal on demand.

No: The crucial distinction, and the crucial way to decide what is part of the money supply, must focus on whether a certain claim is withdrawable instantly *on demand*. The fact that any bank may be able legally to exercise a fine-print option to wait 30 days to redeem a savings deposit is meaningless, for no one takes that fine print seriously. Everyone treats a savings deposit *as if* it were redeemable instantly on demand, and so it should be included as part of estimates of the money supply.

The test, then, should be whether or not a given bank claim is redeemable genuinely and in fact, on demand at par in cash. If so, it should be included in the money supply. The counter-argument is that noncheckable deposits are transferred more slowly than checking. Indeed, we saw above how commercial banks were able to engineer credit inflation in the 1920s by changing from demand to alleged time deposits, which legally required much lower reserves. We also saw how several bank runs on these savings deposits occurred during the 1930s. Everyone treated these deposits as if they were redeemable on demand, and began to redeem them *en masse* when the banks insisted on the fine-print wait of 30 days.

The test, then, should be whether or not a given bank claim is redeemable, genuinely and in fact, on demand at par in cash. If so, it should be included in the money supply. The counter-argument that noncheckable deposits are transferred more slowly than checking accounts and therefore should not be "money" is an interesting but irrelevant fact. Slower-moving money balances are also part of the money supply. Suppose, for example, in the days of the pure gold coin standard, that individuals habitually had kept some coins in their house to be used for day-to-day transactions, while others were locked up in vaults and used only rarely. Weren't both sets of gold coins part of their money stocks? And clearly, of course, the speed of spending the active balances is deeply affected by how much money people have in their slower-moving accounts. The two are closely interrelated.

On the other hand, while savings deposits are really redeemable on demand, there now exist genuine time deposits which should not be considered as part of the money supply. One of the most heartwarming banking developments of the past two decades has been the "certificate of deposit" (CD), in which the bank flatly and frankly borrows money from the individual for a specific term (say, six months) and then returns the money plus interest at the end of the term. No purchaser of a CD is fooled into believing—as does the savings bank depositor—that his money is *really* still in the bank and redeemable at par at any time on demand. He knows he must wait for the full term of the loan.

A more accurate money supply figure, then, should include the current M-1 plus savings deposits in commercial banks, savings banks, and savings and loan associations.

The Federal Reserve, however, has not proved very helpful in arriving at money supply figures. Its current M-2 includes M-1 plus savings deposits, but it also illegitimately includes "small" time deposits, which are presumably genuine term loans. M-2 also includes overnight bank loans; the term here is so short for all intents and purposes as to be "on demand." That is acceptable, but the Fed takes the questionable step of including in M-2 money market mutual fund balances.

This presents an intriguing question: Should money market funds be incorporated in the money supply? The Fed, indeed, has gone further to bring money market funds under legal reserve requirements. The short-lived attempt by the Carter administration to do so brought a storm of complaints that forced the government to suspend such requirements. And no wonder: For the money market fund has been a godsend for the small investor in an age of inflation, providing a safe method of lending out funds at market rates in contrast to the cartelized, regulated, artificially low rates offered by the thrift institutions. But are money market funds money? Those who answer Yes cite the fact that these funds are mainly checkable accounts. But is the existence of checks the only criterion? For money market funds rest on short-term credit instruments and they are not legally redeemable at par. On the other hand, they are economically redeemable at par, much like the savings deposit. The difference seems to be that the public holds the savings deposit to be legally redeemable at par, whereas it realizes that there are inevitable risks attached to the money market fund. Hence, the weight of argument is against including these goods in the supply of money.

The point, however, is that there are good arguments either way on the money market fund, which highlights the grave problem the Fed and the Friedmanites have in zeroing in on one money supply figure for total control. Moreover, the money market fund shows how ingenious the market can be in developing new money instruments which can evade or make a mockery of reserve or other money supply regulations. The market is always more clever than government regulators.

The Fed also issues an M-3 figure, which is simply M-2 plus various term loans, plus large denomination (over $100,000) time deposits. There seems to be little point to M-3, since its size has nothing to do with whether a deposit is a genuine time loan, and since term loans should not in any case be part of the money supply.

The Fed also publishes an L figure, which is M-3 plus other liquid assets, including savings bonds, short-term Treasury bills, commercial paper, and acceptances. But none of the latter can be considered money. It is a grave error committed by many economists to fuzz the dividing line between money and other liquid assets. Money is the *uniquely* liquid asset because money is the final payment, the medium of exchange used in virtually all transactions to purchase goods or services. Other nonmonetary assets, no matter how liquid—and they have different degrees of liquidity—are simply goods to be sold for money. Hence, bills of exchange, Treasury bills, commercial paper, and so on, are in no sense money. By the same reasoning, stocks and bonds, which are mainly highly liquid, could also be called money.

A more serious problem is provided by U.S. savings bonds, which are included by the Fed in L but not in M-2 or M-3. Savings bonds, in contrast to all other Treasury securities, are redeemable at any time by the Treasury. They should therefore be included in the money supply. A problem, however, is that they are redeemable not at par, but at a fixed discount, so that total savings bonds, to be accurately incorporated in the money supply would have to be corrected by the discount. Still more problems are proffered by another figure not even considered or collected by the Fed: life insurance cash surrender values. For money invested for policyholders by life insurance companies are redeemable at fixed discounts in cash. There is therefore an argument for including these figures in the money supply. But is the Fed then supposed to extend its regulatory grasp to insurance companies? The complications ramify.

But the problems for the Fed, and for Friedmanite regulators, are not yet over. For should the Fed keep an eye on, and try to regulate or keep growing at some fixed rate, a *raw* M-1, or M-2 or whatever, or should it try to control the seasonally adjusted figure?

In our view, the further one gets from the raw data the further one goes from reality, and therefore the more erroneous any concentration upon that figure. *Seasonal adjustments* in data are not as harmless as they seem, for seasonal patterns, even for such products as fruit and vegetables, are not set in concrete. Seasonal patterns change, and they change in unpredictable ways, and hence seasonal adjustments are likely to add extra distortions to the data.

Let us see what some of these recent figures are like. For March 1982, the nonseasonally adjusted figure for M-1 was $439.7 billion. The figure for M-2 was $1,861.1 billion. If we deduct money market mutual funds we get $823 billion as our money supply figures for March 1982. There are at this writing no savings bonds figures for the month, but if we add the latest December 1981 data we obtain a money supply figure of $891.2 billion. If we use the seasonally adjusted data for March 1982, we arrive at $835.9 billion for the corrected M-2 figure (compared to $823.1 billion without seasonal adjustments) and $903.6 billion if we include seasonally adjusted savings bonds.

How well the Reagan Fed has been doing depends on which
of these Ms or their possible variations we wish to use. From
March 1981 to March 1982, seasonally adjusted, M-1 increased at
an annual rate of 5.5 percent, well within Friedmanite parameters,
but the month-to-month figures were highly erratic, with M-1
from December 1981 to February 1982 rising at an annual rate of
8.7 percent. Seasonally adjusted M-2, however, rose at a whop-
ping 9.6 percent rate for the year March 1981–March 1982.

The numerous problems of new bank instruments and how to
classify them, as well as the multifarious Ms, have led some economists, including some monetarists, to argue quite sensibly that
the Fed should spend its time trying to control its *own* liabilities
rather than worrying so much about the activities of the commercial banks. But again, more difficulties arise. *Which* of its own
actions or liabilities should the Fed try to control? The Friedmanite favorite is the *monetary base*: Fed liabilities, which consist of
Federal Reserve notes outstanding plus demand deposits of commercial banks at the Fed. It is true that Federal Reserve actions,
such as purchasing U.S. government securities, or lending reserves
to banks, determine the size of the monetary base, which, by the
way, rose by the alarmingly large annual rate of 9.4 percent from
mid-November 1981 to mid-April 1982. But the problem is that
the monetary base is not a homogeneous figure: It contains two
determinants (Federal Reserve notes outstanding + bank reserves)
which can and do habitually move in opposite directions. Thus, if
people decide to cash in a substantial chunk of their demand
deposits, FRN in circulation will *increase* while bank reserves at
the Fed will *contract*. Looking at the aggregate figure of the monetary base cloaks significant changes in the banking picture. For
the monetary base may remain the same, but the contractionist
impact on bank reserves will soon cause a multiple contraction in
bank deposits and hence in the supply of money. And the con-
verse happens when people deposit more cash into the commercial banks.

A more important figure, therefore, would be total bank
reserves, which now consist of Federal Reserve notes held by the

banks as vault cash plus demand deposits at the Fed. Or, looked at another way, total reserves equal the monetary base minus FRN held by the nonbank public.

But this does not end the confusion. For the Fed now *adjusts* both the monetary base and the total reserve figures by changes in reserve requirements, which are at the present changing slowly every year.

Furthermore, if we compare the growth rates of the adjusted monetary base, adjusted reserves, and M-1, we see enormous variations among all three important figures. Thus, the Federal Reserve Bank of St. Louis has presented the following table of growth rates of selected monetary aggregates for various recent periods:[7]

Period	Adj. Monetary Base	Adj. Reserves	M-1
6/81–8/81	4.0 %	1.3 %	3.8 %
8/81–10/81	-2.1	-14.2	2.5
10/81–12/81	9.3	9.4	11.6
12/81–2/82	10.7	19.3	8.7

While total reserves is a vitally important figure, its determination is a blend of public and private action. The public affects total reserves by its demand for deposits or withdrawals of cash from the banks. The amount of Federal Reserve notes in the hands of the public is, then, completely determined by that public. Perhaps it is therefore best to concentrate on the one figure which is totally under the control of the Fed at all times, namely *its own* credit.

Federal Reserve Credit is the loans and investments engaged in by the Fed itself, any increase of which tends to increase the

---

[7]Federal Reserve Bank of St. Louis, *Monetary Trends* (March 25, 1982), p. 1.

monetary base and bank reserves by the same amount. Federal
Reserve Credit may be defined as the assets of the Fed minus its
gold stock, its assets in Treasury coin and foreign currencies, and
the value of its premises and furniture.

Total Fed assets on December 31, 1981 were $176.85 billion.
Of this amount, if we deduct gold, foreign currency, Treasury cash
and premises, we arrive at a Federal Reserve Credit figure of
$152.78 billion. This total consists of:

1. float-cash items due from banks which the Treasury
   has not yet bothered to collect: $10.64 billion
2. loans to banks: $1.60 billion
3. acceptances bought: $0.19 billion
4. U.S. government securities: $140.4 billion

Clearly, loans to banks, despite the publicity that the discount
(or rediscount) rate receives, is a minor part of Federal Reserve
Credit. Acceptances are even more negligible. It is evident that by
far the largest item of Federal Reserve Credit, amounting to 79
percent of the total, is U.S. government securities. Next largest is
the float of items that the Fed has so far failed to collect from the
banks.

Changes in Federal Reserve Credit may be shown by compar-
ing the end of 1981 figures with the data two years earlier, at the
beginning of 1980. Total Reserve Credit, on the earlier date, was
$134.7 billion, a rise of 13.4 percent in two years. Of the partic-
ular items, loans to banks were $1.2 billion in the earlier date, a
rise of 33.3 percent in this minor item. The float's earlier figure
was $6.2 billion, a rise in this important item of 71.0 percent for
the two years. The major figure of U.S. government securities had
been $126.9 billion two years earlier, a rise of 10.6 percent in this
total.

If we take gold as the original and proper monetary standard,
and wish to see how much inflationary pyramiding our Federal
Reserve fractional reserve banking system has accomplished on

top of that gold, we may note that the Fed's total of gold certificates on December 31, 1981 was $11.15 billion. On this figure, the Fed has pyramided liabilities (Federal Reserve notes plus demand deposits at the Fed) of $162.74 billion, a pyramiding of 14.6:1 on top of gold. On top of *that*, however, the banking system had created a money supply totaling $444.8 billion of M-1 for that date, a pyramiding of 2.73:1 on top of the monetary base, or, an ultimate pyramiding of 38.9:1 on top of the Fed's stock of gold.

3. How to Return to Sound Money

Given this dismal monetary and banking situation, given a 39:1 pyramiding of checkable deposits and currency on top of gold, given a Fed unchecked and out of control, given a world of fiat moneys, how can we possibly return to a sound noninflationary market money? The objectives, after the discussion in this work, should be clear: (a) to return to a gold standard, a commodity standard unhampered by government intervention; (b) to abolish the Federal Reserve System and return to a system of free and competitive banking; (c) to separate the government from money; and (d) *either* to enforce 100 percent reserve banking on the commercial banks, or at least to arrive at a system where any bank, at the slightest hint of nonpayment of its demand liabilities, is forced quickly into bankruptcy and liquidation. While the outlawing of fractional reserve as fraud would be preferable if it could be enforced, the problems of enforcement, especially where banks can continually innovate in forms of credit, make free banking an attractive alternative. But how to achieve this system, and as rapidly as humanly possible?

First, a gold standard must be a true gold standard; that is, the dollar must be redeemable on demand not only in gold bullion, but also in full-bodied gold coin, the metal in which the dollar is defined. There must be no provision for *emergency* suspensions of redeemability, for in that case everyone will know that the gold standard is phony, and that the Federal government and its central bank remain in charge. The currency will then still be a fiat paper currency with a gold veneer.

But the crucial question remains: For there to be a gold standard the dollar must be defined as a unit of weight of gold, and *what* definition shall be chosen? Or, to put it in the more popular but erroneous form, at what *price* should gold be fixed in terms of dollars? The old definition of the dollar as 1/35 gold ounce is outdated and irrelevant to the current world; it has been violated too many times by government to be taken seriously now. Ludwig von Mises proposed, in the final edition of his *Theory of Money and Credit*, that the current *market price* be taken as the definition of gold weight. But this suggestion violates the spirit of his own analysis, which demonstrates that gold and the dollar are not truly separate commodities with a *price* in terms of the other, but rather simple definitions of unit of weight. But *any initial* definition is arbitrary, and we should therefore return to gold at the most conveniently defined weight. *After* a definition is chosen, however, it should be eternally fixed, and continue permanently in the same way as the defined unit of the meter, the gram, or the pound.

Since we must adopt *some* definition of weight, I propose that the most convenient definition is one that will enable us, *at one and the same time* as returning to a gold standard, to denationalize gold and to abolish the Federal Reserve System.

Even though, for the past few years, private American citizens have once again been allowed to own gold, the gold stolen from them in 1933 is still locked away in Fort Knox and other U.S. government depositories. I propose that, in order to separate the government totally from money, its hoard of gold must be *denationalized*; that is, returned to the people. What better way to denationalize gold than to take every aliquot dollar and redeem it concretely and directly in the form of gold? And since demand deposits are part of the money supply, why not also assure 100 percent reserve banking at the same time by disgorging the gold at Fort Knox to each individual and bank holder, directly redeeming each aliquot dollar of currency and demand deposits? In short, the new dollar price of gold (or the weight of the dollar), is to be defined so that there will be enough gold dollars to redeem every Federal Reserve note and demand deposit, one for one. And *then*, the Federal Reserve System is to liquidate itself by disgorging the actual gold in exchange for Federal Reserve notes, and by giving the banks enough gold to have 100 percent reserve of gold behind their demand deposits. After that point, each bank will have 100 percent reserve of gold, so that a law holding fractional reserve banking as fraud and enforcing 100 percent reserve would not entail any deflation or contraction of the money supply. The 100 percent provision may be enforced by the courts and/or by free banking and the glare of public opinion.

Let us see how this plan would work. The Fed has gold (technically, a 100 percent reserve claim on gold at the Treasury) amounting to $11.15 billion, valued at the totally arbitrary price of $42.22 an ounce, as set by the Nixon administration in March 1973. So why keep the valuation at the absurd $42.22 an ounce? M-1, at the end of 1981, including Federal Reserve notes and checkable deposits, totaled $444.8 billion. Suppose that we set the price of gold as equal to $1,696 dollars an ounce. In other words that the dollar be defined as 1/1696 ounce. If that is done, the Fed's gold certificate stock will immediately be valued at $444.8 billion.

I propose, then, the following:
1. That the dollar be defined as 1/1696 gold ounce.
2. That the Fed take the gold out of Fort Knox and the other Treasury depositories, and that the gold then be used (a) to redeem outright all Federal Reserve Notes, and (b) to be given to the commercial banks, liquidating in return all their deposit accounts at the Fed.
3. The Fed then be liquidated, and go out of existence.
4. Each bank will now have gold equal to 100 percent of its demand deposits. Each bank's capital will be written up by the same amount; its capital will now match its loans and investments. At last, each commercial bank's loan operations will be separate from its demand deposits.

5. That each bank be legally required, on the basis of the general law against fraud, to keep 100 percent of gold to its demand liabilities. These demand liabilities will now include bank notes as well as demand deposits. Once again, banks would be free, as they were before the Civil War, to issue bank notes, and much of the gold in the hands of the public after liquidation of Federal Reserve Notes would probably find its way back to the banks in exchange for bank notes backed 100 percent by gold, thus satisfying the public's demand for a paper currency.

6. That the FDIC be abolished, so that no government guarantee can stand behind bank inflation, or prevent the healthy gale of bank runs assuring that banks remain sound and noninflationary.

7. That the U.S. Mint be abolished, and that the job of minting or melting down gold coins be turned over to privately competitive firms. There is no reason why the minting business cannot be free and competitive, and denationalizing the mint will insure against the debasement by official mints that have plagued the history of money.

   In this way, at virtually one stroke, and with no deflation of the money supply, the Fed would be abolished, the nation's gold stock would be denationalized, and free banking be established, with each bank based on the sound bottom of 100 percent reserve in gold. Not only gold and the Mint would be denationalized, but the *dollar* too would be denationalized, and would take its place as a privately minted and noninflationary creation of private firms.[8]

---

[8]For a summary and explanation of this plan, see Murray N. Rothbard, "To the Gold Commission," *The Libertarian Forum*, XVI, 3 (April 1982), testimony delivered before the U.S. Gold Commission on November 12, 1981; and a brief abstract of the testimony in *Report to the Congress of the Commission on the Role of Gold in the Domestic and International*

Our plan would at long last separate money and banking from the State. Expansion of the money supply would be strictly limited to increases in the supply of gold, and there would no longer be any possibility of monetary deflation. Inflation would be virtually eliminated, and so therefore would inflationary expectations of the future. Interest rates would fall, while thrift, savings, and investment would be greatly stimulated. And the dread specter of the business cycle would be over and done with, once and for all.

To clarify how the plan would affect the commercial banks, let us turn, once more, to a simplified T-account. Let us assume, for purposes of clarity, that the commercial banks' major liability is demand deposits, which, along with other checkable deposits, totaled $317 billion at the end of December 1981. Total bank reserves, either in Federal Reserve notes in the vaults or deposits at the Fed, were approximately $47 billion. Let us assume arbitrarily that bank capital was about $35 billion, and then we have the following aggregate balance sheet for commercial banks at the end of December 1981 (Figure 17.1).

Commercial Banks

Assets		Equity & Liabilities	
Loans and investments	$305 billion	Demand deposits	$317 million
		Equity	$35 billion
Reserves	$47 billion		
Total Assets	$352 billion	Equity plus total liabilities	$352 billion

Figure 17.1 — The State of the Commercial Banks: Before the Plan

---

Monetary Systems (Washington, D.C., March 1982), vol. II, pp. 480–81. The only plan presented before the Commission (or anywhere else, as far as I know) similar in its sweep is that of Dr. George Reisman, in ibid., vol. II, pp. 476–77.

We are proposing, then, that the federal government disgorge its gold at a level of 100 percent to total dollars, and that the Fed, in the process of its liquidation, give the gold pro rata to the individual banks, thereby raising their equity by the same amount. Thus, in the hypothetical situation for all commercial banks starting in Figure 17.1, the new plan would lead to the following balance sheet (Figure 17.2):

Commercial Banks

Assets		Equity & Liabilities	
Loans and investments	$305 billion	Demand deposits	$317 million
		Equity	$305 billion
Reserves	$317 billion		
Total Assets	$622 billion	Equity plus total liabilities	$622 billion

FIGURE 17.2 — THE STATE OF THE COMMERCIAL BANKS: AFTER THE PLAN

In short, what has happened is that the Treasury and the Fed have turned over $270 billion in gold to the banking system. The banks have written up their equity accordingly, and now have 100 percent gold reserves to demand liabilities. Their loan and deposit operations are now separated.

The most cogent criticism of this plan is simply this: Why should the banks receive a gift, even a gift in the process of privatizing the nationalized hoard of gold? The banks, as fractional reserve institutions are and have been responsible for inflation and unsound banking.

Since on the free market every firm should rest on its own bottom, the banks should get no gifts at all. Let the nation return to gold at 100 percent of its Federal Reserve notes only, runs this criticism, and then let the banks take their chances like everyone else. In that case, the new gold price would only have to be high enough to redeem outfight the existing $131.91 billion in Federal Reserve notes. The new gold price would then be, not $1,690, but $500 an ounce.

There is admittedly a great deal of charm to this position. Why *shouldn't* the banks be open to the winds of a harsh but rigorous justice? Why shouldn't they at last receive their due? But against this rigor, we have the advantage of starting from Point Zero, of letting bygones be bygones, and of insuring against a wracking deflation that would lead to a severe recession and numerous bankruptcies. For the logic of returning at $500 would require a *deflation* of the money supply down to the level of existing bank reserves. This would be a massive deflationary wringer indeed, and one wonders whether a policy, equally sound and free market oriented, which can avoid such a virtual if short-lived economic holocaust might not be a more sensible solution.

Our plan differs markedly from other gold standard plans that have been put forward in recent years. Among other flaws, many of them, such as those of Arthur Laffer and Lewis Lehrman, retain the Federal Reserve System as a monopoly central bank. Others, such as that of F.A. Hayek, doyen of the Austrian School of Economics, abandon the gold standard altogether and attempt to urge private banks to issue their own currencies, with their own particular names, which the government would allow to compete with its own money.[9] But such proposals ignore the fact that the public is now irrevocably used to such currency names as the dollar, franc, mark, and so on, and are not likely to abandon the use of such names as their money units. It is vital, then, not

---

[9]On the Lehrman, Laffer, and similar plans, see Joseph T. Salerno, "An Analysis and Critique of Recent Plans to Re-establish the Gold Standard" (unpublished manuscript, 1982). On Hayek's plan to "denationalize money," see Murray N. Rothbard, "Hayek's Denationalized Money," *The Libertarian Forum* XV, nos. 5–6 (August 1981–January 1982): 9.

only to denationalize the issuing of money as well as the stock of gold, but also to denationalize the dollar, to remove the good old American dollar from the hands of government and tie it firmly once again to a unit of weight of gold. Only such a plan as ours will return, or rather advance, the economy to a truly free market and noninflationary money, where the monetary unit is solidly tied to the weight of a commodity produced on the free market. Only such a plan will totally separate money from the pernicious and inflationary domination of the State.

APPENDIX:
THE MYTH OF FREE
BANKING IN SCOTLAND

Professor White's *Free Banking in Britain* has already had a substantial impact on the economics profession. The main influence has been exerted by one of the book's major themes: the "wonderful" results of the system of free banking in Scotland, a system that allegedly prevailed from 1716 (or 1727) until suppressed by the Peel Act in 1845.[1] White's Scottish free-banking thesis consists of two crucial propositions. The first is that Scottish banking, in contrast to English, was free during this era; that while the English banking system was dominated by the Bank of England, pyramiding their notes and deposits on top of the liabilities of that central bank, the Scottish system, in stark contrast, was free of the Bank of England. In White's words, Scotland "rather maintained a system of 'each tub on its own bottom.' Each bank held onto its own specie reserves."[2]

---

[1]On "wonderful" results, see White, *Free Banking*, p. xiii.

[2]Ibid., p. 43.

The second part of the syllogism is that this free system in some way worked much better than the English. Hence, the triumphant conclusion: that free banking in Scotland was far superior to centrally controlled banking in England. White claims that the salutary effects of free banking in Scotland have been long forgotten, and he raises the hope that current public policy will heed this lesson.

The influence of White's thesis is remarkable considering the paucity of his research and the thinness of his discussion. In a brief book of less than 200 pages, only 26 are devoted to the Scottish question, and White admits that he relies for facts of Scottish banking almost solely on a few secondary sources.[3] And yet, White's thesis on Scottish banking has been hastily and uncritically accepted by many diverse scholars, including the present writer.[4] This has been particularly unfortunate because, as I shall demonstrate, both parts of Professor White's syllogism are wrong. That is, the Scottish banks were (1) not free—indeed, they too pyramided upon the Bank of England—and (2) not surprisingly, they worked no better than the English banks.

Let me take the second part of Professor White's syllogism first. What is his basis for the conclusion that the Scottish banks worked significantly better than the English banks? Remarkably, there is not a word that they were significantly less inflationary; indeed, there is no attempt to present any data on the money supply, the extent of bank credit, or prices in England and Scotland

---

[3]Most of the White book, indeed, is devoted to another question entirely—a discussion and analysis of free-banking theorists in Britain during the first half of the nineteenth century. I shall deal with that part of his book subsequently.

[4]Murray N. Rothbard, *The Mystery of Banking* (New York: Richardson & Snyder, 1983), pp. 185–87. Also see the report on a forthcoming *Journal of Monetary Economics* article by Milton Friedman and Anna Jacobson Schwartz in *Fortune* (March 31, 1986), p. 163. I did have grave preliminary doubts about his Scottish thesis in an unpublished comment on Professor White's paper in 1981, but unfortunately, these doubts did not make their way into the *Mystery of Banking*.

during this period. White does say that the Scottish banks were marked by greater "cyclical stability," but it turns out that he does not mean that they generated less inflation in booms or less contraction during recessions. By cyclical stability, White means solely that the extent of Scottish bank failures was less than in England. Indeed, this is Professor White's *sole* evidence that Scottish banking worked better than English.

But why should lack of bank failure be a sign of superiority? On the contrary, a dearth of bank failure should rather be treated with suspicion, as witness the drop of bank failures in the United States since the advent of the FDIC. It might indeed mean that the *banks* are doing better, but at the expense of society and the economy faring *worse*. Bank failures are a healthy weapon by which the market keeps bank credit inflation in check; an absence of failure might well mean that that check is doing poorly and that inflation of money and credit is all the more rampant. In any case, a lower rate of bank failure can scarcely be accepted as any sort of evidence for the superiority of a banking system.

In fact, in a book that Professor White acknowledges to be the definitive history of Scottish banking, Professor Sydney Checkland points out that Scottish banks expanded and contracted credit in a lengthy series of boom-bust cycles, in particular in the years surrounding the crises of the 1760s, 1772, 1778, 1793, 1797, 1802–03, 1809–10, 1810–11, 1818–19, 1825–26, 1836–37, 1839, and 1845–47.[5] Apparently, the Scottish banks escaped none of the destabilizing, cycle-generating behavior of their English cousins.

Even if free, then, the Scottish banking system worked no better than central-bank-dominated English banking. But I turn now to Professor White's central thesis on Scottish banking: that it, in contrast to English banking, was free and independent, with each bank resting on its own specie bottom. For Scottish banking to be

---

[5]Sydney G. Checkland, *Scottish Banking: A History, 1695–1973* (Glasgow: Collins, 1975).

"free," its banks would have to be independent of central banking, with each redeeming its notes and deposits on demand in its
own reserves of gold.

From the beginning, there is one embarrassing and evident
fact that Professor White has to cope with: that "free" Scottish
banks suspended specie payment when England did, in 1797,
and, like England, maintained that suspension until 1821. Free
banks are not supposed to be able to, or want to, suspend specie
payment, thereby violating the property rights of their depositors
and noteholders, while they themselves are permitted to continue
in business and force payment upon *their* debtors.

White professes to be puzzled at this strange action of the
Scottish banks. Why, he asks, did they not "remain tied to specie
and let their currency float against the Bank of England note?"
His puzzlement would vanish if he acknowledged an evident
answer: that Scottish banks were *not* free, that they were in no
position to pay in specie, and that they pyramided credit on top
of the Bank of England.[6] Indeed, the Scottish banks' eagerness for
suspension of their contractual obligations to pay in specie might
be related to the fact, acknowledged by White, that specie
reserves held by the Scottish banks had averaged from 10 to 20
percent in the second half of the eighteenth century, but then had
dropped sharply to a range of less than 1 to 3 percent in the first
half of the nineteenth. Instead of attributing this scandalous drop
to "lower costs of obtaining specie on short notice" or "lower risk
of substantial specie outflows," White might realize that suspension meant that the banks would not have to worry very much
about specie at all.[7]

---

[6]In a footnote, Professor White grudgingly hints at this point, while not
seeming to realize the grave implications of the facts for his own starry-eyed
view of Scottish banking. Note, then, the unacknowledged implications of
his hint that London was "Britain's financial centre," that the Scottish banks
depended on funds from their correspondent banks and from sales of securities in London, and that Britain was an "optimal currency area." White,
Free Banking, p. 46 n. 12.

[7]White, *Free Banking*, pp. 43–44, n. 9.

Professor Checkland, indeed, presents a far more complete and very different account of the suspension crisis. It began, not in 1797, but four years earlier, in the banking panic that struck on the advent of the war with France. Representatives of two leading Scottish banks immediately went to London, pleading for government intervention to bail them out. The British government promptly complied, issuing Treasury bills to "basically sound" banks, of which £400,000 went to Scotland. This bailout, added to the knowledge that the government stood ready to do more, allayed the banking panic.

When the Scottish banks followed the Bank of England in suspending specie payments in 1797, White correctly notes that the suspension was illegal under Scottish law, adding that it was "curious" that their actions were not challenged in court. Not so curious, if we realize that the suspension obviously had the British government's tacit consent. Emboldened by the suspension, and by the legality of bank issue of notes under £1 after 1800, a swarm of new banks entered the field in Scotland, and Checkland informs us that the circulation of bank paper in Scotland doubled from 1793 to 1803.

Before the Scottish banks suspended payment, all Scottish bank offices were crowded with depositors demanding gold and small-note holders demanding silver in payment. They were treated with contempt and loathing by the bankers, who denounced them as the "lowest and most ignorant classes" of society, presumably for the high crime of wanting their money out of the shaky and inherently bankrupt banking system. Not only the bankers, but even elite merchants from Edinburgh and throughout Scotland complained, in 1764, of "obscure people" demanding cash from the banks, which they then had the effrontery to send to London and profit from the rate of exchange.[8] Particularly interesting, for more than just the 24 years of the

---

[8]See Charles A. Malcolm, *The Bank of Scotland, 1695–1945* (Edinburgh: R.&R. Clark, n.d.).

British suspension, was the reason the Scottish banks gave for turning to suspension of specie payments. As Checkland summed up, the Scottish banks were "most gravely threatened, for the inhibitions against demanding gold, so carefully nurtured in the customers of Scottish banks, was rapidly breaking down."[9]

Now I come to the nub: that, as a general rule, and not just during the official suspension period, the Scottish banks redeemed in specie in name *only*; that, in substance, depositors and note holders generally could not redeem the banks' liabilities in specie. The reason that the Scottish banks could afford to be outrageously inflationary, i.e. keep their specie reserves at a minimum, is that, in practice, they did not really have to pay.

Thus, Professor Checkland notes that, long before the official suspension, "requests for specie [from the Scottish banks] met with disapproval and almost with charges of disloyalty." And again:

> The Scottish system was one of continuous partial suspension of specie payments. No one really expected to be able to enter a Scots bank . . . with a large holding of notes and receive the equivalent immediately in gold or silver. They expected, rather, an argument, or even a rebuff. At best they would get a little specie and perhaps bills on London. If they made serious trouble, the matter would be noted and they would find the obtaining of credit more difficult in future.[10]

At one point, during the 1750s, a bank war was waged between a cartel of Glasgow banks, which habitually redeemed in London bills rather than specie, and the banks in Edinburgh. The Edinburgh banks set up a private Glasgow banker, Archibald Trotter, with a supply of notes on Glasgow banks, and Trotter demanded that the banks of his city redeem them, as promised, in specie. The Glasgow banks delayed and dragged their feet, until

---

[9]Checkland, *Scottish Banking*, p. 221.
[10]Checkland, *Scottish Banking*, pp. 184–85.

Trotter was forced to file a law suit for damages for "vexatious delay" in honoring his claims. Finally, after four years in court, Trotter won a nominal victory, but could not get the law to force the Glasgow banks to pay up. *A fortiori,* of course, the banks were not shut down or their assets liquidated to pay their wilfully unpaid debts.

As we have seen, the Scottish law of 1765, providing for summary execution of unredeemed bank notes, remained largely a dead letter. Professor Checkland concludes that "this legally impermissible limitation of convertibility, though never mentioned to public inquiries, contributed greatly to Scottish banking success."[11] No doubt. Of one thing we can be certain: this condition definitely contributed to the paucity of bank failures in Scotland.

The less-than-noble tradition of nonredeemability in Scottish banks continued, unsurprisingly, after Britain resumed specie payments in 1821. As the distinguished economic historian Frank W. Fetter put it, writing about Scotland:

> Even after the resumption of payments in 1821 little coin had circulated; and to a large degree there was a tradition, almost with the force of law, that banks should not be required to redeem their notes in coin. Redemption in London drafts was the usual form of paying noteholders. There was a core of truth in the remark of an anonymous pamphleteer [writing in 1826] "Any southern fool [from south of the Scottish-English border] who had the temerity to ask for a hundred sovereigns, might, if his nerves supported him through the cross examination at the bank counter, think himself in luck to be hunted only to the border.[12]

---

[11]Ibid., p. 186.

[12]Frank W. Fetter, *Development of British Monetary Orthodoxy, 1797–1875* (Cambridge, Mass.: Harvard University Press, 1965), p. 122. The anonymous pamphlet was *A Letter to the Right Hon. George Canning* (London, 1826), p. 45. Also see Charles W. Munn, *The Scottish Provincial Banking Companies, 1747–1864* (Edinburgh: John Donald Pubs., 1981), pp. 140ff.

If gold and silver were scarcely important sources of reserves or of grounding for Scottish bank liabilities, what was? Each bank in Scotland stood not on its own bottom, but on the very source of aid and comfort dear to its English cousins—the Bank of England. As Checkland declares: "the principal and ultimate source of liquidity [of the Scottish banks] lay in London, and, in particular, in the Bank of England."[13]

I conclude that the Scottish banks, in the eighteenth and first half of the nineteenth centuries, were neither free nor superior, and that the thesis to the contrary, recently revived by Professor White, is but a snare and a delusion.

A similar practice was also prevalent at times in the "free-banking" system in the United States. After the "resumption" of 1817, obstacles and intimidation were often the fate of those who tried to ask for specie for their notes. In 1821, the Philadelphia merchant, economist and state Senator Condy Raguet perceptively wrote to David Ricardo:

> You state in your letter that you find it difficult to comprehend why persons who had a right to demand coin from the Banks in payment of their notes, so long forebore to exercise it. This no doubt appears paradoxical to one who resides in a country where an act of parliament was necessary to protect a bank, but the difficulty is easily solved. The whole of our population are either stockholders of banks or in debt to them. It is not in the interest of the first to press the banks and the rest are afraid. This is the whole secret. An independent man, who was neither a stockholder or debtor, who would have ventured to compel the banks to do justice, would have been persecuted as an enemy of society. (Quoted in Murray N. Rothbard, *The Panic of 1819: Reactions and Policies*, New York: Columbia University Press, 1962, pp. 10–11)

There is unfortunately no record of Ricardo's side of the correspondence.

[13]Checkland, *Scottish Banking*, p. 432. Also see S.G. Checkland, "Adam Smith and the Bankers," in A. Skinner and T. Wilson, eds., *Essays on Adam Smith* (Oxford, England: Clarendon Press, 1975), pp. 504–23.

THE FREE-BANKING THEORISTS RECONSIDERED

The bulk of *Free Banking in Britain* is taken up, not with a description or analysis of Scottish banking, but with analyzing the free-banking controversies in the famous monetary debates of the two decades leading up to Peel's Act of 1844. The *locus classicus* of discussion of free versus central banking in Europe is the excellent work by Vera C. Smith, *The Rationale of Central Banking.*[14] While Professor White makes a contribution by dealing in somewhat more depth with the British controversialists of the era, he unfortunately takes a giant step backward from Miss Smith in his basic interpretation of the debate. Miss Smith realized that the currency school theorists were hard-money men who saw the evils of bank credit inflation and who tried to eliminate them so that the money supply would as far as possible be equivalent to the commodity standard, gold or silver. On the other hand, she saw that the banking school theorists were inflationists who favored bank credit expansion in accordance with the "needs of trade." More importantly, Miss Smith saw that for both schools of thought, free banking and central banking were contrasting means to arrive at their different goals. As a result, she analyzes her monetary writers according to an illuminating 2x2 grid, with "currency school" and "banking school" on one side and "free banking" and "central banking" on the other.

In *Free Banking in Britain*, on the other hand, Professor White retreats from this important insight, misconceiving and distorting the entire analysis by separating the theorists and writers into

---

[14]Vera C. Smith, *The Rationale of Central Banking* (London: P.S. King 8t Sons, 1936). This book was a doctoral dissertation under F.A. Hayek at the London School of Economics, for which Miss Smith made use of Hayek's notes on the subject. See Pedro Schwartz, "Central Bank Monopoly in the History of Economic Thought: a Century of Myopia in England," in P. Salin, ed., *Currency Competition and Monetary Union* (The Hague: Martinus Nijhoff, 1984), pp. 124–25.

three distinct camps, the currency school, banking school, and free-banking school. By doing so, he lumps together analysis and policy conclusions, and he conflates two very distinct schools of free bankers: (1) those who wanted free banking in order to promote monetary inflation and cheap credit and (2) those who, on the contrary, wanted free banking in order to arrive at hard, near-100 percent specie money. The currency school and banking school are basically lumped by White into one group: the pro-central-banking faction. Of the two, White is particularly critical of the currency school, which supposedly all wanted central banks to levy "arbitrary" restrictions on commercial banks. While White disagrees with the pro-central-banking aspects of the banking school, he is clearly sympathetic with their desire to inflate bank credit to supply the "needs of trade." In that way, White ignores the substantial minority of currency school theorists who preferred free banking to central bank control as a way of achieving 100 percent specie money. In addition, he misunderstands the nature of the inner struggles to find a correct monetary position by laissez-faire advocates, and he ignores the vital differences between the two wings of free bankers.

On the currency school, it is true that most currency men believed in 100 percent reserves issued either by a central bank monopoly of note issue or by an outright state bank monopoly. But, as Smith pointed out, the aim of the currency men was to arrive at a money supply equivalent to the genuine free market money of a pure specie commodity (gold or silver). And furthermore, since currency men tended to be laissez-faire advocates distrustful of state action, a substantial minority advocated free banking as a better political alternative for reaching the desired 100 percent gold money than trusting in the benevolence of the state. As Smith notes, Ludwig von Mises was one of those believing that free banking in practice would approximate a 100 percent gold or silver money. Free banking and 100 percent metallic money advocates in the nineteenth century included Henri Cernuschi and Victor Modeste in France, and Otto Hübner in

Germany.[15] Mises' approach was very similar to that of Otto Hübner, a leader of the German Free Trade Party. In his multivolume work, *Die Banken* (1854), Hübner states that his ideal preference would have been a state-run monopoly 100 percent specie reserve bank, along the lines of the old Banks of Amsterdam and Hamburg. But the state cannot be trusted. To quote Vera Smith's paraphrase of Hübner's position:

> If it were true that the State could be trusted always only to issue notes to the amount of its specie holdings, a State-controlled note issue would be the best system, but as things were, a far nearer approach to the ideal system was to be expected from free banks, who for reasons of self-interest would aim at the fulfillment of their obligations.[16]

------

[15]After quoting favorably Thomas Tooke's famous dictum that "free trade in banking is free trade in swindling," Mises adds:

> However, freedom in the issuance of banknotes would have narrowed down the use of banknotes considerably if it had not entirely suppressed it. It was this idea which Cernuschi advanced in the hearings of the French Banking Inquiry on October 24, 1865: "I believe that what is called freedom of banking would result in a total suppression of banknotes in France. I want to give everybody the right to issue banknotes so that nobody should take banknotes any longer." (Ludwig von Mises, *Human Action: A Treatise on Economics*, 3rd rev. ed., Chicago: Henry Regnery, 1966, p. 446)

[16]Smith, *Rationale*, p. 101. Mises, after endorsing the idea of 100 percent reserves to gold of banknotes and demand deposits (the latter unfortunately overlooked by the currency school in Britain), decided against it because of the "drawbacks inherent in every kind of government interference with banking." And again:

> Government interference with the present state of banking affairs could be justified if its aim were to liquidate the unsatisfactory conditions by preventing or at least seriously restricting any further credit expansion. In fact the chief objective of present-day government interference is to intensify further credit expansion. (Mises, *Human Action*, p. 443, 448)

Henri Cernuschi desired 100 percent specie money. He declared that the important question was not monopoly note issue versus free banking, but whether or not bank notes should be issued at all. His answer was no, since "they had the effect of despoiling the holders of metallic money by depreciating its value." All bank notes, all fiduciary media, should be eliminated. An important follower of Cernuschi's in France was Victor Modeste, whom Vera Smith erroneously dismisses as having "the same attitude" as Cernuschi's. Actually, Modeste did not adopt the free-banking policy conclusion of his mentor. In the first place, Modeste was a dedicated libertarian who frankly declared that the state is "the master . . . the obstacle, the enemy" and whose announced goal was to replace all government by "self-government." Like Cernuschi and Mises, Modeste agreed that freely competitive banking was far better than administrative state control or regulation of banks. And like Mises a half-century later (and like most American currency men at the time), Modeste realized that demand deposits, like bank notes beyond 100 percent reserves, are illicit, fraudulent, and inflationary as well as being generators of the business cycle. Demand deposits, like bank notes, constitute "false money." But Modeste's policy conclusion was different. His answer was to point out that "false" demand liabilities that pretend to be but cannot be converted into gold are in reality tantamount to fraud and embezzlement. Modeste concludes that false titles and values, such as false claims to gold under fractional-reserve banking, are at all times

> equivalent to theft; that theft in all its forms everywhere deserves its penalties . . . that every bank administrator . . . must be warned that to pass as value where there is no value . . . to subscribe to an engagement that cannot be accomplished . . . are criminal acts which should be relieved under the criminal law.[17]

---

[17]Victor Modeste, "Le Billet des banques d'emission est-il fausse monnaie?" [Are Bank Notes False Money?] *Journal des economistes* 4 (October 1866), pp. 77–78 (Translation mine). Also see Henri Cernuschi, *Contre le billet de banque* (1866).

The answer to fraud, then, is not administrative regulation, but prohibition of tort and fraud under general law.[18]

For Great Britain, an important case of currency men not discussed by Smith are the famous laissez-faire advocates of the Manchester school. Hobbled by his artificial categories, Professor White can only react to them in total confusion. Thus, John Benjamin Smith, the powerful president of the Manchester Chamber of Commerce, reported to the chamber in 1840 that the economic and financial crisis of 1839 had been caused by the Bank of England's contraction, following inexorably upon its own earlier "undue expansion of the currency." Simply because Smith condemned Bank of England policy, White chides Marion Daugherty for putting J.B. Smith into the ranks of the currency school rather than the free bankers. But then, only four pages later, White laments the parliamentary testimony during the same year of Smith and Richard Cobden as revealing "the developing tendency for adherents of laissez-faire, who wished to free the currency from discretionary management, to look not to free banking but to restricting the right of issue to a rigidly rule-bound state bank as the solution." So what were Smith, Cobden, and the Manchesterites? Were they free bankers (p. 71) or—in the same year—currency men (p. 75), or what? But how could they have been currency men, since White has defined the latter as people who want total power to accrue to the Bank of England? White avoids this question by simply not listing Smith or Cobden in his

---

[18]This policy conclusion is completely consistent with Mises' objective: "What is needed to prevent any further credit expansion is to place the banking business under the general rules of commercial and civil laws compelling every individual and firm to fulfill all obligations in full compliance with the terms of the contract." Mises, *Human Action*, p. 443. For more on fractional-reserve banking as embezzlement, see Rothbard, *Mystery of Banking*, pp. 91–95.

[19]White, *Free Banking*, pp. 71, 75, 135. Also see Marion R. Daugherty, "The Currency-Banking Controversy, Part I," *Southern Economic Journal* 9 (October 1942), p. 147.

table of currency-banking–free-banking school adherents (p. 135).[19]

White might have avoided confusion if he had not, as in the case of Scottish banking, apparently failed to consult Frank W. Fetter's *Development of British Monetary Orthodoxy*, although the book is indeed listed in his bibliography. Fetter notes that Smith, in his parliamentary testimony, clearly enunciates the currency principle. Smith, he points out, was concerned about the fluctuations of the commercial banks as well as of the Bank of England and flatly declared his own currency school objective: "it is desirable in any change in our existing system to approximate as nearly as possible to the operation of a metallic currency; it is desirable also to divest the plan of all mystery, and to make it so plain and simple that it may be easily understood by all."[20] Smith's proposed solution was the scheme derived from Ricardo, of creating a national bank for purposes of issuing 100 percent reserve bank notes.

The same course was taken, in his testimony, by Richard Cobden, the great leader of the Manchester laissez-faire movement. Attacking the Bank of England and any idea of discretionary control over the currency, whether by the Bank or by private commercial banks, Cobden declared:

> I hold all idea of regulating the currency to be an absurdity; the very terms of regulating the currency and managing the currency I look upon to be an absurdity; the currency should regulate itself; it must be regulated by the trade and commerce of the world; I would neither allow the Bank of England nor any private banks to have what is called the management of the currency. . . . I would never contemplate any remedial measure, which left it to the discretion of individuals to regulate the amount of currency by any principle or standard whatever.[21]

---

[20]Quoted in Fetter, *Development*, p. 176.
[21]Ibid.

In short, the fervent desire of Richard Cobden, along with other Manchesterians and most other currency school writers, was to remove government or bank manipulation of money altogether and to leave its workings solely to the free-market forces of gold or silver. Whether or not Cobden's proposed solution of a state-run bank was the proper one, no one can deny the fervor of his laissez-faire views or his desire to apply them to the difficult and complex case of money and banking.

Let me now return to Professor White's cherished free-banking writers and to his unfortunate conflation of the very different hard-money and soft-money camps. The currency school and the free bankers were both launched upon the advent of the severe financial crisis of 1825, which, as usual, was preceded by a boom fueled by bank credit. The crisis brought the widespread realization that the simple return to the gold standard, as effected in 1821, was not enough and that something more had to be done to eliminate the instability of the banking system.[22]

---

[22]One measure of partial reform accomplished by the British government was the outlawing, in 1826, of small-denomination (under £5) bank notes (an edict obeyed by the Bank of England for over a century), which at least insured that the average person would be making most transactions in gold or silver coin. Even Adam Smith, the leading apologist for Scottish "free" banking, had advocated such a measure. But it is instructive to note, in view of Professor White's admiration for Scottish banking, that political pressure by the Scottish Tories gained the Scottish banks an exemption from this measure. The Tory campaign was led by the eminent novelist, Sir Walter Scott. Hailing the campaign, the spokesman for Scottish High Toryism, Blackwood's *Edinburgh Magazine*, published two articles on "The Country Banks and the Bank of England" in 1827–28, in which it wove together two major strains of archinflationism: going off the gold standard and praising the country banks. Blackwood's also attacked the Bank of England as overly restrictionist (!), thus helping to inaugurate the legend that the trouble with the bank was that it was too restrictive instead of being itself the major engine of monetary inflation. In contrast, the *Westminster Review,* the spokesman for James Mill's philosophic radicals, scoffed at the Scots for threatening "a civil war in defense of the privilege of being plundered" by the banking system. See Fetter, *Development*, pp. 123–24.

Among four leading free-banking advocates of the 1820s and early 1830s—Robert Mushet, Sir John Sinclair, Sir Henry Brooke Parnell, and George Poulett Scrope—Professor White sees little difference. And yet they were split into two very different camps. The earlier writers, Mushet and Parnell, were hard money men. Mushet, a long-time pro-gold-standard "bullionist" and clerk at the Royal Mint, set forth a currency-principle type of business cycle theory in 1826, pointing out that the Bank of England had generated an inflationary boom, which later had to be reversed into a contractionary depression. Mushet's aim was to arrive at the equivalent of a purely metallic currency, but he believed that free rather than central banking was a better way to achieve it. Once again, White's treatment muddies the waters. While admitting that Mushet took a currency school approach toward purely metallic money, White still chooses to criticize Daugherty for classifying Mushet with the currency school, since he opted for a free—rather than a central—banking method to achieve currency goals (p. 62n). The more prominent Parnell was also a veteran bullionist writer and Member of Parliament, who took a position very similar to Mushet's.[23]

Sir John Sinclair and George Poulett Scrope, however, were horses of a very different color. White admits that Sinclair was not a pure free-banking man, but he characteristically underplays Sinclair's fervent lifelong views as being concerned with "preventing deflation" and calls Sinclair a "tireless promoter of agricultural

---

[23]Professor White has performed a valuable service in rescuing Parnell's work from obscurity. Parnell's tract of 1827 was attacked from a more consistent hard-money position by the fiery populist radical, William Cobbett. Cobbett averred that "ever since that hellish compound Paper-money was understood by me, I have wished for the destruction of the accursed thing: I have applauded every measure that tended to produce its destruction, and censured every measure having a tendency to preserve it." He attacked Parnell's pamphlet for defending the actions of the country banks and for praising the Scottish system. In reply, Cobbett denounced the "Scottish monopolists" and proclaimed that "these ravenous Rooks of Scotland . . . have been a pestilence to England for more than two hundred years."

interests" (p. 60 and 60n). In truth, Sinclair, a Scottish nobleman and agriculturist, was, all his life, a determined and fanatical zealot on behalf of monetary inflation and government spending. As soon as the pro-gold-standard, anti-fiat paper Bullion Committee Report was issued in 1810, Sir John wrote to Prime Minister Spencer Perceval urging the government to reprint his own three-volume proinflationist work, *History of the Public Revenues of the British* (1785–90), as part of the vital task of rebutting the Bullion Committee. "You know my sentiments regarding the importance of paper Circulation," Sinclair wrote the Prime Minister, "which is in fact the basis of our prosperity." In fact, Sinclair's *Observations on the Report of the Bullion Committee*, published in September 1810, was the very first of many pamphlet attacks on the Bullion Report, most of them orchestrated by the British government.

When Britain went back to the gold standard in 1819–21, Sinclair, joining with the proinflationist and pro-fiat money Birmingham school, was one of the most energetic and bitter critics of resumption of specie payments. It is no wonder that Frank Fetter should depict Sinclair's lifelong enthusiasm: "that more money was the answer to all economic problems."[24] It is also no wonder that Sinclair should have admired the Scottish "free" banking system and opposed the currency principle. But one would have thought that Professor White would feel uncomfortable with Sinclair as his ally.

Another of Professor White's dubious heroes is George Poulett Scrope. While Scrope is also characterized as not a pure or mainstream free-banking man, his analysis is taken very seriously by White and is discussed numerous times. And he is mentioned prominently in White's table as a leading free banker. Scrope's inveterate inflationary bent is handled most gently by

[24]Fetter, *Development*, p. 22. Among his other sins, Sinclair, an indefatigable collector of statistics, in the 1790s published the 21-volume *A Statistical Account of Scotland* and actually introduced the words statistics and statistical into the English language.

White: "Like Sinclair, he [Scrope] placed higher priority on combating deflation" (p. 82 n). In fact, Scrope not only battled against the return to the gold standard in 1819–21, he was also the leading theorist of the fortunately small band of writers in Britain who were ardent underconsumptionists and proto-Keynesians. In his *Principles of Political Economy* (written in 1833, the same year as his major pro-free-banking tract), Scrope declared that any decline in consumption in favor of a "general increase in the propensity to save" would necessarily and "proportionately diminish the demand as compared with the supply, and occasion a *general glut*".

Let us now turn to the final stage of the currency school–banking school–free-banking controversy. The financial crisis of 1838–39 touched off an intensified desire to reform the banking system, and the controversy culminated with the Peel Acts of 1844 and 1845.

Take, for example, one of Professor White's major heroes, James William Gilbart. Every historian except White has included Gilbart among the members of the banking school. Why does not Professor White? Despite White's assurance, for example, that the free-banking school was even more fervent than the currency school in attributing the cause of the business cycle to monetary inflation, Gilbart held, typically of the banking school, that bank notes simply expand and contract according to the "wants of trade" and that, therefore, issue of such notes, being matched by the production of goods, could not raise prices. Furthermore, the active causal flow goes from "trade" to prices to the "requirement" for more bank notes to flow into circulation.

Thus said Gilbart:

> If there is an increase of trade without an increase of prices, I consider that more notes will be required to circulate that increased quantity of commodities; if there is an increase of commodities and an increase of prices also, of course, you would require a still greater amount of notes.[25]

---

[25]Quoted in White, *Free Banking*, p. 124.

In short, whether prices rise or not, the supply of money must always increase! Putting aside the question of who the "you" is supposed to be in this quote, this is simply rank inflationism of the banking school variety. In fact, of course no increase of money is "required" in either case. The genuine causal chain is the other way round, from increased bank notes to increased prices, and *also* to increased money value of the goods being produced.

Professor White may not be alive to this distinction because he, too, is a follower of the "needs of trade" (or "wants of trade") rationale for bank credit inflation. White's favorable discussion of the needs-of-trade doctrine (pp. 122–26) makes clear that he himself is indeed a variant of banking-school inflationist. Unfortunately, White seems to think all this to be consonant with the "Humean-Ricardian" devotion to a purely metallic currency (p. 124). For one thing, White does not seem to realize that David Hume, in contrast to his banking-school friend Adam Smith, believed in 100 percent specie reserve banking.

While Professor White, in the previous quote from Gilbart, cites his Parliamentary testimony in 1841, he *omits* the crucial interchange between Gilbart and Sir Robert Peel. In his testimony, Gilbart declared not only that country bank notes increase solely in response to the wants of trade and, therefore, that they could never be overissued. He *also* claimed—in keeping with the tenets of the banking school—that even the Bank of England could never overissue notes so long as it only discounted commercial loans! So much for Professor White's claims of Gilbart's alleged devotion to free banking! There followed some fascinating and revealing colloquies between Peel and the alleged free banker (i.e., pro-free-banking, pro-gold-standard) James Gilbart. Peel sharply continued his questioning: "Do you think, then, that the legitimate demands of commerce may always be trusted to, as a safe test of the amount of circulation under all circumstances?" To which Gilbart admitted: "I think they may." (Note: nothing was said about exempting the Bank of England from such trust.)

Peel then asked the critical question. The banking school (followed by Professor White) claimed to be devoted to the gold standard, so that the "needs of trade" justification for bank credit would *not* apply to inconvertible fiat currency. But Peel, suspicious of the banking school's devotion to gold, then asked: In the bank restriction [fiat money] days, "do you think that the legitimate demands of commerce constituted a test that might be safely relied upon?" Gilbart evasively replied: "That is a period of which I have no personal knowledge"—a particularly disingenuous reply from a man who had written *The History and Principles of Banking* (1834). Indeed, Gilbart proceeded to throw in the towel on the gold standard: "I think the legitimate demands of commerce, even then, would be a sufficient guide to go by." When Peel pressed Gilbart further on that point, the latter began to back and fill, changing and rechanging his views, finally once more falling back on his lack of personal experience during the period.[26]

Peel was certainly right in being suspicious of the banking school's devotion to the gold standard—whether or not Professor White was later to reclassify them as free bankers. In addition to Gilbart's revelations, Gilbart's fellow official at the London &c Westminster Bank, J.W. Bosanquet, kept urging bank suspensions of specie payment whenever times became difficult. And in his popular tract of 1844, *On the Regulation of Currencies*, John

---

[26]The interchange between Peel and Gilbart may be found in the important article by Boyd Hilton, "Peel: A Reappraisal," *Historical Journal* 22 (September 1979), pp. 593–94. Hilton shows that Peel (far from being the unprincipled opportunist he had usually been portrayed as by historians) was a man of increasingly fixed classical liberal principles, devoted to minimal budgets, free trade, and hard money. Not understanding economics, however, Hilton characteristically brands Peel's questioning of Gilbart as "inept" and sneers at Peel for scoffing at Gilbart's patent dodge of lacking "personal knowledge."

Moreover, not being a classical liberal, Hilton ridicules Sir Robert Peel's alleged inflexible dogmatism on behalf of laissez-faire. It is most unfortunate that White, in his eagerness to censure Peel's attack on inflationary bank credit, praises Hilton's "insightful account of Peel's little-recognized dogmatism on matter of monetary policy" (p. 77n). Does White also agree with Hilton's denunciation of Peel's "dogmatism" on free trade?

Fullarton—a banker in India by then retired in England and a key leader of the banking school—gave the game away. Wrote Fullarton:

> And, much as I fear I am disgracing myself by the avowal, I have no hesitation in professing my own adhesion to the decried doctrine of the old Bank Directors of 1810, "that so long as a bank issues its notes only on the discount of *good* bills, at not more than sixty days' date, it cannot go wrong in issuing as many as the public will receive from it.[27]

Fullarton was referring, of course, to the old antibullionist position that so long as any bank, even under an inconvertible currency, sticks to short-term real bills, it cannot cause an inflation or a business-cycle boom. It is no wonder that Peel suspected all opponents of the currency principle to be crypto-Birmingham men.[28]

The only distinguished economist to take up the free-banking cause is another one of Professor White's favorites: Samuel Bailey, who had indeed demolished Ricardian value theory in behalf of subjective utility during the 1820s. Now, in the late 1830s and early 1840s, Bailey entered the lists in behalf of free banking. Unfortunately, Bailey was one of the worst offenders in insisting

---

[27]Quoted in Fetter, *Development*, p. 193.

[28]Neither is the example of James Wilson reassuring. Wilson, founding editor of the new journal, *The Economist*, was dedicated to laissez-faire and to the gold standard. He entered the monetary debate quite late, in spring 1845, becoming one of the major leaders of the banking school. Though of all the banking school, Wilson was one of the friendliest to free banking and to the Scottish system, he also claimed that the Bank of England could never overissue notes in a convertible monetary system. And though personally devoted to the gold standard, Wilson even made the same damaging concession as Gilbart, though far more clearly and candidly. For, of all the major banking school leaders, Wilson was the only one who stated flatly and clearly that no banks could ever overissue notes if they were backed by short-term, self-liquidating real bills, even under an inconvertible fiat standard. See Lloyd Mints, *A History of Banking Theory in Great Britain and the United States* (Chicago: University of Chicago Press, 1945), p. 90.

on the absolute passivity of the British country and joint-stock banks as well as in attacking the very idea that there might be something worrisome about changes in the supply of money. By assuring his readers that competitive banking would always provide a "nice adjustment of the currency to the wants of the people," Bailey overlooked the fundamental Ricardian truth that there is never any social value in increasing the supply of money, as well as the insight that bank credit entails a fraudulent issue of warehouse receipts to nonexistent goods.

Finally, Professor White ruefully admits that when it came to the crunch—the Peel Acts of 1844 and 1845 establishing a Bank of England monopoly of note issue and eliminating the "free" banking system of Scotland—his free-banking heroes were nowhere to be found in opposition. White concedes that their support of Peel's acts was purchased by the grant of cartelization. In short, in exchange for Bank of England monopoly on note issue, the existing English and Scottish banks were "grandfathered" into place; they could keep their existing circulation of notes, while no new competitors were allowed to enter into the lucrative note-issuing business. Thus, White concedes:

> He [Gilbart] was relieved that the [Peel] act did not extinguish the joint-stock banks' right of issue and was frankly pleased with its cartelizing provisions: "Our rights are acknowledged—our privileges are extended—our circulation guaranteed—and we are saved from conflicts with reckless competitors." (p. 79)

Very well. But White avoids asking himself the difficult questions. For example: what kind of a dedicated "free-banking" movement is it that can be so easily bought off by cartel privileges from the state? The answer, which White sidesteps by avoiding the question, is precisely the kind of a movement that serves simply as a cloak for the interests of the commercial bankers.

For, with the exception of the older, hard-money free-banking men—such as Mushet (long dead by 1844) and Parnell (who died in the middle of the controversy in 1842)—virtually all of

White's free bankers were themselves officials of private commercial banks. Gilbart had been a bank official all his life and had long been manager of the London & Westminster Bank. Bailey was chairman of the Sheffield Banking Company. Consider, for example, the newly founded *Bankers' Magazine*, which White lauds as a crucial organ of free-banking opinion. White laments that a writer in the June 1844 issue of *Bankers' Magazine*, while critical of the currency principle and monopoly issues for the Bank of England, yet approved the Peel Act as a whole for aiding the profits of existing banks by prohibiting all new banks of issue.

And yet, Professor White resists the realization that his entire cherished free-banking movement—at least in its later inflationist "need of trade" manifestation—was simply a special pleading on behalf of the inflationary activities of the commercial banks. Strip away White's conflation of the earlier hard-money free-banking theorists with the later inflationists, and his treasured free-banking movement turns out to be merely special pleaders for bank chicanery and bank credit inflation.

Index

Austrian business cycle theory, 209

Bagehot, Walter, 133, 149, 185
Bailey, Samuel, 289–90
bailment, deposit banking and, 87
balance of payments, deficit in, 121
balance sheet, 76–83
   warehouse receipts appearing on, 87
bank cartels, free market incentives
   against, 123
bank deposits. *See* demand deposits
bank notes
   fractional reserve banking and, 104
   monopoly privilege of issuing, 125,
     181, 182, 187, 193, 235
   outlawing of small-denomination, 283
Bank of England
   origin of, 177–83
   reform of, 186–89
   role in Scotland, 269–70
Bank of North America, 191–93
bank runs
   threat against credit expansion,
     112–14
   under central banking, 133
Banking School, 151n, 277–78
banking
   extent of, 112
   branch, 216, 226
   central
     100 percent reserve, 187
     bankers' bank function of, 126
     coordinated credit expansion
       under, 133–36
     determining total reserves of,
       141–60
     gold standard and, 126, 132, 133
     history of, xv, xix
     lender of last resort function of,
       133, 149–53, 230
     limits on credit expansion
       removed by, 125–39

the National Banking System,
   219–34
operations of, xix
origins of, 177–90
origins in the United States,
   191–206
process of bank credit expansion,
   161–76
proponents of, 232 34
Treasury and, 170–76
in the United States up to the
   Civil War, 207–18
commercial, 98, 107
deposit, 85–110
   100 percent reserve, 95, 187,
     263–64, 280
   embezzlement and, 90–94
   law on, 91–93
free
   definition of, 111
   limits on bank credit inflation
     under, 111–24
   school, 278, 283–91
   Scotland and, 183–86, 189–90,
     269–91
   in the United States, 197,
     214–15, 276n
fractional reserve, 93, 94–103
   business cycle and, 103, 114,
     120–22
   counterfeiting in, 98
   deflationary pressures on,
     101–03
   fight against, 214
   fraud in, 96–97
   gold coin standard vs., 103
   inflationary, 97–98, 100–01, 210
   as mix of deposit and loan bank-
     ing, 107–10
   money warehouse receipts and,
     104–10
   time structure of assets under,
     98–99

293